Japan's ASEAN Policy

In Search of Proactive Multilateralism

The **Institute of Southeast Asian Studies (ISEAS)** was established as an autonomous organization in 1968. It is a regional centre dedicated to the study of socio-political, security and economic trends and developments in Southeast Asia and its wider geostrategic and economic environment. The Institute's research programmes are the Regional Economic Studies (RES, including ASEAN and APEC), Regional Strategic and Political Studies (RSPS), and Regional Social and Cultural Studies (RSCS).

ISEAS Publishing, an established academic press, has issued more than 2,000 books and journals. It is the largest scholarly publisher of research about Southeast Asia from within the region. ISEAS Publishing works with many other academic and trade publishers and distributors to disseminate important research and analyses from and about Southeast Asia to the rest of the world.

Japan's ASEAN Policy

In Search of Proactive Multilateralism

by **Sueo Sudo**

ISEAS

INSTITUTE OF SOUTHEAST ASIAN STUDIES
Singapore

First published in Singapore in 2015 by
ISEAS Publishing
Institute of Southeast Asian Studies
30 Heng Mui Keng Terrace
Pasir Panjang
Singapore 119614

E-mail: publish@iseas.edu.sg
Website: <http://bookshop.iseas.edu.sg>

The responsibility for facts and opinions in this publication rests exclusively with the author and his interpretations do not necessarily reflect the views or the policy of the publishers or their supporters.

ISEAS Library Cataloguing-in-Publication Data

Sudo, Sueo.
  Japan's ASEAN policy : in search of proactive multilateralism.
  Japan—Foreign relations—Southeast Asia.
  Southeast Asia—Foreign relations—Japan.
  Japan—Foreign relations—1989–
  Regionalism—East Asia.
  Title.
DS525.9 J3S941   2015

ISBN 978-981-4519-02-1 (soft cover)
ISBN 978-981-4519-78-6 (e-book, PDF)

Typeset by Superskill Graphics Pte Ltd
Printed in Singapore by Markono Print Media Pte Ltd

CONTENTS

FIGURES AND TABLES

Figures

Tables

PREFACE

The central puzzle in the study of Japanese foreign policy has been why Japan has continued to play a passive role in international affairs, despite its impressive economic and political power. Challenging this central puzzle, the core argument of this study is to present an alternative path for the study of Japanese foreign policy. In fact, in recent years Japanese foreign policy has become less dependent on the United States, more strategic towards Asia, and more energetic towards international and regional institutions. One of the main features is multilateralism in Japanese foreign policy, as shown by Japan's active participation in the regional institutions. In pursuing multilateralism, Japan cooperated closely with the only durable regional body in Southeast Asia, to wit, the Association of Southeast Asian Nations (ASEAN). Given the fact that East Asian regionalism has been driven by ASEAN, it is of utmost urgency to investigate the emerging partnership between Japan and ASEAN. My central thesis in this study is thus to put Japan's ASEAN policy into a proper perspective by asserting that Japan's new policy initiatives towards ASEAN are not reactive, nor are they exceptions in a broader framework of merely reactive foreign policy.

In writing this book, I have fortunately received enormous support and assistance from individuals and institutions. To begin with, I have received financial support from two institutions to carry out my book project. They are a three-year research subsidy by the Japanese government and Pache Research Subsidy of Nanzan University. Without these sources of financial assistance, it would not have been possible to undertake extensive field research in Japan and Southeast Asia. In undertaking my field research, I am especially indebted to the following institutions. In Bangkok, Chulalongkorn University's Institute of Asian Studies gave me a special opportunity to conduct my field research based in Bangkok. For this, I am grateful to Dr Khien Theeravit and Ms Saikew Thipakorn. In Singapore,

I am indebted to the staff of the ASEAN Studies Centre for their time and assistance: Mr Rodolfo Severino, Dr Termsak Chalermpalanupap, and Ms Moe Thuzar. Also at the ASEAN Secretariat in Jakarta, I owe a great deal of thanks to the following staff who were kind enough to answer my questions: Alexander Lim, Bala Palaniappan, and Kris Sandhi Soekartawi.

I have also been assisted immensely by ongoing projects. First is Meijo University's East Asia Project, working closely with South Korea's Kyung Hee University and China's Fudan University. For this, I would like to thank Dr Kwangwook Kim, Professor Susumu Hida and Professor Yuri Sadoi for their support and assistance. Second, Thammasat University's East Asian project has always inspired me since 2011. For this, I am especially grateful to Dr Siriporn Wajjwalku who asked me to join. I have greatly benefited from the discussions with our group members, Kuik Cheng Chwee, Md. Nasrudin Md. Akhir, Yulius Purwadi Hermawan, Nguyen Quoc Viet, Yasushi Katsuma, Sachiko Hirakawa, and Alice Ba.

Special thanks go to Professors Chaiwat Khamchoo, Lee Poh Ping, Aziz Hitam, Mayako Ishii, Masashi Nishihara, Makoto Iokibe, Setsuho Ikehata, Kazuo Kawanishi, Toyoji Tanaka, Chang Hammo, Lee Hong Pyo, Lee Geumdong, Ichiro Inoue, Hitoshi Hirakawa, Kazushi Shimizu, Yoshihiro Tsuranuki, Masaki Takahashi, and Hiro Katsumata for their unceasing encouragement and support.

At Nanzan, Professors Yoko Yoshikawa, David Potter, Robert Croker, and Masahiro Hoshino have provided their valuable time and assistance in the completion of this book. Especially since the publication of our joint work in 2003, Potter-san's ideas of Japanese foreign policy have always inspired my work on Japan-ASEAN relations. As a leading Southeast Asian specialist in Japan, Yoshikawa-san's support and guidance have also made my work much easier. I am also grateful for research assistance rendered by Ms Merryn Black and Ms Yow Min Min.

Finally, as is always the case, without thanking my wife and the family the book project cannot be complete. Whenever I do my research in Southeast Asia I regard Bangkok as home ground and always feel at home due to my wife's family. For this, I am deeply indebted to the Tangpoonsinthana family for having warmly embraced me as a part of their family. Equally important is my wife who has been always with me, sharing hardship and joys. It is to you that I dedicate this work.

ABBREVIATIONS

ABMI	Asian Bond Markets Initiative
ACMECS	Ayeyawady–Chao Phraya–Mekong Economic Cooperation Strategy
ACT	ASEAN Committee in Tokyo
ADB	Asian Development Bank
AEC	ASEAN Economic Community
AEM	ASEAN Economic Ministers
AEM-METI	ASEAN-Japan Economic Ministers' Meeting
AFTA	ASEAN Free Trade Area
AICO	ASEAN Industrial Cooperation
AJCEP	ASEAN-Japan Comprehensive Exchange Program
AJDF	ASEAN-Japan Development Fund
AMBDC	ASEAN Mekong Basin Development Cooperation
AMEICC	ASEAN Economic Ministers–MITI Economic and Industrial Cooperation Committee
AMRI	ASEAN Ministers Responsible for Information
AMRO	APT Macroeconomic Research Office
ANRPC	Association of Natural Rubber Producing Countries
APC	ASEAN Promotion Center
APEC	Asia-Pacific Economic Cooperation
APT	ASEAN Plus Three
APTERR	ASEAN Plus Three Emergency Rice Reserve
ARF	ASEAN Regional Forum
ASA	Association of Southeast Asia
ASA	ASEAN Swap Arrangement
ASEAN	Association of Southeast Asian Nations
ASEAN-ISIS	ASEAN-Institute of Strategic and International Studies
ASEM	Asia-Europe Meeting

ASPAC	Asia-Pacific Council
BBC	brand-to-brand complementation
BIMP-EAGA	Brunei, Indonesia, Malaysia, Philippines, East Asian Growth Area
CEPEA	Comprehensive Economic Partnership in East Asia
CGIM	Credit Guarantee and Investment Mechanism
CLMV	Cambodia, Laos, Myanmar and Vietnam
CLV	Cambodia, Laos and Vietnam
CMIM	Chiang Mai Initiative Multilateralization
COCI	Committee on Culture and Information
CSCAP	Council for Security Cooperation in the Asia-Pacific
CSCE	Conference on Security and Cooperation in Europe
DAC	Development Assistance Committee
DPJ	Democratic Party of Japan
DRV	Democratic Republic of Vietnam
EAC	East Asian Community
EAEC	East Asian Economic Caucus
EAS	East Asia Summit
EAVG	East Asia Vision Group
EC	European Community
EMM	Economic Ministers' Meeting
ERIA	Economic Research Institute of ASEAN and East Asia
EU	European Union
EWEC	East-West Economic Corridor
FCDI	Forum for Comprehensive Development of Indochina
FDI	Foreign direct investments
FTAF	Financial Technical Assistance Fund
GAM	Gerakan Aceh Merdeka (Free Aceh Movement)
GMS	Greater Mekong Sub-region
GSP	General Scheme of Preference
G8	Group of Eight
IAI	Initiative for ASEAN Integration
ICORC	International Conference on the Reconstruction of Cambodia
IDEA	Initiative for Development in East Asia
IGGI	Inter-Government Group for Indonesia
IMF	International Monetary Fund
IMO	International Maritime Organization

IMT	International Monitoring Team
ISC	Information Sharing Center
JACEP	Japan-ASEAN Comprehensive Economic Partnership
JAF	Japan-ASEAN Forum
JAFTAF	Japan-ASEAN Financial Technical Assistance Fund
JAIF	Japan-ASEAN Integration Fund
JBIC	Japan Bank for International Cooperation
JCG	Japan Coastal Guard
JENESYS	Japan East-Asia Network of Exchange for Students and Youths
JICA	Japan International Cooperation Agency
JSEPA	Japan and Singapore Economic Partnership Agreement
JSDF	Japan Self-Defense Force
Keidanren	Federation of Economic Organizations
LDP	Liberal Democratic Party
MAFF	Ministry of Agriculture, Forestry and Fisheries
Maphilindo	Malaya-Philippines-Indonesia
MCEDSEA	Ministerial Conference for the Economic Development of Southeast Asia
METI	Ministry of Economy, Trade and Industry
MITI	Ministry of International Trade and Industry
MJ-CI	Mekong-Japan Economic and Industrial Cooperation Initiative
MOF	Ministry of Finance
MOFA	Ministry of Foreign Affairs
NAFTA	North American Free Trade Agreement
NAID	New Asia Industrial Development Plan
ODA	official development assistance
PKO	peacekeeping operation
PMC	Post-Ministerial Conference
PTA	preferential trade agreement
ReCAAP	Regional Cooperation Agreement on Combating Piracy and Armed Robbery against Ships in Asia
SDF	Self-Defense Forces
SEATO	Southeast Asian Treaty Organization
SEC	Southern Economic Corridor
SLORC	State Law and Order Restoration Council
SRV	Socialist Republic of Vietnam

TAC	Treaty of Amity and Cooperation
UNAMET	United Nations Mission in East Timor
UNTAC	United Nations Transitional Authority in Cambodia
UNTAET	United Nations Transitional Administration in East Timor
WTO	World Trade Organization
ZOPFAN	Zone of Peace, Freedom and Neutrality

INTRODUCTION

Japan's engagement with the outside world in general, and its Asian neighbours in particular, is characterized by large swings. After 250 years of seclusion, Japan opted to go "out of Asia and into the West" in the late nineteenth century. Then, after fighting fiercely with the United States, Japan opted to form a close alliance with its former adversary in 1945. Since opening to the world, Japan's Asian policy has tended to fluctuate from aggressive engagement to indifferent detachment, depending on the available strategic choices the national government faced at each critical moment in time. In fact, consummating the Meiji Restoration in 1868, modern Japan vigorously engaged in an aggrandizing foreign policy under the banner of "a rich nation and a strong army" (*Fukoku kyohei*). In that spirit, Japan entered the international system through a series of acquisitions of foreign territories — Taiwan, Korea, Manchukuo and Southeast Asia. As an extension of its expansionistic foreign policy many Japanese had unrealistically believed that a modernized Japan would be able to reign over the entire Asian region; that is, they shared the illusory hope for the Greater East Asian Co-prosperity Sphere.

It is generally construed that the Japanese occupation of Southeast Asia during World War II was the result of last-minute improvization rather than long-term military planning. Nevertheless, the Japanese fought ruthlessly in the region for their own interest, seeking the region's abundant raw materials. Consequently, as Takashi Inoguchi explains, Japan lost all its credentials in building rapport with Asian neighbours when it wanted to start again from the ashes at the end of the war. The negative consequences of the Japanese war against the West left very deep and wide-ranging scars on the nation. Japan's Asian policy was very difficult to envisage after its defeat in the war and the allied powers' occupation. Japan's Asian policy was merely a derivative of Japan's American policy for a long time to come, even after it regained independence in 1952. In other words, Japan's Asian policy was long an antidote to its mainstream policy of a security alliance with the United States, free trade, and practice of the free market.[1]

Seen from another angle, post-war Japanese foreign policy in a way displays a unique feature of its own, to wit, being dependent exclusively on the United States in its orientation. It was during the Yoshida Doctrine period (1950s and 1960s) that Japan's U.S.-dependent economic foreign policy flourished and induced Japan to become an economic giant. Japan's success also meant that Japan's pro-U.S. orientation could serve it well without the need to pursue an autonomous Asian policy or multilateralism. Understandably, during the Yoshida Doctrine period, Japan's Asian policy was largely devoid of meaningful interactions. In other words, although international relations in the Asian region was full of events, including reparation negotiations, the Bandung conference, normalizations with South Korea and China, and the Vietnam war, Japan's policy of separating politics from economics averted its involvement in regional affairs. Regionalism in Japanese foreign policy is thus a sensitive and delicate issue. For whatever the Japanese do, Asian leaders tend to refer to the memories of the Greater East Asian Co-prosperity Sphere. Accordingly, to the Japanese, regionalism is really a concept by which "we measure our pain". The main purpose of this book is to explain how Japan has overcome the historically derived predicament and transformed its one-dimensional foreign policy.

THREE STREAMS OF JAPANESE FOREIGN POLICY

In order to grasp fully the significance of Japan's regional policy, we need to understand three streams of Japanese foreign policy.[2] They are the mainstream, alternative stream and intermediate stream. The first stream is the mainstream of Japanese foreign policy, characterized by its exclusive emphasis on the alliance with the United States. Its origin was the advent of Yoshida Shigeru as the most influential conservative leader in 1948. At the onset of the Cold War, Japan's options were limited and Yoshida's decision was to rely on the hegemon of the day. As the term "Yoshida School" insinuates, the prominent conservative leader Shigeru Yoshida educated young bureaucrats to become mainstream leaders, including Hayato Ikeda and Eisaku Sato who carried out the Yoshida Doctrine vigorously. Since the mainstream presupposes a one-dimensional foreign policy, Southeast Asia is mainly regarded as only a supplier of raw materials.

The second is the alternative stream, which emerged when an anti-Yoshida group leader Nobusuke Kishi came to power and initiated his autonomous foreign policy, exemplified by his proposal for the Southeast Asian Development Fund in 1957. As the term "anti-Yoshida group" suggests, political leaders in this group tended to do whenever possible what the pro-Yoshida Doctrine group did not advocate, including the revision of the constitution and the invigoration of Asian diplomacy. In particular, the role of the Kishi faction in the Liberal Democratic Party was critically important in promoting an autonomous Asian policy and establishing an equal partnership with the United States.[3]

The third is the intermediate stream, which came to be recognized when Foreign Minister Takeo Miki proposed his diplomatic vision of the Asia-Pacific in 1967. Given the difficulty associated with the second stream's Asia-only orientation, policymakers hesitated to embrace an Asia-only regionalism. Instead, they found a broader region of the Asia-Pacific to be more useful and acceptable to the United States. Although the concept of "open regionalism" is the key to the intermediate stream, this image of Japan is apparently built on an overemphasis of the trade aspect of regionalism; for, in the strictest sense of the term, no regional organization has so far enacted "openness" in terms of membership.[4]

Among the three, the second is the most underdeveloped and thus least explored in the study of Japanese foreign policy.[5] The reasons for this lack in the literature are obviously the dominant role of the United States in Japanese foreign policy and political instability in Southeast Asia. Given the asymmetry of the relationship between Japan and Southeast Asian countries and the uncertainty associated with the enigmatic regional body, the Association of Southeast Asian Nations (ASEAN), the study of Southeast Asia and ASEAN in Japan remains less attractive.

MULTILATERAL FOREIGN POLICY AND JAPAN-ASEAN RELATIONS

In this study, the thesis of Japan's unique diplomatic style as outlined in the second stream described above, will be developed. In the words of Thomas Berger, "the long standing critique of the lack of Japanese 'agency' in international affairs, which argues that Japan is not an independent actor in international affairs and has no agenda of its own, is no longer valid, if it ever was. In fact, it is possible to discern a distinctively Japanese approach to international relations and with it a Japanese 'liberal' set of values."[6] A distinctively Japanese approach can be found in Japan's ASEAN policy.

The question to be asked here is when and why Japan began to implement proactive multilateralism in its foreign policy. In answering the question, there could be two obvious points to be reckoned with. First, Japan's multilateral foreign policy was initiated by the Fukuda Doctrine in 1977, as Hisashi Owada explains: "Prime Minister Fukuda recognized that the creation of a regional identity and solidarity of ASEAN, which were being buttressed by a cooperative undertaking in Japan, would open up new opportunities for useful collaboration, thus, further strengthening solidarity."[7]

Second, due to the special Japan-ASEAN relationship, Japan's foreign policy has become proactive, as Masaru Kohno explains: "In 1977, Prime Minister Takeo Fukuda presented his long-term vision of Japan-Southeast Asia relations. In retrospect, the ensuing 'Fukuda Doctrine' was the first attempt by Japan to present a proactive foreign policy stance since the end of the Second World War."[8] Since 1977, Japan's policy towards Southeast Asia has anchored ASEAN and nurtured ASEAN's regional governance within the framework of political, economic and cultural dimensions. When the third doctrine was announced in 1997, Japan-ASEAN relations began to embrace East Asian countries, thereby attesting to the fact that the Japan-ASEAN partnership has become the hub of East Asian regionalism. As such, it is also true that "the strengthening of Japanese-ASEAN relations is one of the outstanding achievements of postwar Japanese diplomacy."[9] After many years of interaction, therefore, ASEAN has become a concept by which we measure Japan's contributions to East Asia.

STRUCTURE OF THE BOOK

This book is divided into six chapters. Chapter 1 explains a framework for analysing Japan's ASEAN policy, which incorporates ideas, institutions and proactive multilateralism. While critically evaluating the traditional model of reactive foreign policy, this study will explore the reasons for multilateralism. Our central thesis in this study is thus to put Japan's ASEAN policy into a proper perspective by asserting that Japan's new policy initiatives towards ASEAN are not reactive, nor are they exceptions in a broader framework of merely reactive foreign policy. In doing so, the chapter begins by critically examining the definition of a reactive state. Then, it introduces alternative perspectives on Japanese foreign policy, discusses the implications for Japan's ASEAN policy and finally constructs a framework for explaining Japan's proactive multilateral policy towards ASEAN.

Chapter 2 explores the origins of Japan-ASEAN relations and the evolution of the relationship until 1976. The earlier relations were conducted under the framework of the Yoshida Doctrine, which led to Japan's aggressive resource acquisition diplomacy. By the early 1970s, however, Japan was unable to pursue its Southeast Asian policy due to the unexpected withdrawal of the United States from Asia and the rise of anti-Japanese movements in Southeast Asia. Given the failure of Japan's economic diplomacy, to wit, the limitation of the mainstream, Tokyo began to formulate a new framework of regional order. Joined by ASEAN, a mutual quest for a viable partnership finally began.

Chapters 3 to 6 will explicate the dynamic evolution of Japan-ASEAN relations since 1977. Chapter 3 focuses on the Fukuda Doctrine, which laid the foundation for broader relations between Japan and ASEAN, including political, economic and cultural dimensions. This chapter closely looks at new developments in Japanese foreign policy from a different perspective, focusing on how Japanese policymakers came to define Japan's new role in a turbulent region, while pursuing multilateral policies towards ASEAN instead of traditional bilateral economic policies. Japan's new role can be seen in the process of forging the very first foreign policy doctrine in 1977. In fact, designating ASEAN as a pillar of Japanese foreign policy, Japan went through a significant experiment in playing a proactive political role in Southeast Asia between 1977 and 1986.

Chapter 4 traces the development of Japan-ASEAN relations since the proclamation of the Takeshita Doctrine in 1987. This second phase shows the consolidation of this relationship. Against this background, Japan also responded positively to stability in Southeast Asia. As with Fukuda's overtures, Prime Minister Noboru Takeshita attended the Third ASEAN Summit in Manila and never failed to recognize the importance of ASEAN as a partner. Seizing the opportunity to officially proclaim another doctrine in 1987, Japan's ASEAN policy entered a new phase. In particular the end of the Cold War necessitated new initiatives from Japan. Japan's political role was required to resolve the Cambodian conflict and to offer reconstruction assistance after the conflict in Indochina. Japan's economic role was also needed to boost ASEAN economies following the Cambodian conflict. It was also important for Japan to further strengthen mutual understanding by promoting cultural exchanges. Following the effects of the Fukuda Doctrine, this chapter observes closely how Japan reinforced political, economic and cultural relations with ASEAN in the post–Cold War period.

Chapter 5 explores the rationales for the expansion of Japan-ASEAN relations since the Hashimoto Doctrine in 1997. The third phase shows the relationship expanding beyond Southeast Asia. Although the goals of ASEAN Plus Three and the East Asia summit overlap, it is clear that the Japan-ASEAN strategic partnership serves as a hub of East Asian regionalism. Against this background, Japan has also shown some notable initiatives in its foreign policy. It is notable because for the first time Japan has identified itself as part of East Asia. In particular, it was unprecedented that the Japanese government proposed the formation of an East Asian version of the International Monetary Fund in order to deal with the contagious financial crisis, despite American objections. When a populist premier began his domestic and foreign policy, however, Japan's East Asian policy turned around, thus adversely affecting Japan-ASEAN relations. In particular, worsening Japan-China relations, caused mainly by Prime Minister Junichiro Koizumi's controversial visit to the Yasukuni Shrine, could serve as a testing ground for closer Japan-ASEAN relations in the twenty-first century. While closely following the footsteps of the Takeshita Doctrine, this chapter focuses on how Japan managed to cope with the transitional period of the late 1990s and early 2000s.

Chapter 6 examines the post-2007 development of Japan-ASEAN relations until 2011, with special focus on the new administration under the Democratic Party. ASEAN's new direction hinged on its Charter, and Japan's new quest for viable regionalism hinged on the formation of a peaceful regime in East Asia, bridging the two with the shared idea of community building. Thus, beginning in 2007, Japan-ASEAN relations have entered a new phase; although whether a new ASEAN and a new Japan under the Democratic Party continue to serve as a hub of East Asian regionalism remains to be seen. In this last chapter, ASEAN's quest for three-pillars' community building and Japan's greater contributions to East Asian regionalism through a sustainable Japan-ASEAN partnership will be explored.

In conclusion, after acknowledging what this unique relationship between Japan and ASEAN brought about and how well it has been contributing to the construction of the East Asian community, the question of where Japan-ASEAN relations are heading will be discussed.

Notes

1. Takashi Inoguchi, "Japan Goes Regional", in *Japan's Asian Policy: Revival and Response*, edited by Takashi Inoguchi (London: Palgrave Macmillan, 2002), pp. 3, 15. See also Taizo Miyagi, "Sengo Nihon no chiiki chitsujo koso", in *EU to Higashiajia no Chiikikyodotai*, edited by Masaharu Nakamura and Yves Schemeil (Tokyo: Jochidaigaku shuppan, 2012), pp. 265–83 for Japan's attempts to pursue its regional policies.

2. For general discussions of the mainstreams of Japanese foreign policy, see especially Keiko Hirata, "Gaiko", in *Akusesu Nihonseiji ron*, edited by Hiroshi Hirano and Masaru Kono (Tokyo: Nihon keizai hyoron sha, 2003), pp. 236–58 and Masaru Kono, "Gaiko seisaku", in *Gendai Nihon no seiji*, edited by Ikuo Kume and Masaru Kono (Tokyo: Hosodaigaku kyoiku shinkokai, 2011), pp. 173–85.

3. Thus, the cycle of excluding and including the United States in Asian regionalism transpires. See Shintaro Hamanaka, "Regionalism Cycle in Asia (-Pacific): A Game Theory Approach to the Rise and Fall of Asian Regional Institutions", ADB Working Paper Series on Regional Economic Integration, no. 42, February 2010.

4. Shintaro Hamanaka, *Asian Regionalism and Japan: The Politics of Membership in Regional Diplomatic, Financial and Trade Groups* (London: Routledge, 2009), p. 7.

5. There are only a few book-length studies in Japanese. They are Khoontong Intarathai, *ASEAN to Nihon* (Tokyo: Yazawa shobo, 1982), Toshiaki Arai, *ASEAN to Nihon* (Tokyo: Nicchu shuppan, 2003) and Sumio Hatano and Susumu Sato, *Gendai Nihon no Tonanajia seisaku 1950–2005* (Tokyo: Wasedadaigaku shuppanbu, 2007).

6. Thomas Berger, "The Pragmatic Liberalism of an Adaptive State", in *Japan in International Politics*, edited by Thomas Berger, Mike Mochizuki and Jitsuo Tsuchiyama (Boulder, CO: Lynne Rienner, 2007), p. 290.

7. Hisashi Owada, "Japan-ASEAN Relations in East Asia", speech delivered at Hotel New Otani, Singapore, 16 October 2000 <http://www.jiia.or.jp/report/owada/Singapore>.

8. Masaharu Kohno, "In Search of Proactive Diplomacy: Increasing Japan's International Role in the 1990s", CNAPS Working Paper (Center for Northeast

Asian Policy Studies, the Brookings Institution, 1999) <http://www.brookings.edu/papers/1999/fall_japan_kohno.aspx>.

9.   Yoichi Funabashi, *New Challenges, New Frontier: Japan and ASEAN in the 21st Century* (Singapore: Institute of Southeast Asian Studies, 2003), p. 39. For a latest account of Japan-Southeast Asian relations, see Nicholas Tarling, *Southeast Asia and the Great Powers* (London: Routledge, 2010), pp. 93–113.

1

ASEAN IN JAPANESE MULTILATERAL FOREIGN POLICY

It is almost a cliché that Japan's external behaviour is characterized by profound puzzles. Thus, it is no wonder that to many students of international relations, Japanese foreign policy remains an enigma. For instance, Japan provided the largest financial contribution to the 1991 Gulf War, but was never fully blessed by the United Nations. In a similar vein, despite its status as the second-largest economy (third since 2010) in the world, Japan has never tried to translate its economic power into political influence. Japan's position as the second-largest contributor to the United Nations' budget has not yielded any matching role in the international community. Most of all, due to these gaps in perception between Japan's significant economic power and its influence on international events, Japan used to be labelled as an "economic giant and political pigmy".[1] After all these years, have these profound puzzles been resolved to the effect that treating Japan as an enigma is no longer tenable?

The central puzzle in the study of Japanese foreign policy has been why Japan has continued to play a passive role in international affairs, despite its impressive economic and political power. It is no doubt that the study of Japanese foreign policy has advanced remarkably in recent years. Especially noteworthy are the works by Glenn Hook et al. and Michael Green.[2] Hook et al.'s textbook, for instance, is quintessential in the sense that it covers a vast array of information about Japan's diplomacy and economic and security relations in the post-war period. In addition to containing sufficient international relations theory, the works of the four authors offer a unique framework to explain the distinctive style of Japanese foreign policy. The "quiet diplomacy" characterization focuses on a range of consistently low-risk and low-profile international initiatives and is premised on a long-term view of Japan's national interests. In a similar vein, Green's book succinctly explains major changes in post–Cold War Japanese foreign policy. As he stressed, Japanese foreign policy has become more independent from the United States, more strategic towards Asia, and more energetic towards international and regional institutions. Japan's shift towards reluctant realism can be explained by changing international and domestic circumstances, such as the security concerns about China, domestic economic paralysis, and changes in political leaders.

One of the main features to emerge from the recent works is the apparent multilateralism in Japanese foreign policy, as shown by Japan's active participation in the Asia-Pacific Economic Cooperation (APEC), ASEAN Regional Forum (ARF), Asia-Europe Meeting (ASEM), ASEAN Plus Three (APT) and East Asia Summit (EAS). It is interesting to note here that in organizing these institutions, Japan cooperated closely with the only regional body in Southeast Asia, to wit, the Association of Southeast Asian Nations (ASEAN). Why is it that Japan's post–Cold War foreign policy has become more Asia-oriented, independent from the United States? Why has Japan's independent regional policy been more oriented towards ASEAN? In view of the fact that East Asian regionalism has been driven by ASEAN, it is of utmost urgency to investigate the emerging partnership between Japan and ASEAN.

The central thesis of this study is thus to put Japan's ASEAN policy into a proper perspective by asserting that Japan's new policy initiatives towards ASEAN are not reactive, nor are they exceptions in a broader framework of merely reactive foreign policy. The study begins by critically examining the definition of a reactive state. It then introduces alternative perspectives on Japanese foreign policy, discusses the implications for Japan's ASEAN policy, and finally constructs a framework for explaining Japan's proactive multilateral policy towards ASEAN.

REACTIVE FOREIGN POLICY AND THE YOSHIDA DOCTRINE

Ever since the conclusion of the San Francisco Peace Treaty in 1951, Japan's traditional foreign policy has hinged on its alliance with the United States, while resolving wartime issues of reparations and normalization of diplomatic relations with adversary countries. In analysing Japan's normalization with the Soviet Union, reparations negotiations and other post-war foreign policy issues, Donald Hellmann cogently characterized Japan's unique style of conducting foreign relations: "Throughout the postwar period, Japan has flourished in an international greenhouse that was almost totally made in America. Japan was and still remains essentially a passive actor on the world political stage, more a trading company than a nation-state, a nation without a foreign policy in the usual sense of the word."[3]

The Yoshida Doctrine as a Mainstream of Japanese Foreign Policy

Within the framework of the "San Francisco System", based on the peace treaty and the Japan-U.S. Security Treaty, Japanese foreign policy became a function of the following crucial factors: first, U.S. military protection and its reliable commitments in Asia; second, free access to raw materials and export markets in order to reinforce Japan's tainted economy; and third, a stable political framework in which the conservative ruling party can pursue a consistent "economic foreign policy". Most of all, the bipolar international structure and the alliance with the United States set the parameters of Japanese foreign policy during the Cold War simply because the United States provided Japan with necessary military protection and critical access to the American market, technology and foreign aid.

A standard definition of the doctrine includes (1) placing the alliance with the United States as the cornerstone of Japan's foreign policy through which Japan ensures its security, (2) maintaining Japan's defence capabilities at a low level, (3) channelling the extra resources saved by these security arrangements to economic activities so that Japan can thrive as a trading state.[4] Dwelling on this, Yonosuke Nagai popularized the concept in the 1980s. As a result, the Yoshida Doctrine contained three basic elements: first, continued reliance on the alliance with the United States to ensure Japan's security; second, emphasis on economic relations overseas to assist in the reconstruction of the domestic economy; and third, maintenance of a low profile in international politics. Accordingly, these characteristics led to the three pillars of the doctrine: light armaments, an economy-first policy, and the separation of economics and politics.[5]

A few points deserve our attention regarding the historical evolution of the concept of the Yoshida Doctrine. Masashi Nishihara conceptualized the Yoshida Doctrine as a set of principles and working rules. While pointing out three principles — to honour pacifist constitutional restraints and pursue trade-oriented diplomacy; to encourage the establishment of an economically viable (Southeast) Asia; and to support a strong United Nations — he acknowledged that these principles were "little more than guiding principles" and that the actual behaviour of Japan diverged from them from time to time. This led him to introduce five working rules: "(a) to expand the overseas market (for *boeki rikkoku*), (b) to avoid more than minimal defense spending, (c) to avoid involvement in international political disputes, (d) to avoid resorting to the use of force if involved in disputes, and (e) to reduce actual or potential international tensions through diplomatic means". Nishihara argued that these guidelines were only tacit, but they constituted a "fine blending of political passivity and economic positiveness" consciously developed by Yoshida and other leaders.[6]

Calder Model of Reactive State

In 1988 Kent Calder wrote a seminal essay on the reactive nature of Japanese foreign policy, focusing essentially on economic issues.[7] Subsequently, however, the reactive state thesis has been used to analyse Japan's foreign policy in general. Calder's essay was influential because, at the time when Japan appeared poised to pass the United States in gross national product (GNP) and possibly take over leadership of the international economy, he predicted that the country could not or would not take up the responsibilities of hegemonic leadership. The collapse of communism in the Soviet Union and Eastern Europe and the concomitant end of the Cold War inaugurated a lacklustre decade for Japan, apparently confirming Calder's thesis. Japan did not enter the 1991 military confrontation in the Persian Gulf that affected its vital resource interests and principal strategic alliance. Nor did it exercise decisive leadership in the early stages of the Asian foreign exchange crisis of 1997. Paralysis internationally was mirrored by political and economic immobility at home, which strengthened the common view of the peculiar Japanese penchant for passivity.

Yet Japan has shown some notable initiatives in its foreign policy in recent years. It has identified itself as part of East Asia, and has directed its energies more clearly in that direction. Most prominently, the government proposed the formation of an East Asian version of the International Monetary Fund in order to deal with the 1997 financial crisis, and followed up with the new Miyazawa plan, which ultimately led to the institutionalization of the Chiang Mai Initiative in 2001.

These contrasting perceptions of Japanese leadership cause us to ponder whether the country has been demonstrating any foreign policy leadership in general, or in Japan–East Asian relations in particular, and if so, what kind. Or does Japanese foreign policy continue to react to changes in the strategic environment, especially American pressures? Were more recent policy initiatives undertaken within the traditional parameters of a reactive Japanese foreign policy? Or are other forces at work?

Calder defines a reactive foreign policy as one where "the impetus to policy change is typically supplied by outside pressure, and reaction prevails over strategy in the relatively narrow range of cases where the two come into conflict."[8] A reactive state has two essential characteristics: first, it fails to undertake major independent foreign economic policy initiatives when it has the power and national incentives to do so; and second, it responds to outside pressures for change, albeit erratically, unsystematically, and often incompletely. In particular, Calder stresses, "Despite the importance of the international environment and considerations of state strategy, Japan's reactive behavior in the international political economy of the late 1980s cannot be explained without reference to Japanese domestic social and political structures. Japanese domestic political structure discourages proactive foreign policy behavior in several respects. Perhaps most importantly, the fragmented character of state authority in Japan makes decisive action more difficult than in countries with strong chief executives, such as the United States."[9]

As a corollary, the notion that Japan is a reactive state, a state that only reacts to external pressure and rarely initiates its own foreign policy, has become prevalent in the study of Japanese foreign policy. Let us see how recent studies depict Japanese foreign policy. Akitoshi Miyashita and Yoichiro Sato most systematically examine the reactive foreign policy thesis in their edited book, *Japanese Foreign Policy in Asia and the Pacific*, which presents ten case studies where some cases support the reactive thesis and others do not. Explanations differ even among the cases of reactive foreign policy. For example, analysing Japan's aid policy towards China and Russia, Miyashita reiterates a version of the reactive state thesis: "Japan is responsive to US pressure, but the responsiveness is a result of choice rather than an inability to act on the part of the Japanese government."[10]

Other authors reject the reactive state thesis more fully. For instance, William Long sees Japan as a proactive state in the case of overseas development aid: "Japan's use of foreign assistance for nonproliferation is an important exercise of power to set agendas, shape international norms, define Japan's identity in the international system, and condition the international environment so as to shape other states' preferences."[11] And C. Yeung concludes: "Japan has carefully nurtured the idea of creating an economically integrated Asia in accordance to its agenda. Japan's role in the making of APEC shows the success of its subtle, but persistent, strategy in Southeast Asia."[12]

Accordingly, the contour of the Yoshida Doctrine has changed as most of the self-binding restrictions associated with the doctrine have been modified, as explained succinctly by Kenneth Pyle: "no dispatch of JSDF (Japan Self-Defense Force) abroad, no collective defense arrangements, no power projection ability, no more than 1% of GNP for defense, no nuclear arms, no sharing of military technology, no exporting of arms, no military use of space. Only the nuclear weapons restriction remains untouched."[13]

ALTERNATIVE EXPLANATION OF JAPANESE FOREIGN POLICY

If Japan's foreign policy is not simply reactive, then what is it? Several models have emerged in recent debates, portraying Japan in terms of reluctant realism and indirect leadership.

Reluctant Realism

The strategic circumstances for Japan have changed since the Cold War. The country has found itself in a new regional security environment, but one that is not necessarily safer. Indeed, the development of Chinese economic and military power threatens Japan in ways it did not previously, while

North Korea is now less constrained by China and Russia. Domestically, Japan has undergone a major political shift that has nearly destroyed the old left, but has not led to a new national foreign policy vision. In this changed regional security environment, Japan has established a new principle that informs the conduct of day-to-day foreign policy. That principle is simply that Japan takes more proactive steps to defend its position on the international stage, and that these steps can no longer be defined by the U.S.-Japan alliance or by facile assumptions about economic interdependence alone, even as alliance and economics remain at the core of Japan's world role.[14] Japan is thus more sensitive to relative power relations, particularly vis-à-vis China; more clearly recognizes the importance of security policy; more realistically assesses national economic resources and the need to get more bang for Japan's shrinking diplomatic buck; and defines its role now as a global civilian power.

Japanese foreign policy converges at significant points with U.S. foreign policy, and the alliance between the two remains the indispensable core of Japan's position in the world. But this still allows for more Japanese initiatives than was the case during the Cold War. Economic instruments remain the primary tools of Japanese foreign policy, while constraints on the use of force remain largely in place. An alternative strategic vision to the status quo has yet to emerge, so Japan nevertheless is still pursuing a foreign policy of reluctant realism. Green stresses the need for a new term: "After years of cautious international behavior and paralyzing domestic debates about security policy, a broad consensus is forming that Japan should assert its national interests more forcefully. While there is not yet a coherent strategy, there is an emerging strategic view — a reluctant realism — that is being shaped by the combination of external material changes in Japan's international environment, insecurity about national power resources, and aspirations for a national identity that moves beyond the legacies of World War II."[15]

Thus there is still recognizable continuity in long-term foreign policy. But new trends — a greater focus on the balance of power in Asia, frayed idealism, a more determined push for an independent foreign policy, and a more fluid policymaking process — all mean that it is time to recognize Japan as an independent actor in Northeast Asia and to assess Japanese foreign policy on its own terms. In a similar vein, Richard Samuels conceptualizes the post–Yoshida Doctrine orientation of Japanese foreign policy: "Amid considerable public debate about contours and objectives, a fourth consensus is now brewing, one that, if successful, should enable Japan to exist securely without being either too dependent on the United States or too vulnerable to China. If it succeeds, this 'Goldilocks consensus' (a grand strategy that is not too hard, but not too soft, not too Asian and not too Western) will strike a balance between national strength and national autonomy to create new security options for Japan."[16]

Indirect Leadership

As Alan Rix explains, Japanese leadership is unique: "It is a style of leadership that aims at creating long-term Japanese influence in the region, and has been a successful form of long-standing 'entrepreneurial' leadership that has carved out a regional role for Japan as investor, trader, aid donor and political actor."[17] Indeed, Japan exercises leadership in intensifying regional cooperation in East Asia, with both state and non-state actors playing an influential role. This leadership, however, is not active in the sense that Japanese political or economic leaders publicly engage in agenda setting and push for the implementation of goals defined by Japan. Rather, as the APEC process has shown, Japanese actors lead from behind, engaging in behind-the-scenes mediation and acting as spokesmen for Asian interests at the international level.

Examining the public debate about the East Asian Economic Caucasus in Japan and the country's position towards regionalism in Asia, Verena Blechinger and Jochen Legewie detect "deliberate ambivalence".[18] Japanese opinion-leaders support a middle way for Japan that continues the close relationship with the United States, but also includes stronger integration with Asia and a readiness to take on a leadership role in the region. Japanese foreign policy making is becoming more pluralistic, with an increasing number of actors taking the opportunity to pursue their own policy agendas. The East Asian economic crisis has not terminated East Asian regionalism. Rather, the impact of economic turbulence on individual economies and the awareness of how intertwined Asian economies have become, have changed the wish for further integration into a necessity to prevent similar events in the future, with Japan playing a leading role in this process.[19]

The thesis of indirect leadership also suggests the possibility of "a very distinct and effective form of Japanese leadership", which is akin to "quiet diplomacy" or "selective leadership in Asia".[20] If this is what constitutes the change in Japanese foreign policy, then we could argue that Japan was never completely reactive and passive; as J. Maswood argues, "the 'reactive state' and 'consensual leadership' models have a similar emphasis on low-key diplomacy but are substantially different".[21] The reactive state is constrained by competing bureaucratic claims to policymaking, whereas consensual leadership allows for purposive foreign policy behaviour carried out in a particular way. In recent years, moreover, Calder's assessment of Japan's role in East Asia has somewhat changed: "It would most likely be hard for Japan to be a leader in the classical proactive Western sense within the current structure of Pacific relations. Yet, the Japanese conception of leadership is distinctive. It is a paradigm of the leader as conciliator, broker, and behind-the-scenes mediator. In that respect, as demonstrated in the Cambodian case, there is substantial scope for Japan to take a larger role in the future."[22]

These characterizations of Japanese foreign policy suggest that Japan has outgrown the Yoshida Doctrine and reactive foreign policy. In Maswood's view, "To the extent that we can identify divergent Japanese interests in pursuing an increased regional role, it is necessary to further modify the reactive state thesis to suit the new conditions. Recognizing that the Japanese government has ambitions of an expanded presence within the region, it still must balance these with the important objective of maintaining close links with the US. In that context, it is appropriate to depict emerging Japanese regional diplomacy as active but constrained."[23]

IMPLICATIONS FOR JAPAN'S ASEAN POLICY

As many observers note, the greatest innovations in Japan's multilateral policy have occurred in relation to Asia. The Cambodian peace process, which provided the venue for the first overseas dispatch of Self Defense Forces personnel, illustrates the potential benefits of Japan's multilateral diplomacy. It allows Japan to play an honest broker role. Indeed, Southeast Asia has been a key region for Japanese foreign policy activism, the area "where Japan has made its most pronounced attempt to establish a different identity from US foreign policy".[24]

Indeed, Japan's diplomatic initiatives in Southeast Asia also have a distinct style: an emphasis on playing a bridging role between regional rivalries, a willingness to promote multilateralism while respecting consensus diplomacy, and a pragmatic realist approach to the promotion of democracy and human rights in the region. As one scholar cogently puts it, "Japan has behaved strategically in its use of economic power vis-à-vis the USA and East Asia. In securing an external environment for its survival and prosperity, Japan has been remarkably strategic and successful."[25]

Therefore, Japan's Southeast Asian policy as the most successful post-war Japanese foreign policy, could provide a prima facie case for the alternative stream. Two elements are worth noting here: the Fukuda Doctrine as a proactive multilateral foreign policy and Japanese-style multilateral diplomacy.

The Fukuda Doctrine as a Proactive Foreign Policy

The Fukuda Doctrine, the first doctrine as such in Japanese foreign policy to be proclaimed by the government, formally states three commitments to Southeast Asia: (1) Japan rejects the role of a military power, (2) Japan will do its best to consolidate the relationship of mutual confidence and trust based on "heart-to-heart" understanding, and (3) Japan will be an equal partner of ASEAN, while attempting to foster mutual understanding with the nations of Indochina. Thus, the three pillars of Japan's Southeast Asian policy may be characterized as having a non-military, cultural and political orientation.[26]

There are three reasons for Japan's active involvement in the region after the promulgation of the doctrine. First, it was because of a declining American security role in the region that the doctrine established a systematic framework for Japan's political conduct in the region, replacing the earlier unregulated process of decision-making regarding policies towards Southeast Asia. Secondly, since the declaration of the doctrine, the Japanese government has actively developed its contacts with ASEAN as a viable regional organization, as evidenced in Japan's support for regional projects, the establishment of a fund for cultural exchange, and regular conferences between Japan and ASEAN's foreign ministers. As such, many political issues have been coordinated through these networks, as well as through the efforts of official envoys sent by Japan to Southeast Asia, an action that had not been considered prior to the enunciation of the doctrine. Thirdly, Japan's policies towards North-South problems have become more constructive since 1978, with the heightening of political pressure from ASEAN and the approach of the fifth United Nations Conference on Trade and Development in Manila.

Why is this then significant? Beginning in 1977 the Japanese government made it a rule to match its support to ASEAN's regional efforts. In particular, when ASEAN celebrates its decade of regional cooperation by holding a summit, Japan announces its "doctrine" as if both events were repeated every ten years, as Table 1.1 amply suggests.

Thus, as the origin of Japan's proactive multilateral foreign policy, the Fukuda Doctrine can be reinterpreted. In fact, the Fukuda Doctrine is considered by some foreign ministry officials as the "real starting point of Japan's post-war diplomacy".[27]

Japanese-style of Multilateral Diplomacy

As Dennis Yasutomo argues, Japanese multilateral diplomacy from the late 1990s, though low-key, is not stagnant but rather active. The question is whether this dynamism constitutes leadership. If we define leadership as setting the international agenda and establishing the rules of the game, Japan has a long way to go. However, it can try to establish footholds in niches such as multilateral institutions, the Asian region, and the environment.[28]

In evaluating Japan's diplomacy in the post-war period, much has been written about Japan's multilateralism not only at the global level such as the United Nations and Group of Eight, but also at the regional level such as the Economic Commission for Asia and the Far East and the Asian Development Bank. In fact, soon after entering the United Nations, Japan set forth its three diplomatic pillars to which it still adheres: a UN-centred

TABLE 1.1
ASEAN's Four Decades and Japan

	1977	1987	1997	2007
ASEAN	10th Anniversary Framing the Region via TAC	20th Anniversary Economic Cooperation	30th Anniversary ASEAN Ten and East Asia	40th Anniversary ASEAN Community and Charter
External Relations	Japan Australia New Zealand	Japan	Japan China South Korea	APT EAS

diplomacy, cooperation with the free (democratic) world, and membership in the Asian community, as specified in the first Diplomatic Bluebook published in 1957. Without any doubt, these principles are all related to the ideals of Japanese diplomacy on multilateralism at both the global and regional level. However, Japanese diplomacy has been constrained since Japan entered into an alliance with the United States while maintaining a national constitution that does not recognize the right of belligerency. A small resource-scarce country, such as Japan, had no option but to follow the dictate of the United States.

In this sense, Japan's policy towards its neighbouring countries in the 1990s was characterized by a tendency towards multilateralism that sought frameworks for dialogue, including security issues.[29] This enthusiasm for multilateral security dialogues in the Asia-Pacific was a result of changing perceptions about bilateral relationships between each country in this region and the United States. Regional-level and global-level multilateralism such as that found in the United Nations, exists in parallel, while most countries allied with the United States in Asia understand the importance of bilateralism; their hub-and-spoke relations are with the United States.

In understanding the Japanese style of multilateralism, two major works by Dennis Yasutomo and Akiko Fukushima are worth noting here. In his pioneering study, Yasutomo explained Japan's active involvement in the regional multilateral institutions.[30] Focusing on three multilateral development banks as a medium for reconsidering prevailing models of the Japanese foreign-policy-making process and the so-called "reactive state" model, he concluded that whilst Japan's foreign policy is moving away from the Yoshida Doctrine and towards taking a higher profile, more assertive, proactive character, it still remains essentially reactive. Yasutomo's attempt was unique in that for the first time the focus was on multilateralism as an element in Japanese foreign policy. According to Yasutomo, multilateralism is the key to the analysis of a reactive-proactive dichotomy. Japanese foreign policy continued to evolve from a reactive state to a more active posture as it attempted to take on a more responsible leadership role among the Organization for Economic Cooperation and Development states and as an intermediary between those states and Asia. If Japan is going to take on a leadership role, regionally or globally, it will necessarily be within a multilateral context.

Fukushima, on the other hand, focuses on Japan's involvement in multilateral institutions and organizations. The main case study deals with Japan's participation in UN activities. She argues that the post–Cold War international environment has given a new lease of life to the rather vacuous phrase "UN-centred diplomacy". Her second case study is on emerging multilateralism in the Asia-Pacific. According to Fukushima, Japan's contribution has been relatively low-key, in part inhibited by memories of its past wartime action, but by operationalizing the concept of cooperative security, Japan may find the route to a higher profile. Fukushima concluded that the era of passive Japanese foreign policy has come to an end.[31]

It is true that Japan's Asian policy began to change in the post–Cold War period. The process of metamorphosis was fuelled by the loosening unipolarity of the United States. As Takashi Inoguchi explains, it is the undermining of the foundations of Japanese and U.S. economic power, and the rise of China, that have prompted Japan to revamp its Asian policy in two major directions. First, it seeks to redress what it perceives as excesses in U.S. unipolarity by multilateralizing its own diplomatic initiatives. Second, awareness of its steadily shrinking economic resources made available for its foreign policy, has led Japan to make more effective use of what resources it does have, requiring the Japanese government to activate the power of ideas and institutions.[32]

ANALYTICAL FRAMEWORK

There are three main factors that constitute Japan's ASEAN policy: ideas, institutions and proactive multilateralism.

Ideas

In this book, ideas are defined as shared beliefs.[33] Ideas are socially constructed because they come from the international and domestic societies in which states are embedded. The point to stress here is that ideas are closely related to material or social reality. As Alexander Wendt has argued, "power and interest have the effects they do in virtue of the ideas that make them up".[34] In other words, ideas give direction, intentionality and purpose to power. When ideas or knowledge become consensual, they would be expected to help decision-makers define their interests. Then, politicians and bureaucrats use their power to translate idea-based interests into policy and programmes.

As a standard definition, Judith Goldstein and Robert Keohane posit a tripartite distinction between different types of ideas, namely, principled beliefs, causal beliefs, and world views, and suggest different effects for each type of idea. Principled beliefs are seen as the normative bases and justifications for particular decisions, while "causal beliefs imply strategies for the attainment of goals because of shared principles". World views, on the other hand, are the entire cognitive framework of an agent and/or cultural repertoires of entire groups and classes. In terms of their impact on policy, three points are worth noting here. First, ideas are seen as functional devices to promote cooperation among agents whose interests are "given" but not yet realizable. Second, ideas become "focal points" for convergence in conditions of multiple equilibriums. Third, ideas are seen as "the normative context that helps define the interests of actors".[35]

The behaviour of states usually not only responds to changes in the international distribution of power but is also reflected in ideational factors such as culture, identities and norms. Ideational factors are usually path-dependent and change slowly and incrementally. Ideas change when the consequences of external shock cast doubt on their ability to interpret political reality. If such discrepancies transpire, it stimulates a critical evaluation and the demands for a reassessment of the prevailing ideas. When such challenges of ideas occur, states react in three different ways: resistance, localization and transformation.[36]

In undertaking a case study based on the ideational approach, the following three features provide a useful framework for exploring how and why ideas affect behaviour of states. First, ideas can be created and changed at certain critical junctures. Critical junctures are defined as major shocks or crises that disrupt the status quo. They generally imply moments of significant change, since external shocks and challenges call into question the existing rules of the game.[37] Second, ideas as road maps explain the sequence of evolutionary processes, particularly in answering why one particular cooperative solution was chosen; shared beliefs act as road maps around which the behaviour of actors converge. Shared beliefs and road maps, however, do not always emerge without conscious efforts on the part of interested actors. Third, the institutionalization of ideas explains sustainability of specific policies and programmes. This means that once ideas are embedded in rules and norms, they constrain policy because they are difficult to dislodge. Thus ideas embedded in institutions specify policy in the absence of innovation by affecting the incentive structures of political actors.[38]

How could ideas be institutionalized and influence policy? The causal effect of ideas on policy is not easily identified, and the measurement of it poses problems for causal modelling. Nevertheless, it can be illustrated by the following case. Japanese political agents such as the Ministry of Foreign Affairs (MOFA) and the Ministry of Economy, Trade and Industry (METI) assisted the institutionalization of ideas through organizational routines. Organizations develop routines based on standard operating procedures and rules. Accordingly, ideas that became embedded in political institutions are well recognized as exerting a critical influence on policy outcomes. As such, in the process of ideational evolution, institutions play a significant role because "powerful individuals are important in the adopting of ideas, but if these ideas do not find institutional homes, they will not be able to sustain themselves over the long term".[39]

Institutions

For all practical reasons, the ruling party monopolizes control of the government, including the process of policy making, yet it relies heavily on senior career bureaucrats for the initiation and implementation of specific foreign policies. Among the various policy-making institutions, MOFA is one of the most influential actors. Within MOFA, the North American Affairs Bureau is the most powerful simply because it supervises the pivotal bilateral relationship with the United States. The second most powerful bureau is the Asian Affairs Bureau, which clashes frequently with the North American Affairs Bureau, reflecting Japan's dual and occasionally conflicting interests with regard to the United States and East Asia.[40]

Moreover, due to the autonomy bestowed upon each ministry, the policymaking process in Japan is highly compartmentalized, thus provoking inter-bureaucratic rivalry. For instance, the infighting over the allocation of national budgets between the Ministry of Finance (MOF) and MOFA is common; the former strives to avoid any action requiring increased expenditure of public funds and thus increase the burden of the national treasury, while the latter advocates an "internationalist" posture of increasing foreign assistance. The Ministry of International Trade and Industry (MITI) also has conflicting interests vis-à-vis MOFA in international economic policy, since MITI's mission is to carry out export promotion drives through foreign economic assistance. Although the functions of these institutions have been well analysed with respect to foreign assistance policy, much less is known concerning their role in Japan–Southeast Asia relations.[41]

The role of institutions in Japanese policymaking has also changed over time. Foreign aid policy, for instance, has been subject to four rival institutions: MOFA, MITI, MOF and the Economic Planning Agency. While MOFA aims at increasing bilateral aid in harmony with Japan's foreign policy objectives, MITI tends to facilitate business interests through tied loans. Through the administrative reforms, however, the four-player system changed substantially in 2001. Now that the Economic Planning Agency has been dissolved, MOFA, MOF and METI share the responsibility for Japan's foreign aid. Accordingly, METI — previously known as MITI — gave up publishing its white paper on foreign aid.[42]

It is also important to note here that rival institutions, like MOFA and MITI, are often involved in the process of regional institution building. APEC in 1989 was a case in point. MOFA or *Gaimusho*, in particular, was characteristically sensitive to ASEAN's wariness of Pacific-wide institutions, and complained that MITI's proposal would limit discussion to trade and investment. Most importantly, "*Gaimusho* could not put up with MITI intruding into their jealously guarded turf, Asian diplomacy".[43] The rivalry between METI and the Ministry of Agriculture over free trade negotiations is another case. While the former advocates greater trade liberalization, the latter strongly opposes the liberalization of agricultural products, especially rice, which once jeopardized APEC's free trade negotiations in 1998.[44]

Since the Cold War, MOF has occupied a critical place in the Japanese foreign policy process, which was traditionally controlled by MOFA and MITI. With its strong confidence in economic development, to wit, the 1993 publication of *East Asian Miracle*, for instance, the Finance Ministry has begun to seek regional policies. Without the quiet cultivation of financial cooperation with ASEAN since 1994, the proposal for the Asian Monetary Fund in 1997 would not have been possible. Due to the stormy financial crisis in 1997, MOF was able to seize the opportunity to play a larger role in directing financial cooperation in East Asia.[45]

Proactive Multilateralism

Since the core focus of this study is on regional multilateralism, the term multilateralism needs to be defined clearly. Multilateralism is a demanding form of international cooperation, which requires a strong sense of collective identity as well as shared interests between the member states. In contrast to bilateralism, multilateral engagement is a form of foreign policy engagement where each member state is given equal representative status. Thus, multilateralism is generally defined as being a coordinated behaviour among three or more states on the basis of defined principles of conduct. Much of the literature on multilateralism focuses on its significance in providing states a forum for coordinating behaviour among its members on the basis of operating principles of conduct.

Multilateralism, according to John Ruggie, is "an institutional form that coordinates relations among three or more states on the basis of generalized principles of conduct", that is, principles which specify appropriate conduct for a class of actions without regard to the particularistic interests of the parties. Its key elements are (1) generalized principles of conduct, (2) indivisibility, and (3) reciprocity.[46] Generalized principles of conduct refer to the belief that policies and activities "ought to be organized on a universal basis, at least for the group concerned. Indivisibility means that decisions made within the multilateral arrangement are binding upon those involved and that a small number of participants cannot block decisions. Reciprocity means that the members expect that the arrangement will "yield a rough equivalence of benefits in the aggregate and over time".

In a more flexible way, Keohane defines multilateralism as "the practice of coordinating national policies in groups of three or more states, through ad hoc arrangements or by means of institutions".[47] Given the ad hoc arrangement, this definition can be applied to Japan-ASEAN relations since Japan is not a member of ASEAN. Why does non-member Japan pursue ASEAN policy? The reason can be found in the benefits of multilateralism, for states find there are advantages in the multilateral process that make it worth pursuing. These advantages include: (1) a state's opportunity to be heard in the process of negotiating or resolving issues; (2) states are given a chance to develop a positive reputation within the membership of states they engage with; (3) states can become part of a community of members that share common interests and identity; (4) states can build a record of credibility; (5) states can contribute to the policymaking process by developing creative incentives for cooperation; (6) states can downplay individualistic approaches; (7) states can engage in leadership positions; (8) states can assess the motives and circumstances of other states; and finally, (9) states can present themselves as part of a democratic process of representation.[48]

There is another incentive for Japan to pursue regional multilateralism because multilateralism can be sought as a counterweight to dependence on the bilateral relationship with the United States. Japan's efforts to influence multilateral institutions have increased in the post–Cold War era, with the ultimate symbol of multilateral influence being a permanent seat on the Security Council. For instance, the U.S.-Japan collision over the Asian Monetary Fund proposal reflected Tokyo's overestimation of its own influence in the international financial order and Washington's underestimation of the need to share leadership of the international economy with Japan. As Green explains, "Japan, eager to play a larger leadership role in the international financial institutions commensurate with its financial contribution, announces a major proposal, backed by promises of billions of dollars of Japanese financing, but vague in the details."[49]

In this study, Japan's ASEAN policy is deemed as proactive multilateralism mainly because proactivity assumes that Japan has its own ideas, interests, and policy objectives. Its policies are not based solely on the expectations of foreign countries nor in response to direct foreign pressure. As Yasutomo contends, Japan is purposive and decisive and its policy process is not afflicted with immobilism. It has a clear conception of its national interests, it knows what it wants, and it seeks to mobilize its citizens and national resources to attain its objectives through the alteration of the external environment. Japan acts rather than reacts.[50]

CONCLUSION

Writing in 2004, Julie Gilson underscored the development of a new and important strand of Japanese foreign policy behaviour: the growing centrality of a regional multilateralism in the face of greater acquiescence from regional partners themselves. The opportunity now exists for the Japanese government — as its rhetoric already promises — to "strategize" its approaches towards Southeast Asia and to begin to define some of the structures that have been prematurely discerned by scholars of its foreign policy.[51]

The argument in this study is quite simple in that Japanese foreign policy towards ASEAN is a typical example of successful multilateral diplomacy. It is uniquely proactive because the Japanese government provided added policy incentives to buttress ASEAN's regional efforts at the critical stages of 1977, 1987, 1997 and 2007. It is thus safe to say that a history of Japan-ASEAN relations is a history of post-war Japan's gaining confidence in exercising proactive multilateralism in East Asia.

Notes

1. For general descriptions of Japanese foreign policy in the post-war period, see Sueo Sudo, *Kokka no taigaikodo* (Tokyo: Tokyodaigaku shuppankai, 2007), chap. 6 and Naoki Ono, *Nihon no taigaikodo* (Kyoto: Mineruba shobo, 2011), chap. 4.

2. Glen Hook, Julie Gilson, Christopher Hughes and Helen Dobson, *Japan's International Relations* (London: Routledge, 2001) and Michael Green, *Japan's Reluctant Realism: Foreign Policy Challenge in an Era of Uncertain Power* (New York: Palgrave, 2001). For a review, see David Potter and Sueo Sudo, "Japanese Foreign Policy: No Longer Reactive?" *Political Studies Review* 1, no. 3 (2003): 317–32.

3. Donald Hellmann, "Japanese Politics and Foreign Policy: Elitist Democracy within an American Greenhouse", in *The Political Economy of Japan: The Changing International Context*, edited by Takashi Inoguchi and Daniel Okimoto (Stanford: Stanford University Press, 1988), pp. 356, 358. For the evolution of post-war Japanese foreign policy, see Makoto Iokibe, ed., *Sengo Nihon gaikoshi* (Tokyo: Yuhikaku, 1999), Toshikazu Inoue, *Nihon no gaiko* (Tokyo: Shinzansha, 2005) and Kazuhiko Togo, *Japan's Foreign Policy 1945–2009: The Quest for a Proactive Policy* (Boston: Brill, 2010).

4. Masataka Kosaka, "Nihon gaiko no bensho", in *Koza kokusai seiji*, vol. 4, edited by Tadashi Aruga et al. (Tokyo: Tokyodaigaku shuppankai, 1989), p. 299. For major works on the Yoshida Doctrine, see Masataka Kosaka, *Saisho Yoshida Shigeru* (Tokyo: Chuokoronsha, 1968) and Kenneth Pyle, *The Japanese Question: Power and Purpose in a New Era* (Washington, DC: AEI Press, 1992).

5. Yonosuke Nagai, *Gendai to senryaku* (Tokyo: Bungei shunju, 1985).

6. Masashi Nishihara, "How Much Longer the Fruits of the 'Yoshida Doctrine'?" in *Korea and Japan: A New Dialogue across the Channel*, edited by Hahn Bae-ho and Yamamoto Tadashi (Seoul: Asiatic Research Center, Korea University, 1978), p. 155.

7. Kent Calder, "Japanese Foreign Economic Policy Formation: Explaining the 'Reactive State'", *World Politics* 40, no. 4 (July 1988): 517–41.

8. Ibid., p. 518.

9. Ibid., p. 528.

10. Akitoshi Miyashita, "Consensus or Compliance? Gaiatsu, Interests, and Japan's Foreign Aid", in *Japanese Foreign Policy in Asia and the Pacific*, edited by Akitoshi Miyashita and Yoichiro Sato (New York: Palgrave, 2001), p. 58.

11. William Long, "Nonproliferation as a Goal of Japanese Foreign Assistance", in *Japanese Foreign Policy in Asia and the Pacific*, edited by Akitoshi Miyashita and Yoichiro Sato (New York: Palgrave, 2001), p. 130.
12. C.K. Yueng, "Japan's Role in the Making of the Asia-Pacific Economic Cooperation (APEC)", in *Japanese Foreign Policy in Asia and the Pacific*, edited by Akitoshi Miyashita and Yoichiro Sato (New York: Palgrave, 2001), p. 138.
13. Kenneth Pyle, "The Primacy of Foreign Policy in Modern Japan", *Asian Policy*, no. 4 (July 2007), p. 209.
14. Green, *Japan's Reluctant Realism*, pp. 31–32.
15. Ibid., p. 8.
16. Richard Samuels, *Securing Japan: Tokyo's Grand Strategy and the Future of East Asia* (Ithaca, NY: Cornell University Press, 2007), p. 9.
17. Alan Rix, "Japan and the Region: Leadership from Behind", in *Pacific Economic Relations in the 1990s*, edited by Richard Higgott, Richard Leaver and John Ravenhill (Boulder, CO: Rienner, 1993), p. 65.
18. Verena Blechinger, "Flirting with Regionalism: Japan's Foreign Policy Elites and the East Asian Economic Caucus", in *Facing Asia: Japan's Role in the Political Economic Dynamism of Regional Cooperation*, edited by Verena Blechinger and Jochen Legewie (Munchen: Iudicium-Verl, 2001), p. 69.
19. Glenn Hook, "The Japanese Role in the Emerging Asia-Pacific Order", in *Facing Asia: Japan's Role in the Political Economic Dynamism of Regional Cooperation*, edited by Verena Blechinger and Jochen Legewie (Munchen: Iudicium-Verl, 2001), pp. 80–82.
20. See Hook et.al., *Japan's International Relations* and Min Wan, *Japan between Asia and the West* (Armonk: Sharpe, 2001).
21. S. Javed Maswood, "Japanese Foreign Policy and Regionalism", in *Japan and East Asian Regionalism*, edited by S. Javed Maswood (London: Routledge, 2001), p. 22.
22. Ibid., p. 19.
23. S. Javed Maswood, "Conclusion", in *Japan and East Asian Regionalism*, edited by S. Javed Maswood (London: Routledge, 2001), p. 134.
24. Green, *Japan's Reluctant Realism*, p. 167.
25. Wan, *Japan between Asia*, pp. 7–8.
26. Sueo Sudo, *The Fukuda Doctrine and ASEAN: New Dimensions in Japanese Foreign Policy* (Singapore: Institute of Southeast Asian Studies, 1992).
27. Akio Watanabe, *Ajia Taiheiyo no Kokusaikankei to Nihon* (Tokyo: Tokyodaigaku shuppankai, 1992), p. 114.
28. Denis Yasutomo, "Japan's Multilateral Assistance Leadership: Momentum or Malaise?" in *Facing Asia: Japan's Role in the Political Economic Dynamism of Regional Cooperation*, edited by Verena Blechinger and Jochen Legewie (Munchen: Iudicium-Verl, 2001), p. 145.

29. For one of the major studies on Japan's multilateral foreign policy, see Philippe Regnier, ed., *Japan and Multilateral Diplomacy* (Aldershot: Ashgate, 2001).

30. Denis Yasutomo, *The New Multilateralism in Japan's Foreign Policy* (New York: St. Martin's, 1995).

31. Akiko Fukushima, *Japanese Foreign Policy: The Emerging Logic of Multilateralism* (London: Macmillan, 1999), p. 169.

32. Takashi Inoguchi, "Japan Goes Regional", in *Japan's Asian Policy*, edited by Takashi Inoguchi (New York: Palgrave Macmillan, 2002), p. 8.

33. Judith Goldstein, *Ideas, Interests, and American Trade Policy* (Ithaca, NY: Cornell University Press, 1993), pp. 9–13.

34. Alexander Wendt, *Social Theory of International Politics* (Cambridge: Cambridge University Press, 1999), p. 135.

35. Judith Goldstein and Robert Keohane, eds., *Ideas and Foreign Policy: Beliefs, Institutions and Political Change* (Ithaca, NY: Cornell University Press, 1993).

36. Amitav Acharya, *Whose Ideas Matter? Agency and Power in Asian Regionalism* (Ithaca, NY: Cornell University Press, 2009), p. 18; Satoshi Oyane, *Kokusai rejimu to Nichi Bei no gaiko koso* (Tokyo: Yuhikaku, 2012), pp. 11–13.

37. John Campbell, *Institutional Change and Globalization* (Princeton, NJ: Princeton University Press, 2004), p. 68.

38. Goldstein and Keohane, *Ideas and Foreign Policy*, pp. 13–24.

39. Kathryn Sikkink, *Ideas and Institutions: Developmentalism in Argentina and Brazil* (Ithaca, NY: Cornell University Press, 1991), p. 248.

40. Hook et al., *Japan's International Relations*, p. 44.

41. On policymaking institutions in Japan, see Kent Calder, "The Institutions of Japanese Foreign Policy", in *The Process of Japanese Foreign Policy: Focus on Asia*, edited by Richard Grant (London: Royal Institute of International Affairs, 1997), pp. 1–24.

42. Regarding Japan's foreign aid, see Akitoshi Miyashita, *Limits to Power: Asymmetric Dependence and Japanese Foreign Aid Policy* (Lanham, MD: Lexington Books, 2003) and Yasutami Shimomura, *Kaihatsuenjo seisaku* (Tokyo: Nihon keizai hyoron sha, 2011).

43. Yoichi Funabashi, *Asia Pacific Fusion: Japan's Role in APEC* (Washington, DC: Institute for International Economics, 1995), p. 213.

44. See especially Jiro Okamoto, ed., *Trade Liberalization and APEC* (London: Routledge, 2004).

45. See Shigeko Hayashi, *Japan and East Asian Monetary Regionalism: Towards a Proactive Leadership* (London: Routledge, 2006).

46. John Ruggie, ed., *Multilateralism Matters: The Theory and Praxis of an Institutional Form* (New York: Columbia University Press, 1993), pp. 10–14.

47. Robert Keohane, "Multilateralism: An Agenda for Research", *International Journal* 45, no. 4 (Autumn 1990): 731–64.

48. James Caporaso, "International Relations Theory and Multilateralism: The Search for Foundations", *International Organization* 46, no. 3 (Summer 1992): 599–632.

49. Green, *Japan's Reluctant Realism*, p. 264.

50. Yasutomo, *The New Multilateralism*, p. 57.

51. Julie Gilson, "Complex Regional Multilateralism: 'Strategising' Japan's Response to Southeast Asia", *Pacific Review* 17, no. 1 (2004): 91.

2

EMBARKING ON
JAPAN'S ASEAN POLICY:
The Limitation of the Mainstream

Immediately after the war, how could Japan secure the freedom of action to advance into Southeast Asia again when ill feelings towards the nation were prevalent? The answer seems to lie in the process of mutual persuasion between Japanese and U.S. decision-makers, who incorporated Prime Minister Shigeru Yoshida's "economics above all" principles and Washington's "superdomino" metaphor, bridging the two with the concept of U.S.-Japan economic cooperation.[1] Consequently, a triangular, mutually reinforcing relationship among the United States, Japan, and Southeast Asia had come into existence and had become integral to American objectives in Asia, as the Joint Chiefs of Staff cogently put it in July 1952:

> United States objectives with respect to Southeast Asia and United States objectives with respect to Japan would appear to be inseparably related. Moreover, the Joint Chiefs of Staff are of the opinion that Japan's security and Western orientation are of such importance to the United States position in the Pacific area that (1) in the implementation of NSC 125/1 and NSC 124/2 the United States must take into account Japan's dependence upon Southeast Asia for her economic well-being, and (2) the

loss of Southeast Asia to the Western World would almost inevitably force
Japan into an eventual accommodation with the Communist controlled
area in Asia.[2]

For Prime Minister Yoshida, U.S.-protected Southeast Asia was simply
a region of abundant natural resources and of lucrative markets for
Japanese products. The region was all the more important for the Yoshida
government as a means through which to bring about economic success
at home, which in turn could guarantee a conservative party's dominance
in Japanese politics. In other words, Southeast Asia was an integral part
of the Yoshida Doctrine, which consisted of three principles of foreign
policy: (1) minimum defence, (2) economic development at home and
economic diplomacy abroad as the ultimate goal, and (3) the separation
of politics from economics. However, the very success of the Yoshida
Doctrine brought home the fact that Japan's economic diplomacy needed
a complete reappraisal in the early 1970s. Through stormy anti-Japanese
movements, Japanese foreign policy was forced to make a gradual shift
from bilateral to multilateral relations. Why and how did Japan decide to
shift its foreign policy orientation? The answer can be found rather easily
if we carefully examine the very first decade of Japan-ASEAN relations.

SOUTHEAST ASIAN REGIONALISM AND ASEAN

Emerging Regionalism in Southeast Asia

The origins of ASEAN cannot be understood without referring to the
decolonization of Southeast Asia in the 1950s and early 1960s, which
were affected by power games at the international level. The experience
of colonialism deeply affected how the states of Southeast Asia perceived
the regional environment. To differing degrees, the leaders of the region
saw the international system as predatory, with powerful states waiting
to exploit the internal weaknesses of other states. This perception of
external threats played a fundamental role in the shaping of regionalism
in Southeast Asia.[3]

Thus, when the first Indochina war broke out between France and
Vietnam, Washington intervened on behalf of France, albeit in a limited way.
The defeat of France at Dien Bien Phu came as a shock to Washington, which
felt compelled to create the Southeast Asian Treaty Organization (SEATO)
in 1954. Although only Thailand and the Philippines joined SEATO, a
rigid American containment policy left little room for Southeast Asian

countries to adjust their own *raison d'etre*, apart from Sukarno's Indonesia and isolated Burma, who organized the first Asia-Africa conference in 1955, better known as the Bandung Conference. Thus, a polarization of Southeast Asia along the lines of East-West rivalry was firmly established, continuing even after the outbreak of the Indochina War between the United States and Vietnam in 1965.

During the early 1960s, two indigenous regional organizations, the Association of Southeast Asia (ASA) and Malaya-Philippines-Indonesia (Maphilindo), were established in 1961 and 1963 respectively. The members of ASA were Malaya, the Philippines, and Thailand. The first indigenous ASA was heralded by many as a milestone in the history of Southeast Asian regionalism. ASEAN's norms can be traced to its institutional predecessor.[4] However, ASA was eventually paralysed by a territorial dispute between Malaya and the Philippines. To fill the void, Maphilindo was proclaimed in August 1963 but also derailed a month later with the formation of the Federation of Malaysia. The Philippines did not recognize Malaysia because of the Sabah dispute. Indonesia vehemently opposed this situation; Sukarno viewed Britain's creation of Malaysia as the case of an imperial power imposing its will and as a result used force against Malaysia. This resulted in Sukarno's *Konfrontasi* policy, which strengthened the impression that the non-interference principle was key to regional stability.[5]

The outbreak of the 30 September incident was a turning point in Southeast Asian regionalism. Sukarno's adventurous *Konfrontasi* caused a heavy toll, as the Indonesian Army, headed by Major General Soeharto, used the opportunity to conduct a massive purge of actual and suspected communists, whom they blamed for the coup. With the Indonesian Communist Party decimated, Soeharto was able to seize the presidency from Sukarno in March 1966 and quickly began to overturn the latter's foreign policies, including renouncing *Konfrontasi*. The change was apparent in the perception of regional leaders who came to recognize the fact that domestic strife could have regional spillover effects, and left them eager to avoid future interference in their domestic affairs, whether from within the region or without.

The Birth of ASEAN

Therefore, as an extension of these indigenous attempts, a loosely structured ASEAN was formed on 8 August 1967, comprising Indonesia, Malaysia, the

Philippines, Singapore and Thailand.[6] Reflecting on the changing nature of regional politics, the goals of ASEAN were rather vaguely spelled out in the Bangkok Declaration:

1. To accelerate the economic growth, social progress and cultural development in the region through joint endeavours in the spirit of equality and partnership in order to strengthen the foundation for a prosperous and peaceful community of Southeast Asian Nations;
2. To promote regional peace and stability through abiding respect for justice and the rule of law in the relationship among countries of the region and adherence to the principles of the United Nations Charter;
3. To promote active collaboration and mutual assistance on matters of common interest in the economic, social, cultural, technical, scientific and administrative fields;
4. To provide assistance to each other in the form of training and research facilities in the educational, professional, technical and administrative spheres;
5. To collaborate more effectively for the greater utilization of their agriculture and industries, the expansion of their trade, including the study of the problems of international commodity trade, the improvement of their transportation and communications facilities and the raising of the living standards of their peoples;
6. To promote Southeast Asian studies;
7. To maintain close and beneficial cooperation with existing international and regional organizations with similar aims and purposes, and explore all avenues for even closer cooperation among themselves.[7]

Without any doubt, the formation of ASEAN was not based on consensus on the part of five constituting members. For Indonesia, joining ASEAN was an opportunity to rebuild trust within the region and take on a leadership role. Malaysia regarded ASEAN as providing a measure of insurance against intra-regional conflict, which was also highlighted by the announcement by the British of the withdrawal of their military from Southeast Asia. The Philippines believed that its membership in an indigenous regional organization would enable it to share more fully in Asian political and economic interactions by helping to offset its heavy dependence on the United States. For Singapore, the problem of the British withdrawal was even more pressing as its size made it vulnerable to attack. Thus the republic saw ASEAN membership as a means to wield greater influence in the region and improve its tense relations with Malaysia. Thailand's intent was to join ASEAN to promote regional collective security with special emphasis on its three Indochinese neighbours.[8]

Although five members had different reasons to join, they subscribed to the rationale of the organization. In fact, since the immediate task for ASEAN was the development of a basis for mutual trust among member states, the Bangkok Declaration did not specify a mechanism for formal dealings regarding regional issues and external powers. The diplomatic rupture between Malaysia and the Philippines caused by the Sabah debacle in 1968 is a case in point. As such, this earlier sub-regional organization was inward looking and did not produce any tangible results until the First ASEAN Summit in 1976, with the exception of a symbolic agreement in November 1971 to pursue a Zone of Peace, Freedom and Neutrality (ZOPFAN).[9] The fact that all member states but Indonesia had foreign bases and supported American aims in Vietnam clearly indicated the nature and limits of the Association. Economically, both ASEAN and non-ASEAN states alike relied upon their patron's assistance and market for their products, in effect strengthening polarization of the region as well as bilateralism.

PRIMACY OF BILATERAL RELATIONS COURTED BY THE YOSHIDA DOCTRINE

When ASEAN was launched in August 1967, the Japanese government looked favourably on the prospect that the Association might invite Japan to join.[10] Whilst this did not happen as ASEAN was identified as an indigenous regional organization, Japanese officials regarded its formation as an affirmation of growing Southeast Asian regionalism, thus giving tacit encouragement to Tokyo's regional development strategy. On the other hand, the Japanese public was totally indifferent to ASEAN and the mass media responded in a relatively negative way. A major economic newspaper *Nihon Keizai Shimbun* stated: "ASEAN could become a pressure group of primary producers."[11] As such, the Japanese did not take ASEAN seriously, and with ASEAN's rejection of Japan's membership, Tokyo's officials turned to the Ministerial Conference for the Economic Development of Southeast Asia, established in March 1966, for Japanese initiatives, and to bilateral relations with Indonesia as the focus of Japanese policy towards the region.[12]

In fact, after Japan regained its independence in 1952, Japan's foreign policy in general and its Southeast Asian policy in particular was predicated on improving bilateral relations.[13] In December 1953 the Yoshida government announced its basic policy for "economic aid" to Southeast Asia in a Cabinet decision that stressed the following seven goals:

1.   To integrate various organizations related to Southeast Asia into the Asia Society, which shall undertake overall research, technical cooperation, and advertisement in order to avoid generating an image of Japan's economic intervention under the name of economic cooperation.
2.   To promote exchanges and training of technicians by concluding official technical accords.
3.   To smooth economic cooperation by avoiding dual taxation.
4.   To preserve the necessary capital and activate the Export-Import Bank in order to promote the exportation of plants, which is the core of economic cooperation.
5.   To take into consideration measures to waive taxes whenever necessary.
6.   To maintain close contact with counterpart agencies in Asian countries and the UN-related agencies.
7.   To undertake the reparations negotiations in good faith to restore diplomatic relations with the recipient countries.[14]

Subsequently, the utmost efforts were devoted to achieving "economic" foreign policy, directed particularly towards the countries of Southeast Asia, whose demands for Japan's goods were very high, yet whose economies were impoverished. Two ministries were especially designated for the success of an economic diplomacy: the Ministry of Foreign Affairs (MOFA) supporting Southeast Asian development through reparations and economic assistance and the Ministry of International Trade and Industry (MITI) promoting Japan's trade with Southeast Asian countries. Therefore, the Japanese, according to Foreign Minister Okazaki, "sought to devise means to increase their purchasing power through payment of reparations, development of resources, investment, setting up joint enterprises, and the purchase by Japan of large quantities of raw materials."[15]

Prime Minister Nobusuke Kishi's trip to Southeast Asia in 1957 is worth mentioning here. The very first visit to the region was significant in that Japan-led Asian regionalism was initiated for the first time. While attempting an autonomous foreign policy, Kishi's intention was to expedite the reparations negotiations and to generate support for his idea of establishing a Southeast Asian Development Fund. Unlike Yoshida's similar proposal of 1954, the proposed fund was relatively rich in specific policies and projects directed towards Southeast Asian development with American capital and Japanese technology.[16] Although the idea did not materialize, due mainly to American as well as Southeast Asian objections, Kishi's Southeast Asian policy marked a new page in Japan's relationship with the region. However, with the fund proposal denied, Japan's Southeast Asian policy evolved mainly on a bilateral basis until 1976. In order to see how Japan–Southeast Asian relations developed, we will focus on five major countries of ASEAN.

Indonesia

Japan's relations with Indonesia were and are probably the closest of all Southeast Asian countries.[17] Indonesia has been the most important partner in the region for Japan because of its reserves of oil and other natural resources, including liquefied natural gas, timber, nickel, bauxite and natural rubber. In fact, Japanese interest in Indonesian oil dates back to the 1930s at a time when the war in China intensified and the production of Chinese resources became unstable, thereby making resources from Southeast Asia imperative for the Japanese military. Japanese interest was epitomized in the late 1960s by the North Sumatra Oil Development Company, that listed four objectives of the "pilot project": (1) to secure a supply of oil; (2) to increase the number of Japanese technicians in the field of oil extraction and refinement; (3) to make Indonesia dependent on Japan to a certain extent; and (4) to expand Japan's political influence generally.[18]

Although the economic motive was predominant, Indonesia's strategic importance undoubtedly played a part in fostering Japanese interest. It is the largest of the Southeast Asian countries in terms of both geographical extent and population. Also, Japan regards Indonesia to be of strategic importance due to its open sea route to Australia, the Indian Ocean and the Middle East. Moreover, while Indonesian memories of the Japanese occupation were mixed — few have forgotten the harsh treatment at the hands of individual Japanese — most realize that these same troops presented them with the opportunity for independence that might otherwise not have come for a long time.

Thus, given the precarious political conditions, Japan settled its reparations with Sukarno's Indonesia rather quickly and played a mediating role in resolving the conflict between Indonesia and Malaysia.[19] Following the coup of 30 September 1965, the significance of Japan's interest was immediately noticed when Japan held the first conference of the members of the consortium to aid Indonesia in Tokyo in September 1966. The event was indeed symbolic in that the Japanese government worked hard to realize the plan, despite the fact that the opposition party in Tokyo loudly deplored Japan's attempts as "imperialistic plotting". In fact, the resultant consortium, called the Inter-Governmental Group on Indonesia (IGGI), continued to serve as an important stimulus for the development of the Indonesian economy, which had become a crucial ingredient of the New Order's success.

By the early 1970s, therefore, Japan had emerged as the top investor and the most important trading partner for Indonesia. However, to the Indonesian elite surveyed, "exploration, not industrial development, was the purpose behind Japanese assistance and investment".[20] It was in this environment that anti-Japanese riots were staged in Indonesia. As one scholar put it, "the expectation that Japan would genuinely help Indonesia's development plan was seen as unrealized: instead, the public discovered a Japan looking for profits, and this was seen within the framework of Indonesia's value system as unethical, since what was articulated was brotherhood relationship between the two nations."[21] This suggests a critical dilemma in Japan's foreign policy because the appreciation of Japan's assistance and the rejection of Japan's larger role in the region are intertwined and seen as both sides of the same coin.

Malaysia

As a country composed of members of many races and cultures, Malaysia's attitude towards the Japanese occupation was also mixed.[22] While the Chinese took up arms against the Japanese and suffered unbearable hardships, the Malay community in the rural areas did not undergo such an ordeal. According to former prime minister Mahathir Mohammad, who operated a food stall and sold fried bananas in relatively peaceful Alor Star in the northeastern state of Kedha during the Japanese occupation, for instance, the Malays in general lived a fairly normal life.[23]

Nonetheless, in 1967 the Japanese government settled its "blood debt" to Malaysia, paying the equivalent of $8.3 million in ships and other capital goods in lieu of reparations. After this agreement, Japanese companies started to get involved in manufacturing, construction of dams and irrigation projects. A symbolic project for a steel mill in Prai, opposite Penang, was launched in 1967, with a 39 per cent stake held by Japanese companies, more than half of which was held by Yawata Steel. As in Indonesia, this development was seen as a long-term investment with the objective of establishing a base in the Malaysian economy and as part of a general expansion of Japanese influence in the region.[24]

In October 1970, as a major natural rubber producer, Malaysia joined the Association of Natural Rubber Producing Countries (ANRPC) together with Indonesia, Thailand and Singapore. In particular, Indonesia, Malaysia and Thailand accounted for about 75 per cent of world exports of natural rubber. Affected by a fluctuating world economy and the production of synthetic rubber by developed countries, including Japan, however, the price of natural rubber had declined substantially by the late 1960s. Malaysia's dissatisfaction with rubber prices had been expressed in talks with Prime Minister Sato in September 1967. As the second-largest synthetic rubber producer, Sato replied that some form of price stabilization mechanism should be sought. When Japan's promise was not delivered, Malaysia openly criticized the Japanese government by threatening to boycott a meeting of the Ministerial Conference for the Economic Development of Southeast Asia.[25]

When Prime Minister Tanaka visited Kuala Lumpur, Malaysian dissatisfaction exploded, although not to the same extent as in Indonesia and Thailand. University students were ready to protest against Japanese economic expansion in a meeting with the Japanese prime minister, yet the planned meeting was cancelled. It is true that Japan did not make a deep impression on Malaysian public consciousness at the time of Tanaka's visit, although the Malaysians viewed the Japanese as being only interested in business and being hard-headed. This view is said to be expressed by former prime minister of Malaysia, Tengku Abdul Rahman, when he remarked, "although Japan furnishes loans, it takes back with its other hand, as if by magic almost twice the amount that it provides".[26]

The Philippines

No other Southeast Asian country expresses more vivid and unpleasant feelings of the Japanese military occupation than the Philippines.[27] As such, Japan-Philippine relations were from the start overshadowed by bitter feelings. At the same time, the Philippines is a close ally of the United States, which occupied a pivotal position in the region with regard to American strategic deployment. Moreover, its location at the centre of the region and proximity to Japan, and its managerial and labour force are considered to be the Philippines' significant advantages. Thus, the bilateral relationship had a stronger politico-strategic component than with any other country, apart from Indonesia, in the region. It was for these reasons that Japan gave priority to its aid programme in the Philippines, as exemplified by the reparations settlement in May 1956. Japan agreed to pay the largest amount of reparations, $550 million, to the Philippines.[28]

Economically, Japanese interest in the Philippines was primarily in resource extraction. Being an important supplier of copper, nickel and zinc ores, Philippine trade with Japan extended rather rapidly until the late 1960s. However, Japan and the Philippines faced the most difficult hurdle soon after the reparations settlement because the Philippine Congress refused to ratify the Treaty of Friendship, Commerce and Navigation, which was perceived as a threat to Philippine sovereignty. The main reason for this was the fear that the treaty would open the door too widely for Japanese goods and businessmen, and that Japan would ultimately dominate the Philippine economy. Although the Japanese had requested Manila to ratify the treaty since 1960, it was only when President Ferdinand Marcos demanded Japan's agreement to channel the greater portion of its economic assistance to the government sector for procurement of monumental and lasting projects that the treaty was ratified, together with the announcement of Martial Law in 1972.[29]

Under the Martial Law regime Japan was one of the most important sources of foreign assistance. At the same time, the Philippines remained Japan's second most important supplier of resources in Southeast Asia. As Narayan Nagesh explains, "During the martial law years, Marcos made efforts to expand economic interaction between the two countries. Political controversies involving Japan were virtually absent during this period. This in turn contributed to a considerable increase in Japanese aid and investment in the Philippines."[30] Understandably, during Prime

Minister Tanaka's visit to Southeast Asia, Manila could maintain rather cordial relations with Japan due mainly to the state of martial law. Rapidly developing closer relations between Japan and the Philippines was one of the reasons why the Japanese government decided to announce its first doctrine in Manila in 1977.

Singapore

Although Singapore went through hardship during the Japanese occupation due to its being a predominantly Chinese country, a post-independent Singapore spared no time building one of the most successful and advanced city-states in Asia.[31] Towards this goal, Singapore, under the leadership of Prime Minister Lee Kuan Yew, adopted an outward-looking pragmatic policy of encouraging foreign, including Japanese, investment, culminating in the pursuit of a "learn from Japan" policy.

Singapore is important in terms of its geopolitical location, since 90 per cent of the oil that keeps Japan's economy running comes through the Strait of Malacca. Given this significance, the Japanese government settled the so-called "blood debt" for Japanese actions during the war in 1967, when Tokyo agreed to loans and grants amounting to $17 million in lieu of reparations. Following this, new Japanese investment began in Singapore in government-sponsored industrial projects or to set up joint ventures with local Chinese. Most of the major Japanese companies first came to the city-state in the late 1960s attracted by tax incentives provided by the government's Economic Development Board of Singapore and Ishikawajima Harima Industries of Japan for the development of Jurong Shipyard, which became one of the most important ship-repair and servicing centres in Asia.[32]

Singapore leaders are well known for their practicality and rationality in the formulation of domestic and foreign policies. Thus, they publicly supported a view that Japan should assume responsibility for its defence, while maintaining the Japan-U.S. security treaty. Overall relations, however, are weighted against Singapore with its huge trade deficits every year.[33] To redress the imbalance over a range of business issues — including technology transfer and access to the Japanese markets during the turbulent years of anti-Japanese movements — therefore, Singapore under the tightly governed Lee Kuan Yew regime was able to maintain rather cordial relations with Japan.

Thailand

Forming an alliance with Japan during the last war, Thailand underwent a unique experience during the Japanese occupation.[34] Without doubt the Japanese occupation produced individual hardships, but it was not the traumatic experience undergone by other Southeast Asian countries. After the war, Japanese capital moved in to take advantage of cheap labour and an expanding market. Japan's business influence began to burgeon around 1964, in part because an agreement was reached in May of the same year on Thai claims arising from wartime yen issued by Japanese occupation banks. And in part, the Sarit government embarked on forging a strong political foundation for the nation's economic development. Japan agreed to pay the equivalent of $27.7 million annually for six years in goods and services — mainly ships, rolling stock, and textile machinery — towards this development plan.

Under the favourable political and economic conditions created by the Thai military regimes and supported by the United States, the Japanese took advantage of the Thai import substitution policy to secure local markets. In so doing, Japanese trading companies played the most pivotal role. There are two notable examples. The first was the automobile assembly plants; most of which were principally Japanese owned. The domination of Japanese enterprises was attributed to the lack of regulations, by which automobiles became one of the leading export items during the 1960s. The second was the textile industry, in which mills financed by Japanese loans spun synthetic yarn form Japan-made fibre, then wove and finished the yarn in various fabrics.[35] However, depending on their long-term credit and loan, Thai business had to purchase components and spare parts from firms in Japan through the trading companies, thereby culminating in severe trade deficits.

As such, Japan's trade and investment relations with Thailand resulted in severe criticism. The aid merely provided a small grant component and its conditions were stringent. Moreover, Japanese aid was accused of promoting Japanese exports and investment as it tied recipient countries to purchasing Japanese products. Besides the question of aid programmes, a rapid flow of Japanese investment into Thailand caused resentment among local people. As in Indonesia, this created adverse situations for Japan-Thai relations because foreign investment is often viewed negatively. In fact, the rapid flow of Japanese investment into Thailand created a dependency syndrome that influenced Thai perceptions of a colonial relationship.

Because of this syndrome, Thais staged the first large-scale anti-Japanese goods movement for ten days in November 1972, while maintaining that aggressive Japanese companies were invading Thailand. In January 1974, more aggressive demonstrations were staged against Prime Minister Tanaka, which together with the Indonesian riots, made Japan reappraise its traditional economic policy.[36]

Table 2.1 clearly suggests that the bulk of Japan's relations with Southeast Asia rest with Indonesia, with its huge oil exports and the major Japanese investment and aid. The table also shows that a clear division exists between the trade-surplus (Indonesia and Malaysia) and trade-deficit countries (Singapore and Thailand). If the occurrence of anti-Japanese movements is a function of adverse trade relations with Japan, then Indonesia needs special explanation.[37]

TABLE 2.1
ASEAN Economic Relations with Japan, 1967–76 (US$ million)

		1967	1970	1973	1976
Indonesia	Export	197	637	2,214	4,091
	Import	155	316	902	1,639
	Investment	52	49	341	928
	Aid	113	126	143	201
Malaysia	Export	335	419	776	1,362
	Import	88	167	448	704
	Investment	4	14	126	54
	Aid	1	2	15	34
Philippines	Export	374	534	820	793
	Import	363	454	620	1,114
	Investment	9	29	43	14
	Aid	62	29	142	76
Singapore	Export	36	87	223	647
	Import	160	423	702	1,531
	Investment	1	9	81	26
	Aid	0.4	6	4	6
Thailand	Export	160	190	394	848
	Import	341	445	720	1,070
	Investment	8	22	30	19
	Aid	4	7	16	43

Sources: MITI, *Tsusho Hakusho*, 1968–77; Ministry of Finance, *Financial Statistics of Japan*, various issues; Ministry of Foreign Affairs, *Waga Gaiko no Kinkyo*, 1968–77.

EMERGING JAPAN'S REGIONAL ROLE: BEYOND THE MAINSTREAM

Japan's indifference to ASEAN gradually changed in the early 1970s. When ASEAN adopted the neutralization scheme in 1971, the Ministry of Foreign Affairs referred to it in the annual White Paper for the first time.[38] Nevertheless, it was in 1973 that Japan's official contact with ASEAN began in order to resolve a nagging issue of the natural rubber trade, which resulted in the establishment of a Japan-ASEAN forum in 1974. As Table 2.2 suggests, however, official relations were critically lacking. There were no top-level contacts. Nor were ministerial channels formalized. In seeking to understand why this was the case, we will examine two major issues of the Ministerial Conference for the Economic Development of Southeast Asia and Japan's decision to normalize relations with North Vietnam.

Pursuing Japan's Regional Initiative: MCEDSEA

In 1964 U.S. President Lyndon Johnson announced a plan of assisting Southeast Asian development through a massive infusion of aid. Spurred particularly by the Johnson plan, the Japanese government proposed a plan to establish the "Ministerial Conference for the Economic Development of Southeast Asia (MCEDSEA)", which was successfully founded in April 1966

TABLE 2.2
Japan-ASEAN Relations, 1967–76

	PM visit	FMM	Forum
1967	(Sato)		
1968			
1969			
1970			
1971			
1972			
1973		(*)	
1974	Tanaka		1st / 2nd
1975			3rd
1976			4th

Note: (*) ASEAN and Japan agreed to resolve the issue of the natural rubber trade through the Foreign Ministers' meeting.

and continued annually until 1974.[39] Therefore, it was during this period that Japanese foreign policy towards the region exhibited an "induced" activism, as exemplified by other initiatives, including the establishing of the Asian Development Bank, joining the Asia-Pacific Council (ASPAC), and hosting the foundation of the IGGI in 1967.[40]

The objective of MCEDSEA was to promote economic development — focusing on agricultural development — the promotion of tourism, the marketing of new products, and regional programmes to develop transport and communication. The original purpose was to set up an informal forum, but it acquired greater standing through the subsequent ministerial conferences. It especially symbolized Japanese commitment to the economic progress of Southeast Asia. Many of the proposals considered at the MCEDSEA depended on Japanese financial and technical assistance. At the first conference, hosted in Tokyo in April 1966 and attended by South Vietnam, Laos, Cambodia, Thailand, the Philippines, Malaysia, Singapore and Indonesia (observer), nine leaders reached several agreements for the establishment of the Economic Development Center, the Economic Development Promotion Center, the Marine Product and Fishery Development Center and the Southeast Asian University.

Why did Japan decide to hold this conference at this moment? A recent study suggests the following reasons: (1) Foreign Minister Takeo Miki, MITI and the business circle played a very important role in hosting the conference. Since the Japanese economy was in serious recession in 1965, these actors tried to help the country recover by strengthening economic relations with Southeast Asian countries; (2) when the conference was held, Japanese political and economic leaders considered that Japan should play the role of a model or guide for Southeast Asian countries to develop their economy.[41] Although the United States and the Southeast Asian countries appeared to welcome Japan's initiative, the reality was that these countries did not accept it, as they felt repulsed by Japan's self-seeking attitude.

The establishment of the MCEDSEA was highly regarded by the Foreign Ministry as Japan's first diplomatic initiative, yet its development was far from smooth sailing.[42] From the very beginning, the proposed conference met with opposition from Indonesia, Malaysia and Singapore. They expressed their fear that Japan's proposal was not neutral and thus could serve as an American instrument of Cold War strategy. The Japanese tried to reassure them, reiterating that the proposal had no political objectives and was aimed strictly at economic cooperation in Southeast Asia. Following this explanation, Southeast Asian leaders further questioned Japan's policy emphasis on agricultural development rather than Japan's support for industrialization of Southeast Asian countries.

The Japanese Foreign Ministry at first tried to propose the creation of an "Advisory Committee on Southeast Asian Development" modelled after the Inter-American Committee on the Alliance for Progress, but faced opposition from the Finance Ministry which preferred the newly created Asian Development Bank under its own initiative to the creation of a new organ proposed by the Foreign Ministry. Notwithstanding the bureaucratic infighting, the Ministerial Conference itself faced difficult hurdles from the beginning. For instance, although the Ministerial Conference discussed development issues and came forward with conclusions — among them agricultural development as a key until the ninth meeting in 1974 — Southeast Asian participants were disinclined to follow Japanese leadership. Indeed, without any further liberalization of Japanese markets and a substantial increase of ODA, dissatisfaction among the participants was rampant.

As such, many proposed projects were seldom carried out and even rejected by Southeast Asian countries. The hospital project was a case in point. At first, Japan's proposal for a hospital project was accepted and its preparation was almost finalized, but Malaysia and Indonesia suddenly changed their position and declared their withdrawal from the project, which ultimately terminated the plan as well as MCEDSEA itself. Thus, in 1975, Singapore, which was supposed to host the tenth MCEDSEA meeting, explained that ASEAN states were busy in preparation for the First ASEAN Summit and they could not afford to continue MCEDSEA.[43]

Normalization with North Vietnam

Affected by the Nixon Doctrine in 1969, the 1970s saw the emergence of new thinking among Japanese foreign policy makers. Gaining confidence from Japan's own rapid economic development in the 1960s and early 1970s, Japanese leaders came to believe that Tokyo should and could play an independent role in Indochina. The first limited attempt was to convene a conference on Cambodia in May 1970, followed by Japan's offer of assistance to the Indochina countries.[44]

Vietnam offered both political and economic opportunities to the Japanese leadership. Japan's main political goal was to induce Vietnam to loosen its ties with the communist bloc and become "a Socialist country of the Yugoslav type, open to the Western world". Japan was particularly interested in contributing to the creation of a new equilibrium between ASEAN and Vietnam to promote peace and stability in Southeast Asia. Tokyo's economic goal was to help bring about the reconstruction of Vietnam's war-damaged economy and promote the incorporation of Indochina into the market economies of Asia. Japanese leaders were convinced that when integrated into the capitalist economies, Vietnam would provide impressive economic opportunities for Japanese firms seeking to expand trade and investment, extract natural resources, and establish offshore manufacturing in Indochina.

Japan began taking independent initiatives to reach these goals well before the liberation of Saigon in 1975 and the establishment of the Socialist Republic of Vietnam (SRV) in the following year. In 1970 the Director General of the First Southeast Asia Division of the Ministry of Foreign Affairs, Wasuke Miyake, contacted North Vietnamese officials in France to explore possibilities of rapprochement with Hanoi. In 1971 the Japanese embassy in Paris continued these discussions and offered to send Miyake to Hanoi in order to negotiate normalization between Japan and Vietnam. In February 1972 Miyake visited Hanoi to expedite negotiations towards normalization. In May 1973, four months after the signing of the Paris Peace Accord, Miyake made another visit to Vietnam to finalize normalization, which led to the official signing of the diplomatic normalization between Japan and the Democratic Republic of Vietnam (DRV) in September 1973.[45]

After the 1973 Paris Accord, diplomatic rapprochement accelerated between Japan and the DRV. Communications between the two countries increased and even Japanese Diet members — traditionally non-participants in foreign policy making — started contacting elected officials in Hanoi. In 1974 Japanese and Vietnamese politicians established the League for Japan-Vietnam Friendship to promote mutual understanding and friendship. The Japanese members included Diet members not only from the pro-Hanoi Socialist and communist parties, but also from traditionally anti-communist parties, such as the Liberal Democratic Party (LDP) and the Democratic Socialist Party. The LDP Secretary General, Yoshio Sakurauchi, was appointed as chairman. Thus even before the establishment of the SRV government, Japanese policymakers had initiated communications with Hanoi. Japan's active outreach towards the SRV that stemmed from this earlier contact with the DRV augured well for bridging the polarized Southeast Asia.[46]

JAPAN'S ENCOUNTER WITH ASEAN: RUBBER NEGOTIATIONS

As a result of Japan's rapid economic penetration of Southeast Asia, ASEAN felt that joint negotiations with Tokyo were necessary. This was a reflection of the growing fear of Japan's economic domination in several countries, exemplified by Thailand's Japanese goods boycott movement in 1972 and Malaysia's criticism of Japanese production and export of synthetic rubber.[47] The latter soon resulted in collective action by ASEAN against Japan on the issue.

Without doubt, ASEAN-Japan negotiations over synthetic rubber as the initial encounter had a major impact on Japan's regional policy. The beginning of negotiations was the sixth ASEAN Foreign Ministers' Meeting held in April 1973 in Pattaya, Thailand where the Malaysian delegation led by Deputy Prime Minister Tun Ismail presented the position paper against "the indiscriminate expansion of the synthetic rubber industry by Japan", which was adopted by the delegates.[48] As the joint statement put it, "The Ministers considered the indiscriminate expansion of the synthetic rubber industry by Japan and the accelerated export of such rubber and recognized that this posed a serious threat to the economies of the ASEAN countries. In expressing their grave concern, they urged Japan to review its policy of indiscriminate expansion and accelerated export of synthetic rubber. They agreed that ASEAN officials would work out appropriate measures to meet this threat."[49] This was the first action towards a non-member country, thus inaugurating the first interaction between Japan and ASEAN as a regional grouping.

In August 1973 ASEAN issued an aide-memoire to Japanese envoys in the ASEAN capitals and, after a two-day meeting of senior officials, agreed to take collective action on behalf of the Association against the export expansion of Japanese synthetic rubber.[50] In response to ASEAN's request, together with anti-Japanese demonstrations in Jakarta, the Japanese government decided to set up a formal dialogue to resolve the issue. The institutionalization of the ASEAN-Japan Forum on Rubber was realized in quite a low-profile way in November 1973, as the joint statement released at the end of the Tokyo meeting merely proclaimed: "As a result of fruitful exchange of views, the Ministers agreed on the establishment of a forum in which a dialogue between ASEAN and Japan on the question of synthetic rubber, including the question of natural rubber in relation thereto, would be continued at the level of government officials and experts."[51] The meeting was deemed highly successful in that ASEAN's joint stand had a unifying effect and could set a precedent for future joint actions.

This soon resulted in the first rubber forum meeting in February 1974 in Kuala Lumpur. At the meeting, Japan showed a positive attitude in guaranteeing that its synthetic rubber production would not adversely affect natural rubber production.[52] At the second forum in March 1974 in Tokyo, furthermore, Japan reiterated that it would ensure that its production of synthetic rubber would be managed so as not to impinge on the natural rubber market. Accordingly, by the time of the 1974 Ministerial Meeting, both Japan and ASEAN had come to a basic understanding for swift resolution, as the joint statement clearly suggested: "The Ministers expressed their satisfaction that the ASEAN joint approach to Japan on the indiscriminate production and accelerated exports of synthetic rubber had resulted in obtaining the Japanese Government's agreement to exercise a restraining influence on the Japanese synthetic rubber industry, so that it will not jeopardize the economies of ASEAN countries. The Ministers welcomed the cooperation and understanding of the Japanese Government in this matter."[53]

In July 1975 Japan agreed to offer its economic and technical assistance by accepting ASEAN's proposed conditions, including governmental guidance and mutual consultation over Japan's synthetic rubber policy, Japan's technological assistance to natural rubber industries in Southeast Asia, and the expansion of Japan's market for natural rubber.[54] As such, the rubber problem was resolved in practical terms due to the ASEAN-Japan interactions within the framework of multilateral negotiations. Responding to this official engagement, furthermore, the Federation of Economic Organizations (Keidanren) announced codes of conduct for Japanese firms in the region, including (1) long-term investment for the benefit of both parties, (2) promotion of business activities based on mutual trust, (3) contribution to local industrialization, (4) promotion of re-investment, and (5) cooperation and harmonization with the recipient countries.[55]

Why did Japan concede at this moment and agree to incorporate ASEAN in the agenda of Japanese foreign policy? There are four main reasons to explain the decision. First of all, the 1973 oil crisis was affecting synthetic rubber production, while at the same time production costs were rising. Second, Japan received notice of complaints from some ASEAN countries regarding their unbalanced trade relations with Japan. Third, Japan was trying to avoid any collision with Indonesia because the country was becoming a major oil supplier to Japan. Fourth, and most importantly, ASEAN displayed its political will as "a test case for ASEAN unity" to resolve the issue. In this respect, it was symbolic that the anti-Japanese demonstrations, whatever the catalyst, were the most threatening at the time of Prime Minister Tanaka's visit to Jakarta in January 1974.

Furthermore, with the end of the war in Vietnam in 1975, new challenges faced ASEAN. The most urgent problem was how to deal with the new communist regimes in Indochina, while at the same time consolidating regional policies. In July 1975 the third forum convened and discussed Japan's assistance for rubber production and technical assistance by the Japan International Cooperation Agency for Thai rubber production. In November 1976 the fourth forum confirmed Japanese assistance for tyre research, and a grant of 600 million yen for this purpose was made to Malaysia.[56]

FROM SATO TO TANAKA: THE FAILURE OF ECONOMIC DIPLOMACY

The first decade of Japan-ASEAN relations was thus characterized as strained and antagonistic due to the failure of Japan's economic diplomacy centred on MITI's resource-first trade policy. In fact, Japan made no secret of its aggressive economic goals for the region. Even its foreign aid objectives reflected them. According to MITI's *Annual Report on Economic Cooperation*, for instance, the main objectives were to "secure access to essential resources", "increase exports and strengthen the international base of Japan's economy", and "fulfill Japan's obligations as the only advanced nation in Asia".[57]

During the height of Japan's economic diplomacy, Prime Minister Eisaku Sato, an exemplar student of the "Yoshida School", visited the Southeast Asian countries in September-October 1967, but regional cooperation through ASEAN was not included in the discussion agenda. Although the journey was designated as a "Southeast Asian trip", Japan's main target was to strengthen economic and political cooperation with India and Australia. The trip was also diplomatically significant because it was quite a tactical step towards effecting the reversion of Okinawa. To put it bluntly, Sato got Okinawa in exchange for an active Southeast Asian policy. It was not until the publication of the 1972 *Diplomatic Blue Book* that Japan explicitly addressed ASEAN as one of the main Asian regional organizations.[58]

Accelerating Japan's Economic Diplomacy and Anti-Japanese Movements

Ensconced behind the American security networks and with added commitments in regional development, Japan concentrated on economic penetration with broader actions and aims, paying little attention to the voices of Southeast Asian countries. In accounting for the role of Japan in the region, therefore, one of the most outspoken scholars in the Philippines had this to say: "Japan's war-time vision of the Greater East Asia Co-Prosperity Sphere is now a peace-time reality, thanks to reparations, John Foster Dulles and the Cold War, the World Bank, IMF, ADB, and other modern instruments for economically dominating formally independent countries, namely: foreign trade, foreign investment and foreign aid."[59]

As Table 2.3 indicates, since 1972 all the economic figures increased rapidly, especially trade and investment.[60] Trade in 1973 almost doubled in a year and investment almost tripled. Why the rapid increase in 1973?

TABLE 2.3
Japan's Economic Relations with ASEAN, 1967–76 ($ million)

	Trade		Investment		ODA	
1967	2.209	(9.9%)	74	(26.9%)	180	(52.8%)
1968	2,440	(9.4%)	60	(10.8%)	135	(43.9%)
1969	3,100	(9.9%)	75	(11.3%)	143	(42.1%)
1970	3,673	(9.6%)	123	(13.6%)	170	(45.8%)
1971	4,159	(9.5%)	152	(17.7%)	177	(41.0%)
1972	4,997	(9.6%)	213	(9.1%)	242	(50.6%)
1973	8,047	(10.7%)	621	(17.8%)	322	(42.1%)
1974	13,369	(11.4%)	564	(23.5%)	360	(40.9%)
1975	12,290	(10.8%)	856	(26.1%)	381	(44.7%)
1976	13,799	(10.5%)	1,041	(30.1%)	360	(40.9%)

Sources: MITI, *Tsusho Hakusho*, 1968–77; Ministry of Finance, *Financial Statistics of Japan*, various issues; Ministry of Foreign Affairs, *Waga Gaiko no Kinkyo*, 1968–77.

It was due to the capital liberalization in Japan that furthered Japan's resource diplomacy in Southeast Asia. In fact, together with the provision of aid, Japan started its aggressive search for resources in Southeast Asia. In particular, Japan's ambition to secure and diversify its oil resources was the primary factor for increasing foreign direct investment.

A closer look at the statistics (Tables 2.1 and 2.3) reveals several unique characteristics of Japan-ASEAN economic relations. First of all, Japanese trade with ASEAN shifted away from Malaysia, the Philippines and Thailand towards Indonesia and Singapore. The figures for Indonesia's trade with Japan indicate that its exports accounted for almost 52 per cent and its imports 27 per cent. Second, Japan's investment rose most rapidly in Indonesia and Singapore, especially in Indonesia where direct investment reached $928 million in 1976, eighteen times higher than in 1967. Accordingly, the lion's share of investment by Japan in ASEAN goes to Indonesia, accounting for 89 per cent of the total.[61] Third, in terms of Japan's investment, ASEAN countries can be classified into two groups: Indonesia and the Philippines as one, and Malaysia, Singapore and Thailand the other. Japan invested mostly in resource development in the former group, and in the manufacturing sector in the latter. Fourth, Japan's official developmental assistance (ODA) went mainly to Indonesia and the Philippines for special reasons, as elaborated by Ikema.

> There seem to be at least three characteristics common to Indonesia and the Philippines from the viewpoint of Japan. First, both countries are recipients of Japanese reparations. Second, both countries are sources of natural resources for Japan. Third, related to the second point, Japan's investment in these countries is biased strongly towards resource development. These three factors together appear to have attracted Japan's bilateral ODA disproportionately to Indonesia and the Philippines.[62]

As such, the Japanese government and the business community vigorously undertook a unified policy of trade expansion, largely derived from Japan's reparations payments and other financial assistance. In particular, MITI and Keidanren mutually supporting and reinforcing, together with the malpractices of Japanese businessmen in the region, contributed to extensive penetration of Southeast Asian economies while creating visible trade imbalances in favour of Japan. Since Japan had not implemented any policy to allay repercussions, the rapid expansion resulted in the eruption of anti-Japanese movements.

For instance, a university in Bangkok formed an "anti-Japanese goods club" in January 1971 and launched a campaign urging the public not to buy Japanese products. The Thai students maintained that they did not have a negative attitude towards the Japanese, but they resented the fact that "aggressive Japanese companies are invading Thailand, and that Japanese products are so pervasive". Demanding Japan remove import barriers on goods from Thailand, Thai students staged a ten-day national boycott of Japanese goods in November 1972.[63]

Prime Minister Tanaka's visit

Japan's economic diplomacy towards resource-rich Southeast Asia was a major success due mainly to the scheme of Japan-U.S. economic cooperation. As a result of Japan's rapid economic penetration into Southeast Asia, however, ASEAN began to feel that joint negotiations with Tokyo were necessary. This was a reflection of the growing fear of Japan's economic domination in several countries in Southeast Asia, exemplified by Thailand's 1972 boycott movement and Malaysia's later criticism of Japanese production and export of synthetic rubber. With the apparent change in American policy towards China and Vietnam, Southeast Asian countries had second thoughts on America's junior partner, that is, Japan's role in the region.

During the height of tensions, Prime Minister Kakuei Tanaka, known as a resource diplomacy promoter, visited five Southeast Asian countries, namely the Philippines, Thailand, Singapore, Malaysia and Indonesia from 7 to 17 January 1974. On the occasion of his visit Tanaka made the following principles clear:

1. Promotion of good relations with the Southeast Asian countries to share peace and prosperity with them.
2. Respect for the independence of those countries.
3. Promotion of mutual understanding with those countries.
4. Contribution to the economic development of those countries without disturbing their economic independence.
5. Respect for voluntary regional cooperation among those countries.[64]

It should be noted here that these principles accrued from Japan's negotiations with ASEAN over the natural rubber issue. The leaders of the host countries all welcomed the Prime Minister's explanations and these principles were incorporated in each of the joint press releases issued by Japan and the respective host country. The leaders also discussed bilateral relations in depth. As for economic cooperation, Japan expressed its preparedness to cooperate positively in the development efforts of the host countries and agreed to give a third tranche of yen credit to Malaysia.[65]

In connection with the oil crisis, the leaders of all the host countries urgently requested that Japan ensure stable supplies of oil-related products, especially fertilizers. In reply, the Prime Minister explained in detail the effects of the oil crisis on the Japanese economy and, at the same time, made it clear that Japan would respect to the greatest extent possible the contracts already made in order to avoid an adverse influence of the oil crisis on the economies of those countries. Given the increasing criticism towards Japan's overwhelming economic presence and the business methods of Japanese enterprises, as well as the behaviour of Japanese residents in those countries, local students and workers staged anti-Japanese demonstrations and riots in Bangkok and Jakarta. Protests also occurred in Malaysia and elsewhere.[66]

When Prime Minister Tanaka visited Southeast Asia in 1974, therefore, unprecedented anti-Japanese movements took place, particularly in Indonesia and Thailand. In Indonesia, for instance, a parade of thousands of students in the streets turned into a riot, burning Japanese cars and damaging more than 50,000 stores and buildings. Since Indonesia was the last stop as well as Japan's most important trading partner in Southeast Asia, the riot finally assured the Tanaka tour of a very negative image both within and outside Japan.

Although the anti-Japanese movements of 1974 were partially induced by various domestic factors within each country, Tokyo was compelled to review its Asian policy — the one it had pursued for more than two decades — as then Deputy Prime Minister Takeo Miki explained: "The time has come for the government to conduct a serious review of the hitherto-taken foreign policy and the way of economic cooperation."[67] Thus, the failure of post-war *Nanshin*, together with the first oil crisis of 1973–74, which mitigated Japan's free access to raw materials and export markets, impelled Japan to formulate initiatives for a "new" Southeast Asian diplomacy. With the end of the Vietnam War, gone was the Cold War environment that had nurtured Japan as the superdomino or the workshop of Asia.

Soon after the visit, Tanaka reported to the National Diet: "Recently I visited five nations in Asia.... I saw with my own eyes and heard with my own ears the complaints and criticisms concerning our relations with them as well as the economic activities of the Japanese enterprises in those countries. I had a strong feeling that although mutual cooperation and understanding are of utmost importance to the peoples and countries, these words are easier said than done."[68] Despite moves to criticize Japan, the common understanding was reaffirmed that it was necessary to promote such relations further in a constructive manner for mutual benefit. This was the reason why Japan inaugurated the Ship for Southeast Asian Youth Program in 1974.[69]

MUTUAL QUEST FOR A VIABLE PARTNERSHIP

ASEAN's Quest for Dialogue Partners

The end of the Vietnam War in 1973 and the partial realization of the domino theory, that is the emergence of the communist bloc in 1975, therefore compelled ASEAN to restructure its basic posture of regional cooperation. This was the first transformation of ASEAN regionalism. Convening the inaugural summit meeting in 1976, the ASEAN countries decided to strengthen the hitherto fragile organizational foundation so as to deal with pressing regional issues. The first Bali summit produced two milestone documents. The ASEAN Concord underscored ASEAN's long-term goal in the following way:

> Member states shall vigorously develop awareness of regional identity and exert efforts to create a strong ASEAN community, respected by all and respecting all nations on the basis of mutually advantageous relationship and in accordance with the principles of self-determination, sovereign equality and non-interference in the internal affairs of nations.

In terms of its external strategy, ASEAN's growing confidence, gained from the rubber negotiations with Japan, was also spelled out in the Concord:

> Member states shall accelerate joint efforts to improve access to markets outside ASEAN for their raw material and finished products by seeking the elimination of all trade barriers in those markets, developing new usage for these products and in adopting common approaches and actions in dealing with regional groupings and individual economic powers.[70]

In a similar vein, under the Treaty of Amity and Cooperation (TAC) also adopted at the Bali meeting of 1976, ASEAN members agreed to abide by the following principles: (1) mutual respect for the independence, sovereignty, equality, territorial integrity, and national identity of all nations, (2) the right of every state to lead its national existence free from external interference, subversion, or coercion, (3) non-interference in internal affairs of one another, (4) settlement of differences or disputes by peaceful means, (5) renunciation of the threat or use of force, and (6) effective cooperation among themselves.[71]

Now that ASEAN had adopted its first binding treaty, ASEAN's viability would be subject to its management of regional conflicts and economic development. This was meant to be a golden opportunity for ASEAN to dispel the long-held image of a ramshackle regime. To invigorate regional stability and economic development, ASEAN leaders began to call for the participation of Indochina countries in the regional body and more importantly Japan's active role in the region as Singapore Prime Minister Lee Kuan Yew "urged Japan to express a firm commitment to ASEAN by extending more aid, and particularly to help their proposed industrial projects".[72]

Japan's Quest for an ASEAN-centred Southeast Asian Policy

Due to stormy political events at the end of 1974, Takeo Miki replaced Prime Minister Tanaka and introduced three policies aimed at improving the LDP's tainted popularity. These were the tightening of the Anti-Monopoly Law, a reform of LDP intra-party elections, and the enactment of a new control law for elections and political funds. In spite of mounting troubles, Miki displayed surprising skill in foreign policy in general and Asian diplomacy in particular. In his policy speech at the National Diet on 24 January 1975, Miki averred that "Japan will endeavor to intensify economic cooperation and cultural as well as personal interchange with the ASEAN countries in order to continue our contribution to stability and prosperity in the Asian region."[73]

When Miki visited the United States in August 1975, moreover, he tried to include his idea of an "Asia-Pacific Forum" in the discussion agenda. Although this attempt was rejected by the Foreign Ministry, Miki expressed his straightforward policy towards Southeast Asia at the Washington National Press Club, which was held soon after the Miki–Ford talks: "Japan will be prepared to extend its positive support to the activities of ASEAN, while respecting the initiatives and aspiration of its member countries".[74] It was a positive signal stressing the importance of the region in the post–Vietnam War era, but Miki's ideas met with little domestic support as a result of his personalized handing of foreign affairs.

A surprising development in late 1975 was the sudden announcement by Miki calling for an Asian "Rambouillet" conference to invigorate economic cooperation among the Asia-Pacific nations. Announcing the rudiments of the scheme in August 1975, Miki disclosed a plan to stabilize export earnings of specific products for the developing countries of the region. Thus, when the 31st LDP convention was held in January 1976, ASEAN was for the first time mentioned as the core actor in Southeast Asia with which Japan could help stabilize the region. In order to carry out Japan-ASEAN high-level talks, Miki sought to attend the First ASEAN Summit in Bali to be held in February. Miki thought that Japan's involvement in the ASEAN Summit would work as if it were an Asian summit.[75] However, this attempt failed due to the fact that the ASEAN countries wanted to hold the very first summit by themselves. Reflecting on this, Foreign Minister Kiichi Miyazawa reiterated Japan's policy towards ASEAN:

> The ASEAN nations, faced with the new situation in Indochina, are strengthening their regional solidarity and building greater self-reliance, while working to increase their respective strength. Our country welcomes these moves and hopes that the summit meeting of ASEAN nations scheduled for late February will be fruitful. The government intends to continue to strengthen our friendly and cooperative relations with the ASEAN nations, with Burma, which borders this region, so that Japan may contribute to peace and development in the whole of Southeast Asia.[76]

In fact, Miki envisaged three plans to improve relations with ASEAN countries: (1) to develop an Asian version of the Lomé Agreement, (2) to triple its official development aid and (3) to contribute to the International Agricultural Development Fund.[77] Although all these plans were abandoned due to opposition from the Ministry of Finance, which had experienced financial difficulties caused by the oil shock and was reluctant to increase expenditure, they were indicative of Miki's keenness to forge improved relations with ASEAN countries.[78]

CONCLUSION

Undoubtedly, the end of the Vietnam War in April 1975 eventually forced Japan to dispel the myth of triangular diplomacy. Why did this take until 1975? It can be inferred that the Japanese leaders, officially and privately, had a long-held hope that as long as the United States stayed in the region Japan could benefit from it. In fact, from the conception of the idea of economic cooperation, Japan depended upon U.S. financial assistance for Southeast Asian economic development. Thus, plans during the first phase were to utilize U.S. capital for Southeast Asian development by employing Japan's technologies and labours as exemplified by Yoshida's $4 billion plan in 1954, Prime Minister Kishi's proposal for the Asian Development Fund in 1957, and MCEDSEA in April 1966 which was induced by President Johnson's $1 billion plan for Southeast Asian development.

However, Japan's aggressive economic diplomacy invited various criticism and repercussions. In particular, the anti-Japanese movements in the early 1970s marked the end of Tokyo's post-war economic diplomacy towards Southeast Asia, and these, *inter alia*, prevented the Japanese government from developing a positive dialogue with ASEAN. It was unfortunate that direct contact between Japan and ASEAN as an organization was established during the high tide of anti-Japanese movements in Southeast Asia.

Most importantly, the changing Southeast Asian power configuration, and especially the dissolution of the war — i.e., the collapse of South Vietnam and the revitalization of ASEAN at the Bali Summit in February 1976 — had a major impact on the Japanese government. In particular, the absence of a predominant American presence in Southeast Asia compelled Tokyo to formulate a new framework of regional order. A new set of diplomatic principles was needed because Japan's previous policy towards the region, based on bilateral economic assistance and strong American security commitments, had become untenable. With the end of the Vietnam War, the regional structure that sustained the mechanism of the Cold War in Southeast Asia — SEATO, ASPAC, and more important to the Japanese, MCEDSEA — had begun to crumble.

From a theoretical viewpoint, it should be noted that through interaction with ASEAN leaders, Japan had begun to learn what had gone wrong in the Japanese approach and what Southeast Asia wanted. The failed MCEDSEA and rubber negotiations particularly brought home the need for ideational change in Japan's attitude towards ASEAN, which led to Tanaka's five principles. The failure of MITI's institutionalized idea of economic diplomacy would be a lesson for MOFA's positive posture towards ASEAN. After ten years of interaction, both actors recognized the importance of helping each other through multilateral collaboration.

By the end of 1976, Japan and ASEAN seemed ready to embark on a new course of regional affairs, thereby kicking off the second phase of Japan-ASEAN relations. Towards this end, the Second ASEAN Summit in Kuala Lumpur in 1977 deserves special attention.

Notes

1. This chapter is largely based on Sueo Sudo, "Nanshin, Superdomino, and the Fukuda Doctrine: Stages in Japan-Southeast Asian Relations", *Journal of Northeast Asian Studies* 5, no. 3 (Fall 1986): 35–51.

2. Department of State, *Foreign Relations of United States 1952–1954*, XIV, pt. 2 (Washington, DC: Government Printing Office, 1985), p. 1290.

3. Shaun Narine, *Explaining ASEAN: Regionalism in Southeast Asia* (Boulder, CO: Rienner, 2002), p. 10.

4. Estrella Solidum, *The Politics of ASEAN: An Introduction to Southeast Asian Regionalism* (Singapore: Eastern University Press, 2003), pp. 79–80.

5. J.A.C. Mackie, *Konfrontasi: Indonesia-Malaysia Dispute 1963–1966* (Kuala Lumpur: Oxford University Press, 1974); Donald Weatherbee, *International Relations in Southeast Asia: The Struggle for Autonomy* (Lanham, MD: Rowman & Littlefield, 2005), pp. 66–67.

6. Major works on early ASEAN are Bernard Gordon, *Toward Disengagement in Asia* (Englewood Cliffs: Prentice-Hall, 1969); Estrella Solidum, *Towards a Southeast Asian Community* (Quezon City: University of the Philippines Press, 1974); Arnfinn Jorgensen-Dahl, *Regional Organization and Order in South-East Asia* (London: Macmillan, 1982) and Nicholas Tarling, *Regionalism in Southeast Asia* (London: Routledge, 2006).

7. *Bangkok Post*, 9 August 1967; ASEAN, "ASEAN Declaration (Bangkok Declaration), Bangkok, 8 August 1967", Jakarta: ASEAN Secretariat <http://www.asean.sec.org/1212.htm>.

8. Interview with former Thai Foreign Minister Thanat Kohman, 18 April 1996 and former Singapore Foreign Minister Rajaratnam, 20 June 1990.

9. Regarding the Sabah issue and ZOPFAN, see especially Heiner Hanggi, *ASEAN and the ZOPFAN Concept*, Pacific Strategic Paper 4 (Singapore: Institute of Southeast Asian Studies, 1991).

10. *Asahi Shimbun*, 31 August 1967; Ikuo Ohama, "Materials on Japan-ASEAN Relations", in *Aspects of ASEAN*, edited by Werner Pfennig and Mark Suh (Munchen: Weltforum Verlag, 1984), p. 331. For post-war Japan's Southeast Asia policy, see Lawrence Olson, *Japan in Asia* (New York: Praeger, 1970), K.V. Kesavan, *Japan's Relations with Southeast Asia, 1952–60* (Bombay: Somaiya, 1972), Chaiwat Khamchoo, "Japan's Southeast Asian Policy in the Post-Vietnam Era 1975–1985" (PhD Dissertation, University of Washington, 1986), Wolf Mendl,

Japan's Asia Policy: Regional Security and Global Interests (London, Routledge, 1995) and Sumio Hatano and Susumu Sato, *Gendai Nihon no Tonanajia seisaku 1950–2005* (Tokyo: Wasedadaigaku shuppanbu, 2007).

11. *Nihon Keizai Shimbun*, 9 August 1967. For the birth of ASEAN, see especially Vincent Pollard, "ASA and ASEAN, 1961–1967", Asian Survey 10, no. 3 (March 1970): 244–55 and Nobuhiro Ihara, "ASEAN setsuritsukatei saiko: Genkameikoku no taiIndoneshia fushin ni chumokushite", *Kokusaiseiji*, no. 164 (2011): 115–28.

12. Foreign Minister Takeo Miki for the first time proposed an idea of Asia-Pacific cooperation together with the establishment of the Pacific Basin Economic Council, supported by the Ministry of International Trade and Industry in 1967. See especially Hatano and Sato, *Gendai Nihon*, pp. 211–13.

13. Concerning Japan's re-entry into Southeast Asia, see Akira Suehiro, "The Road to Economic Re-entry: Japan's Policy toward Southeast Asian Development", Social Science Japan Journal 2, no. 1 (April 1999): 85–105.

14. *Nihon Keizai Shimbun*, 19 December 1953.

15. Katsuo Okazaki, "Japan's Foreign Relations", *Annals of the American Academy,* no. 308 (November 1956), p. 162. For a superb analysis of Japan's economic diplomacy, see Satoshi Oyane, "Keizai gaiko", in *Nihon seiji*, edited by Keiichi Tako (Osaka: Osakadaigaku shuppankai, 2005), pp. 220–44.

16. For Kishi's attempts, see Sayuri Shimizu, *Creating People of Plenty: The United States and Japan's Economic Alternatives, 1950–1960* (Kent, OH: Kent State University Press, 2001), pp. 194–98 and Kwon Yongseok, *Kishiseikenki no Ajiagaiko* (Tokyo: Kokusai shoin, 2008).

17. Yutaka Kawashima, *Japanese Foreign Policy at the Crossroads* (Washington, DC: Brookings Institution Press, 2003), p. 111. Regarding Japan-Indonesia relations, see Masashi Nishihara, *The Japanese and Sukarno's Indonesia: Tokyo-Jakarta Relations, 1951–1966* (Honolulu: University of Hawai'i Press, 1976), Kanichi Goto, *Kindai Nihon to Indoneshia* (Tokyo: Hokuju shuppan, 1989) and Taizo Miyagi, *Sengo Ajia chitsujo no mosaku to Nihon* (Tokyo: Sobunsha, 2004).

18. Olson, *Japan in Asia*, p. 194. For Soeharto's memoir, see "Watashi no rirekisho", *Nihon Keizai Shimbun*, 1–30 January 1998.

19. James Llewelyn, "Japan's Return to International Diplomacy and Southeast Asia: Japanese Mediation in *Konfrontasi*, 1963–66", *Asian Studies Review* 30, no. 4 (December 2006): 355–74.

20. Franklin Weinstein, *Indonesian Foreign Policy and the Dilemma of Dependence* (Ithaca, NY: Cornell University Press, 1976), pp. 266–67.

21. Ragi Adiwoso-Suprapto, "Indonesian Perceptions of Japan and Indonesian-Japan Relations", in *Presence and Perceptions: The Underpinnings of ASEAN-Japan Relations*, edited by Charles Morrison (Tokyo: Japan Center for International Exchange, 1986), p. 42.

22. On Japan-Malaysia relations, see Md Nasrudin Md Akhir, "Five Decades of Malaysia-Japan Relations", in *Japan and the Asia Pacific*, edited by Md Nasrudin Md Akhir and Rohayati Paidi (Kuala Lumpur: Department of East Asian Studies, University of Malaya, 2009), pp. 53–86, K.S. Jomo, ed., *The Sun Also Sets* (Selangor: Institute for Social Analysis, 1983) and K.S. Jomo, ed., *Japan and Malaysia Development: In the Shadow of the Rising Sun* (London: Routledge, 1994).

23. Mahathir Mohamad, "Watashi no rirekisho", *Nihon Keizai Shimbun*, 1–30 November 1995.

24. Mendl, *Japan's Asia Policy*, p. 101.

25. *Straits Times*, 25 June 1973. See also Gerald Tan, *ASEAN Economic Development and Cooperation* (Singapore: Times Academic Press, 1996), pp. 181–82.

26. Lee Poh Ping, "Malaysian Perceptions of Japan before and during the 'Look East' Period", *Asia Pacific Community*, no. 29 (Summer 1985): 98.

27. For Japan-Philippines relations, see Torao Sato, *Filipin to Nihon* (Tokyo: Saimaru shuppan, 1994), Setsuho Ikehata and Lydia Yu Jose, eds. *Philippines-Japan Relations* (Manila: Ateneo de Manila University Press, 2003) and Narayana Nagesh, *Japan's Economic Diplomacy in Southeast Asia* (New Delhi: Lancers Books, 1996).

28. Yoko Yoshikawa, *Nihhi baishogaiko kosho no kenkyu* (Tokyo: Keiso shobo, 1991).

29. Yoko Yoshikawa, "War Reparations Implementation, Reparations-secured Loans and a Treaty of Commerce", in *Philippines-Japan Relations*, edited by Setsuho Ikehata and Lydia Yu Jose (Manila: Ateneo de Manila University Press, 2003), pp. 377–442.

30. Narayana Nagesh, *Japan's Economic Diplomacy*, p. 49. See also Renato Constantino, *The Second Invasion: Japan in the Philippines* (Quezon City: Karrel, 1989) for Filipino perceptions of Japan.

31. Regarding Japan-Singapore relations, see Wee Mon-cheng, *Chrysanthemum and the Orchid* (Singapore: Times Academic Press, 1975) and Ysu Yun Hui, ed., *Japan and Singapore* (Singapore: McGraw-Hill, 2006). Lee's memoir can be found in "Watashi no rirekisho", *Nihon Keizai Shimbun*, 1–30 January 1999.

32. Hiroshi Shimizu and Hitoshi Hirakawa, *Japan and Singapore in the World Economy 1870–1965* (London: Routledge, 1999).

33. Hiroshi Shimizu, *Shingaporu no keizaihatten to Nihon* (Tokyo: Komonzu, 2004). See also Gaimusho (Japan's Ministry of Foreign Affairs), *Outline of Japan's Basic Policies and Japan-Singapore Relations* (Tokyo: Ministry of Foreign Affairs, 1977).

34. On Japan-Thailand relations, see Pasuk Pongpaichit et al., eds, *The Lion and the Mouse* (Bangkok: Chulalongkorn University, 1986), Yoneo Ishii and Toshiharu Yoshikawa, *Nittai Koryu Yonhyakunenshi* (Tokyo: Kodansha, 1987) and Chaiwat

Khamchoo and Bruce Reynolds, eds., *Thai-Japanese Relations in Historical Perspective* (Bangkok: Institute of Asian Studies, Chulalongkorn University, 1988).

35. Sueo Sudo, "The Politics of Thai-Japanese Trade Relations", in *Thai-Japanese Relations in Historical Perspective*, edited by Chaiwat Khamchoo and Bruce Reynolds (Bangkok: Institute of Asian Studies, Chulalongkorn University, 1988), pp. 213–35.

36. Concerning anti-Japanese movements in Thailand, see Eiichi Imagawa and Hiroshi Matsuo, *Nikka haiseki* (Tokyo: Nikkei shinsho, 1973) and Masahide Shibusawa and Shiro Saito, eds., *Tonanajia no Nihon hihan* (Tokyo: Saimaru shuppan, 1974).

37. For Indonesia's domestic problems that affected anti-Japanese movements, see Shizuo Suzuki, "1970 nendaizenhan no Tonanajia niokeru hannichi no ronri", in *Tonanajia to Nihon*, edited by Toru Yano (Tokyo: Kobundo, 1991), pp. 233–47.

38. Gaimusho, *Waga gaiko no kinkyo* (Tokyo: Okurasho insatsukyoku, 1972), p. 99.

39. For the process of establishing MCEDSEA, see Gaimusho, "Tonanajia kaihatsukaigi nitsuite (an), 10 July 1965", copies of documents obtained through Freedom of Information Act, Diplomatic Record Office (Tokyo: Ministry of Foreign Affairs); Kyong-ah Jeong, "60nendai niokeru Nihon no Tonanajia kaihatsu", *Kokusaiseiji*, no. 126 (February 2001): 117–31; Koji Hoshiro, "Tonanajia kaihatsukaigi no kaisai to Nihon gaiko", *Kokusaiseiji*, no. 144 (February 2006): 1–15.

40. On Japan's role in establishing the Asian Development Bank, the Asia Pacific Council and IGGI, see especially Dennis Yasutomo, *Japan and the Asian Development Bank* (New York: Praeger 1983), Shintaro Hamanaka, *Asian Regionalism and Japan: The Politics of Membership in Regional Diplomatic, Financial and Trade Groups* (London: Routledge, 2009), pp. 46–50 and Taizo Miyagi, *Sengo Ajia chitsujo*, pp. 213–37.

41. Fumiaki Nozoe, "Tonanajia kaihatsukakuryokaigi kaisai no seijikeizaikatei", *Hitotsubashi Hogaku* 8, no. 1 (March 2009): 61–99.

42. For various Southeast Asian criticisms, see Jeong, "60nendai niokeru Nihon", p. 123 and Nozoe, "Tonanajia kaihatsukakuryokaigi", pp. 92–96.

43. Hamanaka, *Asian Regionalism*, p. 45.

44. Concerning the Japan–North Vietnam normalization, see especially Masaya Shiraishi, *Japanese Relations with Vietnam: 1951–1987* (Ithaca, NY: Cornell University Press, 1990) and Amiko Nobori, "Japan's Southeast Asian Policy in the Post-Vietnam War", G-Sec Working Paper no. 21 (Global Security Research Institute, Keio University, October 2007).

45. Wasuke Miyake, *Gaiko ni shori wanai* (Tokyo: Fuyosha, 1990).

46. A critical interpretation of the normalization can be found in Seki Tomoda "Nichietsu gaiko kankeijuritsu no keii to shomondai", in *Nihon to Ajia*, edited by Ajiadaigaku Ajia kenkyusho (Tokyo: Ajiadaigaku Ajia kenkyusho, 1995), pp. 93–106.

47. Regarding the Rubber negotiations, see especially Kunisada Kume, "Nihon no Tonanajia gaiko to ASEAN", in *ASEAN womeguru kokusaikankei*, edited by Tatsumi Okabe (Tokyo: Nihon kokusaimondai kenkyusho, 1977), pp. 320–41 and Alan Rix, "ASEAN and Japan: More than Economics", in *Understanding ASEAN*, edited by Alison Broinowski (London: Macmillan, 1982), pp. 169–95.

48. *Straits Times*, 18 April 1973; *Nihon Keizai Shimbun*, 19 April 1973. ASEAN's approach was indeed "a storm signal for Japan". Lim Teck Ghee, "Southeast Asian Perceptions of Japan and the Japanese", in *Japan as an Economic Power and Its Implications for Southeast Asia*, edited by K.S. Sandhu (Singapore: Singapore University Press, 1974), p. 92.

49. ASEAN, "Joint Communique of the Sixth ASEAN Ministerial Meeting, Pattaya, 16–18 April 1973" (Jakarta: ASEAN Secretariat); *Far Eastern Economic Review*, 20 April 1973, p. 72.

50. *Straits Times*, 7 August 1973; *Asahi Shimbun*, 25 August 1973; *Straits Times*, 26 September 1973.

51. Gaimusho, "Joint Press Release on the question of synthetic rubber with the Japanese representatives and the representatives from countries of the Association of South-East Asian Nations, Tokyo, 27 November 1973" (Gaimusho Press Releases, 1974); *Nihon Keizai Shimbun*, 28 November 1973. Foreign Minister Malik stressed that Japan agreed to ASEAN's requests. *Straits Times*, 3 December 1973.

52. *Straits Times*, 22 February 1974; *Asahi Shimbun*, 13 March 1974; Ajiakyoku Chiikiseisakuka, "Goseigomu ni kansuru ASEAN to wagakuni no dai2kai jimureberu kaigo (Tokyo kaigo) nitsuite", Postwar Diplomatic Records, A'-433, Postwar Diplomatic Records, Diplomatic Record Office (Tokyo: Ministry of Foreign Affairs).

53. ASEAN, "Joint Communique of the Seventh ASEAN Ministerial Meeting, Jakarta, 7–9 May 1974" (Jakarta: ASEAN Secretariat, 1974).

54. *Nihon Keizai Shimbun*, 28 July 1975, evening issue; *Straits Times*, 29 July 1975.

55. Keidanren, *Keidanren sanjunenshi* (Tokyo: Keidanren, 1978), pp. 674–86.

56. *Nihon Keizai Shimbun*, 20 November 1976.

57. MITI, *Keizaikyoryoku no genjo to mondaiten* (Tokyo: Okurasho insatsukyoku, 1969), pp. 75–81. Strangely enough, Japan had two white papers on ODA until 2001. The other is *Wagakuni no seifu kaihatsu enjo*, published annually by Gaimusho.

58. On Sato's foreign policy, see especially Frank Langdon, *Japan's Foreign Policy* (Vancouver: University of British Columbia Press, 1973) and Sumio Hatano, ed., *Ikeda-Sato seikenki no Nihon gaiko* (Kyoto: Mineruva shobo, 2004).
59. Constantino, *The Second Invasion*, p. 34.
60. Japan-ASEAN economic relations were substantially documented by Narongchai Akrasanee, ed., *ASEAN-Japan Economic Relations: Trade and Development* (Singapore: Institute of Southeast Asian Studies, 1983) and Sueo Sekiguchi, ed., *ASEAN-Japan Economic Relations: Investment* (Singapore: Institute of Southeast Asian Studies, 1983).
61. From the tables in Sueo Sudo, *The Fukuda Doctrine and ASEAN* (Singapore: Institute of Southeast Asian Studies, 1992), pp. 248–55.
62. Makoto Ikema, "Japan's Economic Relations with ASEAN", in *ASEAN in a Changing Pacific and World Economy*, edited by Ross Garnaut (Canberra: Australian National University Press, 1980), p. 469.
63. Anoosorn Chantapan, "Changing Patterns of Japan-ASEAN Relations (1967–1989)" (PhD dissertation, Johns Hopkins University, 1993), p. 106. For anti-Japanese movements in Southeast Asia, see Friedemann Bartu, *The Ugly Japanese: Nippon's Economic Empire in Asia* (Singapore: Longman, 1992); Raul Manglapus, *Japan in Southeast Asia: Collision Course* (New York: Carnegie Endowment for International Peace, 1976).
64. Concerning Tanaka's visit to the ASEAN countries in 1974, see Ajiakyoku, "Sori no Tonanajia shokoku homonyo hatsugen shiryo, January 1974", Postwar Diplomatic Records, A'1–5–1–16, Diplomatic Record Office (Tokyo: Ministry of Foreign Affairs, 1974).
65. Gaimusho, *Waga gaiko no kinkyo*, vol. 1 (1974), p. 21.
66. *Straits Times*, 13 January 1974: *Nihon Keizai Shimbun*, 15 January 1974.
67. *Asahi Shimbun*, 16 January 1974, evening issue.
68. Gaimusho, *Waga gaiko no kinkyo*, vol. 2 (1974), p. 14.
69. There occurred serious reappraisal of Japan's resource diplomacy towards Southeast Asia in late 1973. *Asahi Shimbun*, 17 and 31 December 1973. For Japan's resource diplomacy, see particularly Shoko Tanaka, *Post-War Japanese Resource Policies and Strategies: The Case of Southeast Asia* (Ithaca, NY: China-Japan Program, Cornell University, 1986).
70. ASEAN, "Declaration of ASEAN Concord, 24 February 1976" (Jakarta: ASEAN Secretariat, 1976).
71. ASEAN, "Treaty of Amity and Cooperation in Southeast Asia, 24 February 1976" (Jakarta: ASEAN Secretariat, 1976).
72. *Far Eastern Economic Review*, 18 February 1977, p. 34.
73. *Mainichi Shimbun*, 26 January 1975.
74. *Asahi Shimbun*, 7 August 1975.
75. *Nihon Keizai Shimbun*, 25 January 1976.

76. Gaimusho, *Waga gaiko no kinkyo* (1976), pp. 21–22.

77. Keiichiro Nakamura, *Miki seiken 747 nichi* (Tokyo: Gyoseimondai kenkyusho, 1981), p. 131.

78. According to a Gaimusho document, the Asian Affairs Bureau almost came to a consensus on Japan's Southeast Asian policy by the end of 1976. See especially Ajiakyoku, "Tai Tonanajia seisaku (an), November 1976", copies of documents obtained through Freedom of Information Act, Diplomatic Record Office (Tokyo: Ministry of Foreign Affairs, 1976).

3

STRAIGHTENING THE ASEAN-INDOCHINA DIVIDE: The Pursuit of the Alternative Stream

The end of the Vietnam War in April 1975 brought about many changes in the international relations of Southeast Asia: rapidly declining American commitments, a growing Soviet influence, and the polarization of Indochina and the Association of Southeast Asian Nations (ASEAN) that was induced by the antagonism between communist countries. It is thus no wonder that Soviet-supported Vietnam invaded and ousted the pro-China Pol Pot regime in Cambodia in December 1978. During the height of a new Cold War, it was ASEAN that seized the opportunity to become a viable regional body by resolving the most critical regional conflict. As a matter of fact, ASEAN has come to develop its political base while pursuing economic cooperation policies with the assistance from outside powers.[1]

Many studies have been undertaken to account for these changes, yet the growing Japanese role in the region has not generated any substantial analysis.[2] One of the reasons for the limited scrutiny of Japan's Southeast Asian policy is the view that Tokyo has never changed its traditional economic policy and that its reactions to the changing regional environment are being induced by external pressures.[3] Also, the consistency of Japan's low-profile economic diplomacy has led many scholars to believe that Japan, without adequate military power, does not stand a chance of playing a significant role in Southeast Asia.

This chapter looks closely at new developments in Japanese foreign policy from a different perspective, focusing on how Japanese policymakers came to define Japan's new role in a turbulent region, while pursuing multilateral policies towards ASEAN instead of traditional bilateral economic policies. Japan's new role can be seen in the process of forging the very first foreign policy doctrine in 1977. In fact, designating ASEAN as a pillar of Japanese foreign policy, Japan went through a significant experiment in playing a proactive political role in Southeast Asia between 1977 and 1986.

ASEAN IN 1977: 10TH ANNIVERSARY AND JAPAN

The year 1977 could be regarded as a turning point in ASEAN regionalism for two reasons. The first is the fact that ASEAN held another summit in a row. The second is that ASEAN incorporated dialogue partners into the framework of the regional cooperation scheme. In fact, having founded a framework for ASEAN's modus operandi in 1976, which was to be based on national and regional resilience, ASEAN decided to hold another summit the following year in 1977 in order to consolidate its foundation for external cooperation. ASEAN began to realize, despite perennial problems and animosity, the importance of Japan's active involvement in the region, thus seeking a new modus vivendi with Japan in 1977. To this end, ASEAN first of all rather hastily chose five ASEAN industrial projects to be financed by Japan as a symbol of upgraded regional cooperation, simply because some of the member countries strongly objected to the alternative idea of "free trade" and ASEAN trade liberalization. ASEAN agreed that the package of five projects was the one substantial element by which relations between ASEAN and Japan could be further strengthened. In other words, the five projects "became one of the props on the stage where Japan was expected to play a major role, written for it by ASEAN".[4]

According to a confidential document adopted at the fourth meeting of the ASEAN economic ministers in June 1977, ASEAN's economic policy towards Japan was formulated for the first time, together with a decision to send an ASEAN mission to Japan.[5] In July 1977 the members of an ASEAN economic mission, headed by Indonesian Trade Minister Radius Prawiro, vigorously negotiated with their Japanese counterparts. Presenting a four-point plan, the mission emphasized that "ASEAN has been giving priority to its economic development since the end of the Indochina war in 1975. In this context the ASEAN states attach importance to relations with Japan."[6] The mission's requests implied the creation of an economic bloc with ASEAN hoping to win special preferential treatment for its exports to Japan. It naturally behoved Japan to respond to this strong call for an active role in the region.

When ASEAN held the second summit in Kuala Lumpur on 4–5 August 1977, with the same heads of government in attendance except for a new Thai Prime Minister, Thanin Kraivichien, widespread attention was cast on ASEAN's meeting with the heads of government from Australia, Japan and New Zealand, which took place on 6–8 August. Reflecting the leaders' shared intention to celebrate the 10th anniversary, the joint communiqué underscored the following:

> The Heads of Government expressed satisfaction that ASEAN countries have made significant progress in building their national resilience through the acceleration and intensification [of] economic, social and cultural cooperation and the strengthening of the foundation of social justice and equity for all within their individual states. In the context of ASEAN consolidation, as laid down in the ASEAN Declaration and the Declaration of ASEAN Concord, ASEAN countries have intensified their collaboration in all fields. This has contributed significantly to the solidarity, cohesion and maturity of ASEAN.[7]

While discussing the major agenda, including regional development; the zone of peace, friendship and neutrality (ZOPFAN); economic cooperation; external relations; cooperation in the social, cultural and other fields; and improvement of the ASEAN machinery, the second summit could not achieve much.[8] However, by continuing to convene top-level meetings with the three external powers, it received new momentum, further recognition, and added stimulus for greater internal unity, thus making a successful beginning for ASEAN's second decade. In this respect, by holding top-level meetings with the three dialogue partners, ASEAN succeeded in obtaining significant concessions and commitments from them, particularly from Japan. As one observer cogently put it, "If this summit on the 10th anniversary of the founding of ASEAN is remembered, it will be for drawing the economic barons from Japan into substantial involvement in the region's future."[9]

PROMULGATION OF THE FUKUDA DOCTRINE

The election of a new prime minister on 23 December 1976 was the beginning of Japan's new Southeast Asian policy with its special emphasis on ASEAN.[10] As a strong Liberal Democratic Party (LDP) leader, but one who also had personal relationships with many top ASEAN leaders, Prime Minister Takeo Fukuda was highly esteemed by government officials as well as by Southeast Asian leaders. Recognizing favourable signals from ASEAN leaders, Fukuda, upon establishing his Cabinet, expressed readiness to promote an Asia-centred diplomacy in his policy speech in January 1977:

> The peace and prosperity of Southeast Asian nations is a major concern of Japan, itself an Asian nation, and it is from this perspective that we intend to extend cooperation to their various efforts to develop themselves in the spirit of self-reliance as seen in the efforts by ASEAN through personal exchanges, active contributions to nation-building and other means.[11]

Unlike his predecessors, Prime Minister Fukuda came into office with clearly defined domestic and foreign policy objectives. His external policies could be epitomized by his support for three concepts: first, Japan's unprecedented experiment as a great economic power without military power; second, the interdependent world community and Japan's responsibility to it; and third, a sense of the world economic crisis and Japan's ability to contribute to world economic recovery and towards solving the North-South problems. Of the three, the first had been a long-cherished policy objective since Fukuda's days as foreign minister.[12]

The initiation for the first doctrine in Japanese foreign policy was undertaken rather quickly, for all policymakers involved in the process held one view in common: that existing Southeast Asian policy was not working.[13] There were three reasons for this conclusion. First, the anti-Japanese movement in 1974 was a decisive counterblow to Japan's resource-based diplomacy. Second, the end of the Vietnam War in 1975 and American withdrawal from the region necessitated Japan's reappraisal of its policy orientation, which had always followed the dictates of the United States. In other words, the power vacuum in Southeast Asia required a new role for Japan in the region. Third, and in relation to the second, ASEAN as a regional organization was becoming a fully fledged actor in the region, exemplified by its first summit in 1976, and it expected strong Japanese support, especially economic support. Special commitments, not vague promises, were demanded by ASEAN in the field of regional economic development. All these factors, including the Tanaka riots, the power vacuum, and ASEAN's demands, provided Japanese policymakers with a unique opportunity to initiate a systematic new Southeast Asian policy.

The basic framework for Tokyo's new diplomacy was discussed for the first time by all concerned policymakers and agreed to by Prime Minister Fukuda, Foreign Minister Iichiro Hatoyama and the Japanese ambassadors to Southeast Asia on 6 March 1977, a few weeks before Fukuda's visit to the United States.[14] The study meeting spent more than three hours dealing with crucial issues involved in the forthcoming Southeast Asian policy, with Fukuda emphasizing his concept of a "heart-to-heart" relationship with the region. With respect to Japan's Indochina policy, however, the meeting was split between the active promoters and the cautious ones. After heated discussion the consensus finally reached was that Japan should actively promote ASEAN-centred policies.[15]

The talks between newly elected Prime Minister Fukuda and President Carter were extraordinary in that both countries declared their particular stress on ASEAN.[16] Suffice it to say that the joint communiqué, which unusually referred to ASEAN and Indochina, reflected what the Asian Affairs Bureau of the Ministry of Foreign Affairs (MOFA) had come up with after a large-scale *nemawashi* (laying the groundwork). It should be stressed here that extraordinary measures had been taken by Fukuda and the MOFA to ensure Japan's unshakable desire for enhanced relations with the ASEAN countries. First, before the Fukuda–Carter conference, Fukuda sent his colleague, Kazuo Tamaki, as an emissary to Indonesia to brief its government on what Japan stood for, and to reflect upon Southeast Asian requests in the forthcoming conference in the United States. Furthermore, after the conference, Fukuda dispatched a special envoy to five ASEAN countries and Burma to demonstrate that Japan's quest for partnership with ASEAN was real and significant, and that Washington would remain a strong supporter of the organization.[17]

However, by July 1977, two problems remained to be solved before formulating systematic Southeast Asian policies. The first was concerned with Japan's posture towards Hanoi. Reflecting the great debate within the government, Takehiko Nishiyama, Director of the Policy Planning Division of the Foreign Ministry's Asian Affairs Bureau, flew to Hanoi in order to explain Japan's forthcoming policies to the Vietnamese leaders and to sound out Vietnam's reactions.[18] The trip, according to Nishiyama, who met with his counterpart in Hanoi, turned out to be successful, thereby paving the way for the new role Japan could play in bridging relations between ASEAN and Indochina. Now Japan found aid to be the only means by which it could play a political role in the region. Nishiyama's trip was crucial in strengthening the activists' position within the policymaking circle. Furthermore, Yosuke Nakae, Director General of the Asian Affairs Bureau, took pains to persuade the pacifists within the government to come to terms with a new reality in the region by pointing to the ASEAN initiatives towards the Indochinese countries.[19]

The second problem was concerned with the content of Japan's commitments. In arriving at a consensus, upon which Prime Minister Fukuda's offer could be based, there existed disagreements among the concerned ministries, although these ministries held a basic understanding that the "historical" talks between Fukuda and ASEAN leaders should not fail. Because of negative attitudes from the concerned ministries, including the Finance, International Trade and Industry (MITI), and Agricultural, Forestry and Fisheries (MAFF), the following agreements were reached in July 1977: first, $1 billion loans for five ASEAN regional projects would be pledged; second, a scheme to establish commodity export earnings (STABEX) and the fund ($400 million) to carry it out would be further discussed; and third, the tariff problems would be examined as part of the Tokyo Round.[20] In short, except for the offer of $1 billion, the concerned ministries could not decide on Fukuda's commitments.

In formulating a new Southeast Asian policy, the Foreign Ministry took the initiative and manipulated the process of decision-making in Japan. In coordination with Prime Minister Fukuda's secretary, Hisashi Owada, a quasi-policy group (Yosuke Nakae, Takehiko Nishiyama, Sumio Edamura, Sakutaro Sumino) within the Foreign Ministry propounded the so-called Fukuda Doctrine, which was originally composed of six principles:[21]

1. The need to forge a cooperative partnership between Japan and Southeast Asian countries for world peace and stability.
2. Declaration of Japan's support for socio-economic development of the ASEAN countries and Burma and ASEAN's regional cooperation.
3. The formation of special trade and commercial relations between Japan and ASEAN-Burma.

4. The advancement of heart-to-heart relations between Japan and ASEAN-Burma.
5. The continuation of top-level dialogues between Japan and ASEAN-Burma.
6. The promotion of ASEAN-Indochina cooperation and the establishment of friendly relations between Japan and Indochina.[22]

More importantly, according to the leading policymaker, the doctrine aimed at giving Japan a political role in Southeast Asia in securing stable coexistence between ASEAN and Indochina.[23] To this end, policymakers sought to use economic aid to Hanoi as a political lever to move Vietnam away from confrontational policies in the region, and away from its close ties to the Soviet Union. Nishiyama considered that Japan could employ three policies: First, simply strengthen ASEAN so that Vietnam would eventually find it more advantageous to improve its relations with ASEAN. Second, promote greater mutual understanding of real intentions by providing a forum where they could talk together. And third, create conditions in which the Indochinese countries could carry out their reconstruction and fulfil their aspiration for national independence without destabilizing the situation in Southeast Asia.[24] At the same time, Japan approached ASEAN as a viable regional organization that could help establish peaceful coexistence and a stable regional order in post–Vietnam War Southeast Asia. Having launched the Japan-ASEAN Forum in March 1977, replacing the old Rubber Forum, the Japanese government vigorously pursued a "special" relationship with the organization.

Japan's "special" relationship with ASEAN deserves a brief explanation. It did not intend to establish an economic bloc, but to forge close "political" coordination between Japan and ASEAN as a regional actor. ASEAN demanded a preferential trade agreement (PTA) for the relationship to be really special. However, due to the domestic difficulties, Japan insisted on an "aid not trade" policy, which meant that Japan disagreed with the formulation of the proposed Japan-ASEAN PTA, although it agreed to study the STABEX system.[25] In other words, while avoiding the difficult task of opening markets for ASEAN products, a special relationship could be established by making political use of economic assistance. This was initially intended as a departure from Japan's usual practice of offering foreign economic assistance. Multilateral and official relations were stressed, as opposed to traditional bilateral and private ones, simply because the latter had been denounced as "the source of corruption and exploitation". Japanese officials thought that the negative image of Japan could be improved if extended cooperation was forged through ASEAN. Another element of the "special" relationship was to forge close diplomatic ties with the organization. More specifically, the Japanese government intended to inform the organization on current developments in international issues that directly affected the member countries. It did so by sending official envoys whenever deemed necessary.

For these reasons Japan and ASEAN, after ten years, chose to recognize each other's calculated interests as a positive relationship. ASEAN needed Japan's economic assistance to reinforce regional cooperation, and Japan needed ASEAN to play its political role in the region and to develop multilateral economic relations. Thus, the Second ASEAN Summit in Kuala Lumpur was an ideal opportunity for Japan's new Southeast Asian policy because it led to the initiation of multilateral foreign policy. Japan's ASEAN policy was formulated as the core of the Fukuda Doctrine and designated as a "national" policy. As a third attempt, the new draft was completed on 22 July, which consisted of the following five principles.

1. [I]n our future Southeast Asia policy, Japan will steadfastly maintain its commitment to peace and its determination not to become a military power.
2. Japan recognizes ASEAN as having been solidly established as an autonomous regional organization in Southeast Asia and, as the closest friend of ASEAN, will extend its positive understanding and cooperation in its efforts toward greater solidarity.
3. Japan will attempt to further strengthen its economic and technical cooperation so that its economic and technical capabilities may be of use to ASEAN members and Burma along the lines of their social and economic developments plans; and at the same time, Japan will seek to develop specially close trade and economic relationships with these countries.
4. [W]ith the ideal of elevating Japan's relationships with ASEAN members and Burma to that of mutual confidence and trust on the basis of true heart-to-heart communication, Japan will take positive steps not only in trade and economic areas but in political, social and cultural fields as well.
5. Japan would like to see maintenance and development of a good neighborly relationship with the nations of Indochina, and would

hope that these nations will grow as peace-loving nations that respect
freedom and independence, and will encourage their efforts for
building peace-loving nationhoods.[26]

With the revised five-principled draft in hand, Prime Minister Fukuda
embarked on his ASEAN tour on 6 August 1977.[27] In many respects,
therefore, the historical meeting between the Japanese prime minister and
the heads of the ASEAN countries was all the more significant because it
was the first meeting in the entire post-war period, and only the second
since the Greater East Asian Conference held in Tokyo in 1943. It was
unprecedented that the joint communiqué of the Kuala Lumpur summit
underscored the special relationship between Japan and ASEAN for the
first time: "The ASEAN Heads of Government and the Prime Minister
of Japan agreed that cooperation between ASEAN and Japan should be
expanded and that Japanese cooperation with ASEAN should be extended
in such a manner as to contribute towards ASEAN's efforts at self-reliance
in order to enhance ASEAN's economic resilience and consolidate further
ASEAN's solidarity. They agreed to develop through such cooperation a
special and close economic relationship between ASEAN countries and
Japan in the spirit of partnership."[28]

However, throughout talks at the summit, and with individual
countries after, the Japanese delegation recognized that there still existed
a sense of suspicion on the part of ASEAN countries, and because of this,
as well as the newspaper leaks of the doctrine,[29] the Manila speech was
rewritten on 15 August, which can be distilled into the following three
principles:

First, Japan, a nation committed to peace, rejects the role of a military
power, and on that basis is resolved to contribute to the peace and
prosperity of Southeast Asia, and of the world community;

Second, Japan, as a true friend of the countries of Southeast Asia, will
do its best to consolidate the relationship of mutual confidence and trust
based on "heart-to-heart" understanding with these countries, in wide-
ranging fields covering not only political and economic areas but also
social and cultural areas;

Third, Japan will be an equal partner of ASEAN and its member countries,
and cooperate positively with them in their own efforts to strengthen their
solidarity and resilience, together with other nations of like mind outside
the region, while aiming at fostering a relationship based on mutual

understanding with the nations of Indochina, and will thus contribute to the building of peace and prosperity throughout Southeast Asia.[30]

All the policymakers recognized Japan's limited offer, particularly with respect to any increase in Japan's imports due to the structural problems in Japanese industry, and made it clear that Japan would have to explain to the ASEAN countries exactly what it could or could not do. Thus, economic assistance was not the core of forging a "special" relationship with ASEAN; rather it was the establishment of closer "political" coordination between Japan and ASEAN as a regional actor that constituted the heart of a "special" relationship.[31] Most intriguing was the change in Japan's approach to foreign assistance in Southeast Asia. The difference was subtle, but the ideas behind the new approach are important in understanding the changes in Japanese attitudes towards the region. As Nakae explained, the amount of Japanese aid had been customarily decided according to the requests of concrete projects, but now the Japanese government decided to offer $1 billion for ASEAN industrial projects in the absence of any concrete projects, hoping that "ASEAN could strive for successful implementation of the projects as quid pro quo for Japan's positive intention".[32] It was not a matter of the amount Japan offered but a matter of change in approach that characterized the doctrine.

In summary, through interaction with ASEAN, the policymakers identified the problems created by Japan's ongoing Southeast Asian policy and tried to find the best solutions to resolve them. Policy ideas were threefold. First, it was hoped that a policy of cultural promotion would compensate for economically skewed relations. Second, playing a political role was the most challenging policy, and it was the best solution in terms of the power vacuum existing in the region. Third, providing economic assistance was to develop regional industrialization projects. As part of this policy, the establishment of a "special" relationship was crucial in furthering Japan's own interests along with ASEAN's demands and interests. In order to institutionalize these policy ideas, the next step was to be consistent in efforts to implement the proclaimed policy.

THE POLITICS OF JAPAN-ASEAN RELATIONS

Japan's political relations with ASEAN have been characterized by prime ministers' visits, regular meetings of foreign ministers, irregular meetings of economic ministers and the Japan-ASEAN Forum (see Table 3.1).

TABLE 3.1
Japan-ASEAN Relations, 1977–86

	PM Visits	Summit	Forum	FMM	EMM
1977	Fukuda	1st	1st/2nd		
1978				1st	
1979			3rd	2nd	1st
1980			4th	3rd	
1981	Suzuki			4th	
1982			5th	5th	
1983	Nakasone		6th	6th	
1984				7th	
1985			7th	8th	2nd
1986			8th	9th	

Prime Ministers' Visits to ASEAN

The year 1978 may be called "ASEAN year", because ASEAN became the focus of international diplomatic activity, with various leaders visiting the region, among them American Vice President Walter Mondale, Soviet Deputy Foreign Minister Nikolai Firyupin, and Chinese Vice President Deng Xiaoping. Japan's political initiative in taking ASEAN seriously was clearly being emulated by other big powers. Following Fukuda's footstep, Prime Minister Zenko Suzuki visited the region (Indonesia, Malaysia, the Philippines, Singapore and Thailand) as his first overseas trip in January 1981. Like Fukuda, Suzuki made a major speech in Bangkok, which stressed the following points: (1) Japan will not play a military role in the international community; (2) Japan will play a political role to help maintain world peace, commensurate with Japan's status in the community of nations; and (3) Japan will stress four areas in its economic cooperation policy, such as rural development, energy resources, human resources, and small and medium-sized enterprises. More than anything else, it was unprecedented that Japan's top leader visited Southeast Asia before meeting with his American counterpart.[33]

Only two years later, in April–May 1983, Prime Minister Yasuhiro Nakasone again paid a visit to ASEAN countries (Indonesia, Malaysia, the Philippines, Singapore and Thailand). In promoting a relationship of mutual trust between the two parties, Nakasone announced three proposals: first, a fifty per cent increase in the ceiling of quotas under the preferential scheme for ASEAN industrial products starting in 1984; second, reactivation of a programme for Japan to assist ASEAN enterprises; and third, an invitation to 150 ASEAN youths to visit Japan every year for a short stay and the launching of Japan-ASEAN scientific and technological cooperation.[34] Thus, by offering new commitments to the region, the momentum generated by the Fukuda Doctrine was maintained (see Table 3.2).

Soon after the visit, however, Nakasone was preoccupied with economic problems as a result of mounting pressures from the United States and Europe. The announcement of an action programme in July 1985 was a case in point. Stressing Japan's new self-image as a member of the West, Nakasone showed strong leadership in resolving economic frictions with the West. This initiative, however, resulted in a "benign neglect" of his ASEAN policy, as underscored by a declining trend in trade and investment. It was unfortunate that the sense of Japan's benign neglect arose just when ASEAN was suddenly feeling vulnerable, faced with the worst economic stagnation in its history.[35]

During the first phase, nevertheless, ASEAN-Japan relations developed remarkably, as seen in the rapid institutionalization of the relationships. This occurred in three main venues: ASEAN-Japan Foreign Ministers' Meeting, ASEAN-Japan Economic Ministers' Meeting and the ASEAN-Japan Forum.

TABLE 3.2
Japanese Prime Ministers' Visits, 1977–86

Premier	Date	Countries visited	Results
Fukuda	August 1977	Thailand, Malaysia, Singapore, Indonesia, Burma, Philippines	(1) The First Japan-ASEAN Summit (2) Fukuda Doctrine (3) Five Regional Projects
Suzuki	January 1981	Philippines, Indonesia, Singapore, Malaysia, Thailand	(1) Human Resource Development (2) ASEAN Regional Studies Promotion Programme
Nakasone	April 1983	Malaysia, Singapore, Thailand, Indonesia, Philippines	(1) Plant Renovation Programme (2) Youth Programme (3) 50% quota increase

Japan-ASEAN Foreign Ministers' Meeting

The first venue is the Japan-ASEAN Foreign Ministers' Meeting. Initiated by Foreign Minister Sunao Sonoda, this political forum between ASEAN and Japan was institutionalized in June 1978 with the intent of expanding later to include the participation of the United States, Australia, New Zealand, and the European Community.[36] It should be stressed here that Japan's proposal for this meeting led to the institutionalization of the Post-Ministerial Conferences (PMC). Since then, ASEAN has held a regular conference with these dialogue partners immediately after each meeting of its foreign ministers. Among other things, the Japan-ASEAN Ministerial Meeting focused on the relevance of Japan's economic aid to Hanoi as a crucial factor in maintaining stability in Southeast Asia. Japan had insisted that its economic assistance was a political lever while ASEAN warned of the danger of strengthening its communist neighbour. Although this disagreement was settled in ASEAN's favour in 1980, many on the Japanese side felt that the further isolation of Vietnam would only result in more adventurism on its part, such as the invasion of Cambodia in 1978.[37]

Since the intervention, Japan supported ASEAN's stand on the Cambodian issue. While following the ASEAN dictate in resolving the conflict, Japan nonetheless maintained its dialogue with Hanoi. In 1979 Japan finally suspended its foreign aid to Hanoi, but maintained its cardinal relations with Vietnam as the only advanced country that could play a mediating role.[38] In this respect, the Kuantan Principle forged by Malaysia and Indonesia in March 1980, provided Japan with a window of opportunity. Reflecting on the "soft approach" to Hanoi, Foreign Minister Saburo Okita proposed the creation of a demilitarized zone in Cambodia in July 1980 while reiterating Japan's engagement policy.[39]

In a similar vein, at the third PMC in June 1981, Foreign Minister Sonoda disclosed Japan's formula for a "comprehensive political settlement" of the Cambodian problem, including (1) the introduction of peace-keeping forces to enforce an immediate ceasefire, (2) the phased withdrawal of Vietnamese forces in accordance with a prearranged schedule, (3) the regrouping of all Cambodian armed elements in designated locations for their disarmament, and (4) the maintenance of peace and order in the country.[40]

Furthermore, by calling for an international conference on Cambodia, Sonoda expressed Japan's readiness to extend as much cooperation as possible in close coordination with ASEAN, if and when the conflict made headway towards a solution in this direction. However, during the following two years there were no signs of settlement of the conflict. As such, Japan became more concerned with economic and financial contributions for the reconstruction of the post-war economies of Indochina.

In 1984 Japan's engagement policy began to bear some fruit. The fact that Japan invited Sihanouk to Tokyo and eventually held talks with Vietnamese Foreign Minister Nguyen Co Thach can be regarded as Japan's visible contributions to settlement of the conflict. Most importantly, Foreign Minister Shintaro Abe spelled out rather vigorously Japan's policy towards the conflict by outlining three principles as follows: (1) Japan will bear the expenses for peace-keeping activities; (2) Japan will provide personnel and facilities for an election to be held under international supervision; and (3) Japan will provide economic assistance to the three Indochinese countries following the realization of peace in Cambodia.[41] These so-called Abe principles augured well for smoothing the process of conflict resolution.

Japan-ASEAN Economic Ministers' Meetings

The second venue is the ASEAN-Japan Economic Ministers' Meeting (EMM), which was first institutionalized in November 1979 on a request basis. The first EMM, held in Tokyo, covered various issues of mutual interest — trade, commodities, investment, transfer of technology, and development assistance — as well as the world economic situation as a whole.[42] The ASEAN side was represented by the economic ministers of each country and the Secretary-General of the ASEAN Secretariat. The Japanese side was composed of five ministers: Foreign Affairs, Finance, Agriculture, International Trade and Industry, and Economic Planning Agency. Presenting three memoranda on trade, commodities and investment, ASEAN asked for vigorous Japanese initiatives to rectify the imbalances in trade patterns between the developed and developing countries. The Japanese government concurred with the ASEAN request to establish the ASEAN Promotion Center for Trade, Investment and Tourism as a symbolic gesture of its cooperation. Beyond this measure, Tokyo failed to give any substantial boost to its economic relations with ASEAN.[43]

Following this inaugural meeting the second meeting was held in June 1985, but failed to achieve any substantial results. ASEAN's emphasis was for greater Japanese cooperation for a more balanced trade structure, improved market-opening measures taking into account ASEAN interests instead of only the interests of developed countries, and better market access for ASEAN exports, particularly for semi-manufactured and manufactured products.[44] The problems of commodity issues, the declining trend of investment flow from Japan to ASEAN, the need for transfer of technology, and research and development were also areas which engaged ASEAN in its relations with Japan. Japan's response, however, was "too little, too late", and ASEAN ministers criticized the atmosphere of the meeting as "overly formal". It cannot be denied that during the Fukuda Doctrine period, there existed a problem of overlapping and complications in these institutional arrangements, most notably between the AJF and the EMM. It was not until the early 1990s that MITI as a single body began to forge its dialogues with ASEAN.

Japan-ASEAN Forum

The third venue is the Japan-ASEAN Forum (JAF) that took over from the Rubber Forum in November 1973 for the purpose of settling problems of the rubber trade. Unlike the previous forum's inclination towards negotiation, the first two meetings of the new forum were to lay the foundation for the discussion of economic and cultural cooperation between ASEAN and Japan. The goals of the inaugural forum in March 1977 were threefold; namely, to formulate decisions based on the areas of cooperation between ASEAN and Japan, to review and monitor the progress of cooperation between the two, and to recommend measures that would achieve the objective of expanding cooperation.[45] The second JAF was held in Tokyo in October, soon after Fukuda's visit to the region. At the meeting, both sides discussed three specific areas of trade, economics and culture and agreed that there would be a continuous examination of other areas of mutual benefit within the framework of expanded cooperation. Yet, no major agreements on these three areas of cooperation were reached; an outcome deplored by one Japanese official as undermining Japanese credibility in responding earnestly to ASEAN demands.[46]

As a Japanese official lamented, Japan has remained reactive, and at best equivocal, in economic cooperation. From the third through the ninth meetings of the JAF, the same pattern has been observed, with ASEAN asking Japan to open its market and to be more generous in foreign aid and technology transfer. Japan's "too little, too late" response has, thus, become the bone of contention at each JAF. As such, the format of the JAF has somewhat changed and come to focus on how much Japan can assist in the economic development of ASEAN countries.

Faced with one of the most difficult economic crises in history and with little response from Japan, ASEAN's frustrations exploded in 1984. At the seventh JAF in October 1984, the ASEAN leaders declared in a strong voice: "In the latest round of tariff reductions of the affected items, ASEAN's share of the total Japanese imports was minimal while the developed countries enjoyed the preponderant share. The ASEAN side stressed that trade was of vital importance to ASEAN and cooperation between ASEAN and Japan on trade matters should be improved."[47] ASEAN's contention was very clear: despite Japan's announcement of a series of market-opening measures, Japan had not addressed the specific ASEAN requests, which had been reiterated over the years of dialogue with Japan.

When the eighth JAF was held in July 1986, ASEAN again stressed the problem of market access for ASEAN exports to Japan and requested an improvement in the Japanese General Scheme of Preference (GSP), the lowering of tariffs and non-tariff barriers, and the expansion of import quotas for products of interest to ASEAN countries. ASEAN also requested that Japan provide a prior consultative session on its market-opening measures and non-tariff barriers so that ASEAN interests could be taken into account in these exercises.[48]

Since 1977, therefore, the JAF had become the vehicle for Japan's ASEAN policy. At the same time, the Japanese government encouraged private initiatives towards a better understanding between Japan and the regional group.

THE ECONOMICS OF JAPAN-ASEAN RELATIONS

Without doubt, Japan's relations with ASEAN have to a large extent been economic in nature. Three economic aspects have been stressed in the relations: trade, investment and aid. Before going into the details of the three components, it would be useful to see the trend in macro-level relations (see Table 3.3). In 1986 Japan's trade with ASEAN was US$28,640 million, or 8.5 per cent of its total trade. ASEAN was Japan's third-largest trading partner after the United States (32.6 per cent) and the European Community (13.3 per cent). Japanese investment in ASEAN accounted for 13.7 per cent of its accumulated total foreign investment between 1951 and March 1986, the second largest after the United States (33.5 per cent), and slightly larger than that of the EC (12.5 per cent). About 30 per cent of Japan's total official development assistance (ODA) is allocated to ASEAN, which has been the largest recipient of Japan's foreign aid.[49] Table 3.3 indicates,

TABLE 3.3
Japan's Economic Relations with ASEAN, 1977–86 ($ million)

	Trade	Investment	ODA
1977	15,730 (10.4%)	636 (22.7%)	266 (29.9%)
1978	18,566 (10.5%)	917 (19.9%)	447 (29.4%)
1979	25,923 (12.1%)	595 (11.9%)	569 (29.8%)
1980	34,245 (13.9%)	927 (19.7%)	701 (35.9%)
1981	36,162 (13.3%)	2,834 (31.8%)	797 (35.4%)
1982	34,304 (14.0%)	801 (10.4%)	682 (28.9%)
1983	32,377 (12.7%)	973 (11.9%)	724 (30.0%)
1984	36,160 (11.8%)	906 (8.9%)	833 (34.3%)
1985	31,462 (10.3%)	935 (7.6%)	800 (31.2%)
1986	28,644 (8.5%)	855 (3.8%)	914 (23.7%)

Note: Brunei is included from 1984.
Sources: MITI, *Tsusho Hakusho*, 1978–87; Ministry of Finance, *Financial Statistics of Japan*, various issues; Ministry of Foreign Affairs, *Waga Gaiko no Kinkyo*, 1978–87.

however, that ASEAN's overall share in the three fields has been on the decline. Should it be judged as a weakening of the relationship? To answer this question, each component must be examined closely.

Japan-ASEAN Trade

Owing to its large import of petroleum, Japan continues to run a deficit in its trade with ASEAN as a whole, which in 1986 reached US$4,390 million. Bilaterally, however, it is another story. Without petroleum exports, all the ASEAN countries would suffer trade deficits with Japan. Japan's trade with Brunei, Indonesia and Malaysia is in the red, but the latter are all exporters of petroleum and liquefied natural gas (LNG), without which they would be unable to achieve a surplus in their trade with Japan. On the other hand, Japan has chronic surpluses in trade with Singapore and Thailand. These trends have continued over the years.

According to the data in Figures 3.1 and 3.2, it is clear that Japan-ASEAN trade has levelled off, and even fallen by 1986. There are many reasons for this decline. Most importantly, economic activity in the ASEAN nations has stagnated as lower growth rates in the United States have brought their exports to this critical market. Japan is partly to blame for this situation, for Japan had been chalking up massive oil reserves,

FIGURE 3.1
Japan's Exports to ASEAN Countries, 1977–86 ($ million)

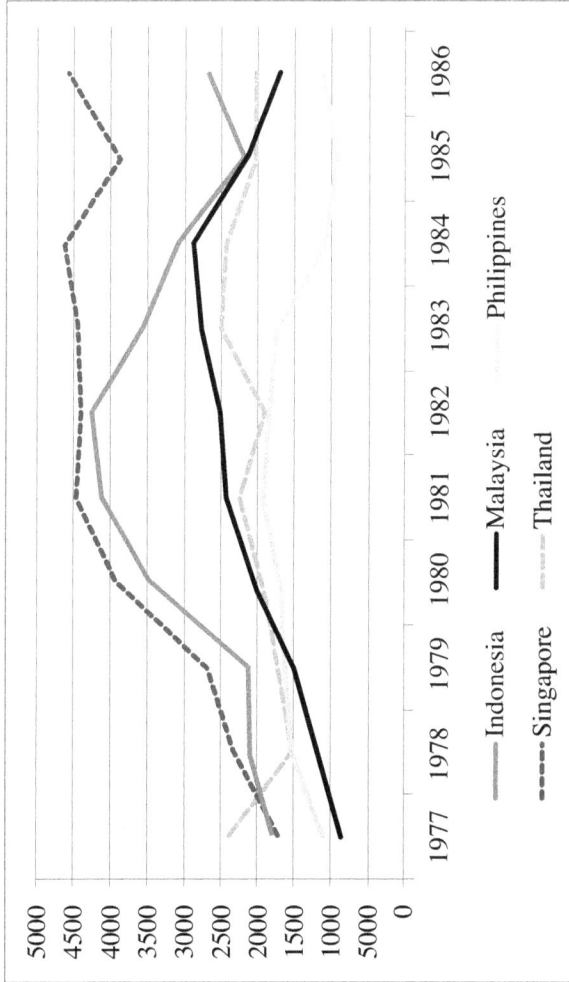

FIGURE 3.2
Japan's Imports from ASEAN Countries, 1977–86 ($ million)

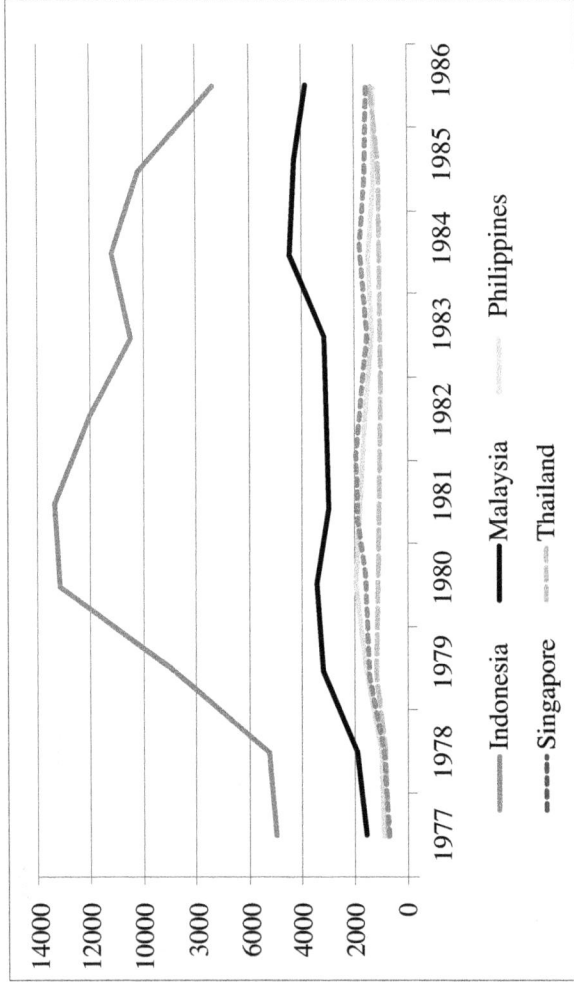

and other primary commodities have fallen markedly, thereby adversely affecting the exporters of raw materials. It should be noted here that energy conservation, technological innovations and other factors reforming the Japanese economy during the 1980s have altered the nation's trade structure. It is now difficult to expect any drastic increase in trade unless ASEAN replaces some of its mainstay exports with items better targeted towards the changing demand in Japan.[50]

Japanese Investment in ASEAN

Japan's cumulative private direct foreign investment in ASEAN reached $13.47 billion at the end of fiscal year 1985, accounting for 16.1 per cent of the nation's total foreign investment. On a sectoral basis, investment in extractive industries represented 47.2 per cent of the ASEAN total at the end of the same fiscal year, compared with 40.5 per cent for investment in manufacturing. Nearly half of Japan's global investment in natural resources development is in the ASEAN region. Until the mid-1980s Japan's investment was characterized by small-scale labour-intensive manufacturing and natural resource development.

New investment in the region was expanded by more than $900 million annually (except 1981) in these years. Yet, the share of ASEAN in Japan's annual total global investment has been shrinking, reaching a low of 7.6 per cent in fiscal year 1985 as a result of shifts in investment emphasis. In the past, Japanese businesses invested heavily in labour-intensive industries such as textiles, a pattern which inevitably drew them to the lower labour costs of ASEAN. Massive investment in 1981 is a case in point (see Figure 3.3).[51] In the later part of the 1980s, however, the intensification of trade friction and the rise of protectionism in developed countries prompted Japanese multilateral enterprises to invest mainly in the advanced countries. Owing to the protective nature of Japanese investment strategy, the so-called export-substitution investment policy — designed to maintain or expand foreign market share through local production — inclined towards the United States and Western Europe, the major export markets for Japan's industrial products. Until 1986 there had been little investment in ASEAN countries for export-oriented production.[52]

In order to cope with these declining economic relations, the Japanese government created an "action programme" in June 1985 to improve market access.[53] This programme was designed to expand trade with foreign

FIGURE 3.3
Japanese Investment in ASEAN, 1977–86 ($ million)

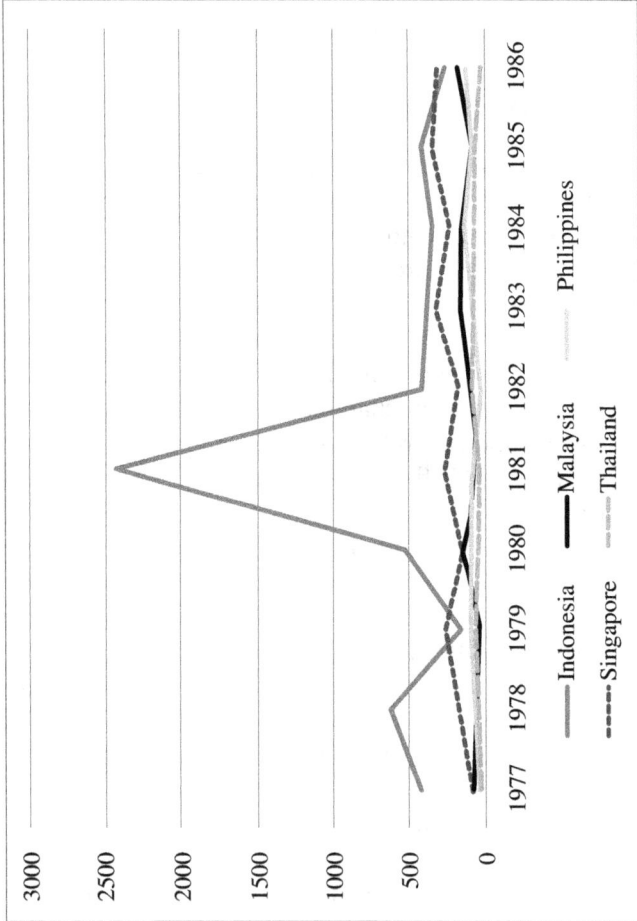

countries, including ASEAN, through further liberalization of the domestic market. Tariff cuts on a variety of products of interest to ASEAN, including boneless chicken and palm oil, were made ahead of schedule, as a political symbol of Japan-ASEAN trade relations. Yet, as explained earlier, Japan's slow and minimal response failed to satisfy ASEAN. As a result, the state of Japan's economic relations with ASEAN caused apprehension throughout the region. Since the action plan was aimed primarily at advanced countries, Japan's response to ASEAN's request for the reduction of tariffs and non-tariff barriers was far from meeting the needs of ASEAN countries.

Japanese Economic Aid to ASEAN

Japan's foreign aid policy since 1977 has been geared towards playing a role in the international community commensurate with its economic status. The Japanese government thus embarked on the so-called "aid-doubling" plan: the first plan between 1978 and 1980, the second between 1981 and 1985, and the third between 1986 and 1992. In undertaking this plan, ASEAN has been at the core of Japan's economic assistance policy: approximately 30 per cent of net disbursements of bilateral official development assistance goes to ASEAN countries. In a sense, the relatively high level of Japan's economic assistance to ASEAN is unique, given the fact that ASEAN countries have been largely successful in their economic development.

In the late 1970s, however, Japan's economic aid policy was expanded, with additional impetus largely due to external pressure. The United States was most vocal in asking the Japanese government to share the burden of buttressing pro-Western developing countries near major conflict areas. It was for this reason that, since 1980, Thailand and the Philippines had received special consideration under the slogan of "strategic assistance", resulting in the high level of Japanese aid to ASEAN as a whole (see Figure 3.4).[54]

Besides this added rationale for foreign aid, Japan's strategy of export promotion has also translated into the promotion of industries in the developing countries. There is still a commercial component to many of Japan's aid programmes, which have been criticized by the recipients for many years. Whether pressured or self-motivated, Japan's total ODA has increased substantially and was placed third among the eighteen DAC (Development Assistance Committee) countries in 1985. Yet, the quality of Japan's aid is far from the status befitting that of a "big donor country".

FIGURE 3.4
Japan's ODA to ASEAN, 1977–86 ($ million)

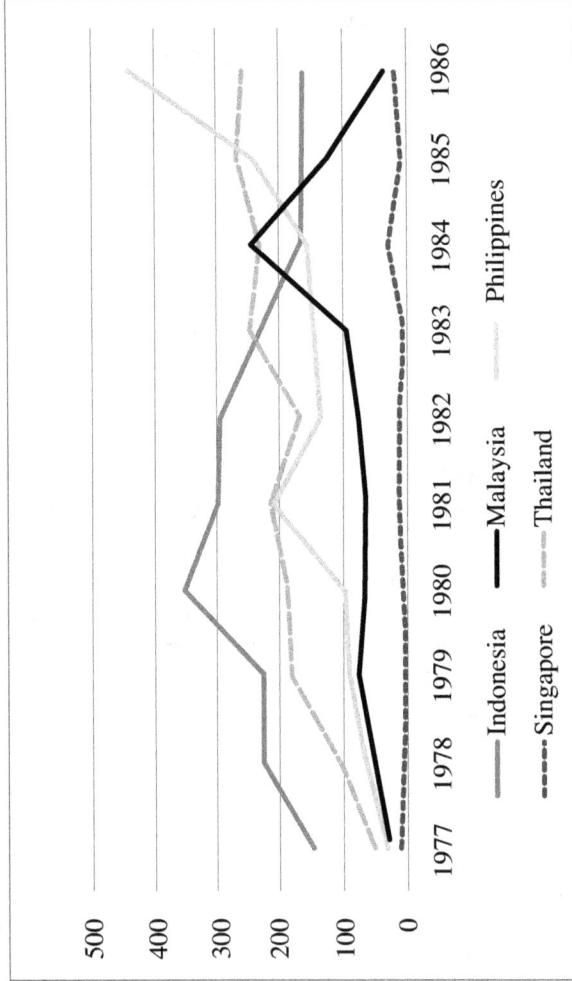

In 1985, for instance, both the grant ratio (47.5 per cent) and grant elements (73.6 per cent) in Japanese aid were the lowest among the DAC countries; despite jumps in the following year to 59.2 per cent and 80.0 per cent respectively, both figures remain well below the average percentages of 80.8 and 91.4. This is mainly due to the fact that Asian countries are the major recipients of Japan's aid, and ODA loans are the leading form of aid extended by Japan to Asian countries in order to meet their high demand for capital. It is perhaps ironic that Japan's aid to ASEAN will be substantially reduced should Japan, in an attempt to improve the quality of its aid, increase the grant element to the same level as that of the other advanced countries.

In summary, without resolving the nagging problems underlying traditional economic relations between Japan and ASEAN, there has been stagnation since the late 1980s. It seems ASEAN will have to live with the "no-win" situation whereby Japan is the only country that is ready or can be manipulated to substantially assist in the region's economic development. Despite the declining economic relations, and growing apprehension, however, Japan has been increasingly called upon to play a more active economic role partly because other ASEAN dialogue partners are not in a position to give a substantial boost to the region's economy. This is the primary reason why the Japanese prime minister was the only top leader invited to the Third ASEAN Summit. As one observer cogently depicted it, Japan has come to be regarded as an "unloved but vital partner".[55]

CULTURAL ASPECTS OF JAPAN-ASEAN RELATIONS

Japan has an image problem in Southeast Asia. Anti-Japanese movements in the early 1970s forced the Japanese government to establish two regional branches of the Japan Foundation in 1972.[56] These two cultural centres, in Bangkok and Jakarta, symbolize the underlying impetus for Japanese cultural co-operation with the region. It has only been since the declaration of a "heart-to-heart" policy by Fukuda that Japan-ASEAN cultural relations have been initiated and become an integral part of ASEAN policy. The main thrust has been to win the hearts and minds of Southeast Asians.

In the past decade, Japanese leaders have proposed many cultural programmes to ASEAN, with Fukuda establishing the ASEAN Cultural Fund in 1978 and Ohira introducing the ASEAN Youth Scholarship in 1980, followed by the Regional Studies Promotion Program in 1982.

Nakasone also founded the 21st Century Friendship Program in 1984. In other words, all Japanese prime ministers since 1977 have been committed to the promotion of cultural cooperation with ASEAN. At the same time, the Japan Foundation has increasingly promoted exchanges of people, supporting ASEAN students studying in Japan and setting up various Japanese language programmes in the ASEAN region. Judging by the number of such programmes, Japan can be said to be very culturally active in the region.[57]

The establishment of the ASEAN Cultural Fund in 1978 also stimulated ASEAN towards cultural cooperation between its members. As part of "heart-to-heart" relations, Japan announced a contribution of five billion yen to the fund in March 1978 as Fukuda's first commitment to be realized, and since then Japan has embarked on active cultural diplomacy in its relations with Southeast Asia. Although the effects of cultural promotion would not emerge in the short run, its positive effect in the long run would bring about a significant change in Japan-ASEAN relations.[58]

This soon resulted in the first cultural body called the ASEAN Committee on Culture and Information (COCI) in October 1978. Its terms of reference are (1) to develop and recommend policies and programmes for regional cooperation in the fields of culture, information and mass communication; (2) to monitor and coordinate the implementation of approved activities of the committee; (3) to create when necessary ad hoc technical or experts' groups and to plan, execute and review approved activities or projects; (4) to formulate, implement and review the approved projects for funding under the Agreement on the Establishment of the ASEAN Cultural Fund; and (5) to initiate and recommend to the appropriate ASEAN authorities cultural and information programmes and projects which require funding by the third countries and/or agencies.[59]

Yet, its effect on mutual understanding is another story. The so-called "cultural transfer", as opposed to cultural exchanges, seems to be predominant, as Japanese goods have permeated the region far beyond the pace of cultural exchange. At the same time as the region was flooded with Japanese "cultural" items through commercial goods, growing relations between Japan and ASEAN tended to incite anti-Japanese feelings that stemmed from the fear of "over-dependence" on one single country. Table 3.4 amply indicates the dismal state of Japan-ASEAN cultural relations. In fact, the total number of ASEAN students in Japan was only 1,138, with the largest number of 408 Thai students in 1986. Without a more balanced cultural exchange scheme between Japan and ASEAN, tensions are likely to occur. Given the high propensity for local politicization of

TABLE 3.4
ASEAN Students Studying Abroad

Indonesia		Malaysia		Philippines		Singapore		Thailand	
US	7,048	US	19,758	US	3,364	US	3,369	US	5,943
Germany	2,260	Australia	5,964	S. Arabia	383	Canada	1,090	Philippines	832
Australia	798	UK	4,922	Vatican	141	UK	1,083	India	767
Netherlands	555	Singapore	3,687	Japan	123	Australia	674	Japan	408
S. Arabia	407	Canada	2,346	Germany	82	NZ	233	France	289
Philippines	347	India	1,726	Australia	81	Japan	67	Germany	238
Canada	288	NZ	784	Canada	74	Germany	49	S. Arabia	212
UK	263	Japan	343	UK	74	India	41	UK	206
Japan	197	France	175	Belgium	39	France	40	Australia	170
Total	12,850	Total	40,493	Total	4,540	Total	6,689	Total	9,496

Source: UNESCO Statistical Yearbook, 1987.

Japan's dominant presence, the worst scenario would be the recurrence of the anti-Japanese movements that "shocked" the Japanese government in the early 1970s.

MAJOR ISSUES FOR CONSOLIDATING JAPAN-ASEAN RELATIONS

A close examination of three aspects of Japan-ASEAN relations reveals major problems and impediments to each of them. Given the mix of declining and growing relations between Japan and ASEAN, what can or should the Japanese government do to invigorate the relationship? It stands to reason that future dialogues should aim at overcoming these impediments. The review of a decade of Japan-ASEAN relations leads one to expect a fresh start should Japan want to play a significant role in the region. Based on the major initiatives undertaken by the Japanese government in recent years, it is possible to propose several measures in three areas: political, economic and cultural.

Political Initiatives

The above analysis shows that before 1977 Japan had played a pre-dominantly economic role in Southeast Asia, avoiding any political or military entanglement. This has been called "Seikei Bunri", eschewing political and military involvement while concentrating on economic affairs. However, a radical change in the politico-military environment of Southeast Asia has made it increasingly difficult for Japan to maintain a purely economic role, hence the announcement of the Fukuda Doctrine. Accordingly, a more vigorous political role was taken by Japan. With the Vietnamese intervention in Cambodia in late 1978, Japan complied with the ASEAN stand and supported the ASEAN-sponsored UN resolution calling for Vietnam to withdraw all of its forces from Cambodia while suspending economic aid to Vietnam.

Against this backdrop, an incident occurred when a leading Japanese trading company, Nissho Iwai, reportedly reached an agreement to extend long-term credit and other economic aid to Vietnam for development projects. ASEAN immediately lodged a protest with Japan. In its aide-memoire, ASEAN urged the Japanese government to discourage private aid to Vietnam as part of international efforts to isolate Hanoi. ASEAN feared that an improved Vietnamese economy would undermine international efforts to have Vietnamese troops pulled out from Cambodia. In particular, disregarding the Japanese company's move would create a de facto endorsement of further commercial deals with Hanoi.

The Japanese government apparently felt concerned about ASEAN's public outcry over the issue and declared that the allegation was unfounded. However, ample reasons seemed to exist for the ASEAN countries to be concerned over implications of increasing trade between Japan and the Indochinese countries. Given the fact that the Thai government was controlling the growing business interests of Thai firms in Indochina, how could Japan justify the mushrooming of its "lucrative" trade with Vietnam? Unlike Japan, Thailand simply could not regard the conflict as "fire across the river". The incident clearly suggests the limitations of Japan's economic approach to the Cambodia issue. Most revealing is the fact that any policy induced by Japan's own economic interests would eventually backfire; a harsh reality that the Japanese government should acknowledge.

If Japan was going to play a significant political role in Southeast Asia, a fresh start would have had to have been made while modifying its economic-oriented policy. The moment seemed ripe for the following reasons. Firstly, ASEAN-Vietnam negotiations had reached a stalemate, thereby requiring a new impetus from a third country. Secondly, Sihanouk had requested that Japan play a mediating role, while embarking upon his own initiatives in resolving the conflict. Thirdly, the prolonged conflict seemed to have forced Vietnam to concentrate on its own reconstruction, as epitomized in the recent statements by Nguen Van Linh. All this points to the fact that the Cambodia issue had reached the crucial stage at which a vigorous initiative could yield fruitful results.

Economic Initiatives

One of the main reasons for declining economic relations is that both Japan and ASEAN had become entangled in the so-called "historical economic adjustment". In Japan, mounting pressure from Western countries to reduce Japan's huge trade surpluses and the precipitous appreciation of the yen since September 1985 had rendered many Japanese manufacturers uneconomical. Simply put, the pattern of Japan's trade and development based upon the traditional vertical division of labour is no longer tenable. At the same time, the world economic stagnation and the accompanying prolonged depression of commodity prices since 1980 had caused huge losses of ASEAN's foreign exchange earnings, soaring debts, and retarded growth. As a result, all the ASEAN countries were forced to undertake painful adjustments and to push for the rapid development of export-oriented industries as a means to overcome their economic difficulties.

In order to carry out economic reforms, both Japan and ASEAN could substantially liberalize their markets. It was abundantly clear that neither ASEAN's preferential trading arrangements (PTA) nor its attempts at industrial cooperation had done much to increase intraregional trade and foreign investment. In fact, the most expected PTA was not yielding any tangible results due to the voluntary nature of the items offered for tariff preferences and a cumbersome exclusion list for sensitive product imports. Without expanded intraregional trade through liberalization, Japan's investment would not be forthcoming. To make it more conducive to intra- and extra-trade, therefore, a Japan-ASEAN free trade agreement could serve as a lever.

Cultural Initiatives

As we have seen above, Fukuda's cultural initiative contributed to awakening the importance of ASEAN's cultural cooperation, which resulted in the establishment of ASEAN COCI in October 1978. In order to further strengthen Japan-ASEAN cultural exchanges, the Japanese government has contemplated some measures to invigorate Japan's cultural relations with the region. It is timely to initiate the restructuring of Japan's cultural exchange programmes which have been plagued by many domestic impediments such as the dearth of public and private institutions to develop and administer cultural exchange; the dismal state of Japanese universities; and the low priority assigned to cultural exchange in the national government budget.

If Japan is to avoid past pitfalls, a new initiative in the cultural field should aim to help nurture feelings of "equal partnership". It is also important to turn Japan into a major study centre for ASEAN students. Since growing economic interdependence and more complex political relationships will inevitably increase the chances for a collision of interests, the most effective way of building a strong foundation for mutually beneficial relations between Japan and ASEAN is to foster more extensive cultural exchanges. Table 3.5 suggests that, as shown by Questions 2 and 3, the history factor still remains an obstacle to forging better relations between

TABLE 3.5
Opinion Poll on Japan, 1987

Q1 Will Japan become a military power?					
	Indonesia	Malaysia	Philippines	Singapore	Thailand
Yes	21%	34%	47%	29%	53%
No	68%	45%	46%	46%	37%
Q2 What do you think about Japanese deeds during World War II?					
Cannot forget	36%	25%	35%	25%	29%
Do not mind	63%	70%	61%	67%	66%
Q3 Does Japan contribute positively to the development of Asian countries?					
Yes	83%	74%	91%	71%	61%
No	11%	12%	7%	14%	31%
Q4 Does Japan's aid contribute to your country's economy?					
Yes	98%	86%	81%	88%	88%
No	—	3%	18%	3%	6%
Q5 How do you evaluate current relations between your country and Japan?					
Friendly	98%	87%	98%	90%	95%
Not friendly	1%	3%	2%	1%	2%

Source: Gaimusho, ASEAN shokoku niokeru tainichi yoronchosa, July 1987.

Japan and ASEAN and to a positive role for Japan in the development of Asian countries, although Japan's relations with individual countries are being viewed positively (Q5).

CONCLUSION

All these developments since the declaration of the Fukuda Doctrine have brought new dimensions to Japanese foreign policy. Centred on ASEAN, Japan's Southeast Asian policy has become more multilateral, and the process of its decision-making on major policies towards the region has become more open, taking into consideration ASEAN's demands and interests. New dimensions are three-fold. Politically, Japan has committed to a bridge-building role. Economically, Japan has pledged to forge much closer and special relations. Culturally, Japan intends to forge "heart-to-heart" relations through the proposed ASEAN Cultural Fund. Although the extent to which ASEAN's demands have been put into action is far from commendable, the trend towards cooperative and joint decision-making seems to be significant and should not be overlooked. If fully developed, this trend would generate a more favourable environment from which truly interdependent relations would accrue.

Has Japan clearly formulated its ASEAN policy? Three main areas of cooperation have been designated by the Foreign Ministry's Asian Affairs Bureau as a framework for conducting and developing Japan's multilateral relations with ASEAN (see Figure 3.5). They are the promotion of mutual relations, mainly contingent upon official as well as private dialogues; enhancing ASEAN's resilience, which requires economic and cultural assistance such as ASEAN industrial projects; the Cultural Fund, and the ASEAN Scholarship and Regional Studies Promotion Program; and strengthening the partnership for dealing with international politico-economic problems as exemplified by Cambodian and North-South issues. Although not well articulated, the figure suggests the emergence of the basic pillars of Japan's ASEAN policy, to wit, political, economic and cultural. The Foreign Ministry has particularly emphasized the partnership for the twenty-first century and suggested that its full potential has yet to be realized.[60]

Insofar as the framework for conducting an active role in the region is retained, or MOFA's institutionalized ideas are upheld, it seems likely that the Fukuda Doctrine will be at the core of Japan's ASEAN policy. In June

FIGURE 3.5
Japan's ASEAN Policy: An Emerging Framework

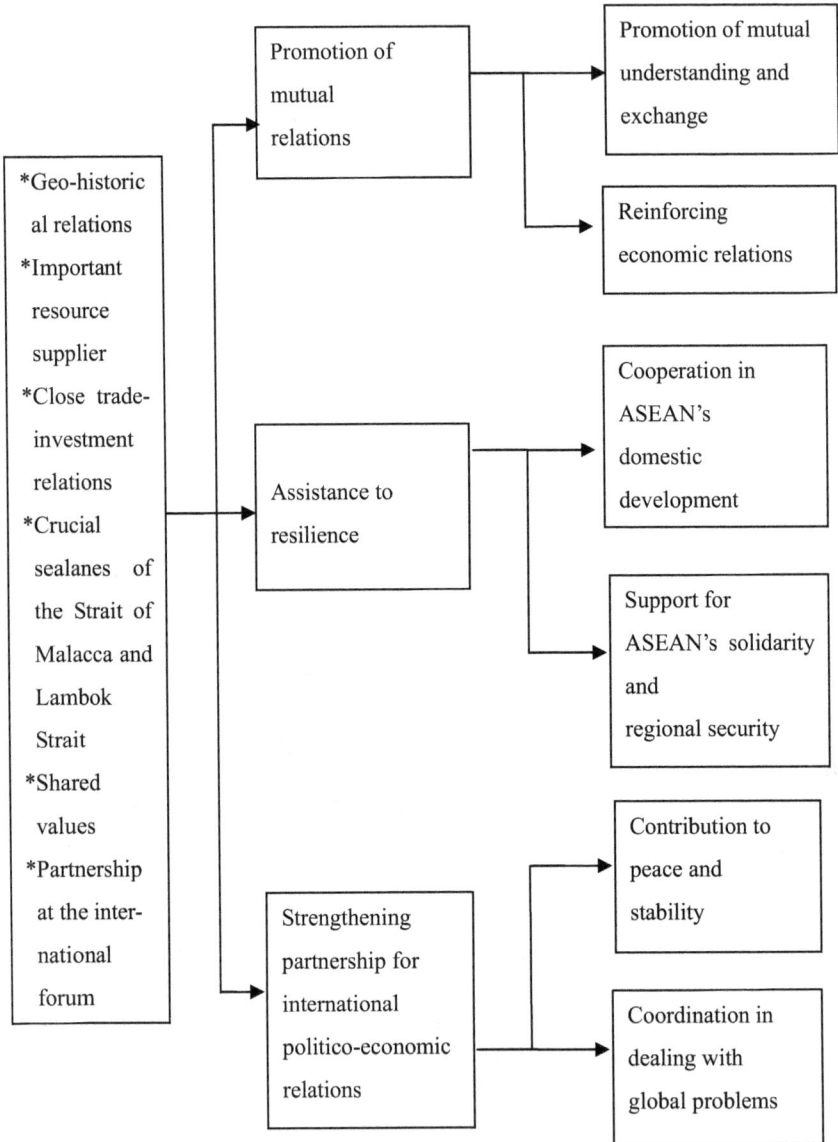

1986, for instance, Foreign Minister Shinzo Abe announced his "doctrine" which was virtually identical to the Fukuda Doctrine. It emphasized Japan's contribution as a peace-loving country, and the establishment of mutual trust and cooperation with ASEAN.[61] In an era of economic cooperation, ASEAN leaders now seem to expect another major Japanese commitment in promoting industrialization of the region. Singapore's Prime Minister Lee epitomized the view when he said: "Now is the time for Japan to offer another major incentive for ASEAN's industrialization, an incentive as substantive as that of 1977."[62]

Having closely delineated the post-doctrine developments, the following significant changes can be seen. To begin with, the foreign-policy-making process was not slow. The Foreign Ministry's Asian Affairs Bureau, more precisely the pseudo action team, swiftly responded to changing Southeast Asian relations with the determined purpose of playing a political role. It was political because Japan attempted to use its aid to Hanoi for smoothing relations between the two blocs. That one of the twin goals of the doctrine failed in 1980 does not imply the end of Japan's pursuit of that strategy. In other words, even after cancelling foreign aid to Hanoi, the Japanese officials still believed that the Soviet presence in Vietnam would only be "temporary" until the threat from China was mitigated and until Hanoi found its place in the West. Japan would be prepared to show readiness to help Hanoi, but without antagonizing ASEAN or the West.

Second, when judged by the way Japanese policymakers defined a "special" relationship with ASEAN, Japan's attempts could be assessed as a success. ASEAN's participation in the process of Japanese foreign policy making could represent a significant development. Consistent efforts along the line of the $1 billion commitment for regional projects seems to have generated important stimuli in strengthening ASEAN as a viable regional organization. Similarly, the Cultural Fund would be able to stimulate ASEAN's cultural cooperation. However, in terms of tangible results of the special relationship for ASEAN countries, it is far from a success.[63] In particular, Japan-ASEAN trade should be better with greater emphasis on opening the Japanese market for the region. A special relationship in a literal sense cannot be built without bringing about a situation of mutual and equitable relations.

Third, we have observed an apparent discrepancy between what the Fukuda Doctrine intended and what Japan has achieved in the post-doctrine period. In other words, we can point out inherent limits in

Japanese foreign policy. Two major impediments Japan has encountered
are the lack of control over the international environment and domestic
factors that attenuate active external policies. In particular, the ad hoc
nature of decision-making leads to an acute policy-oriented problem once
major policymakers are replaced, although it is conducive to implementing
action swiftly.[64]

Fourth, through interaction, Japan and ASEAN began to learn about
each other and adjust their regional policies for mutual benefits. If the
Fukuda Doctrine that succeeded in founding a basic framework is the first
step, then the second step would be to elevate the relationship towards a
special one, which requires "proactive" multilateralism.

Notes

1. This chapter is mainly based on Sueo Sudo, "From Fukuda to Takeshita:
   A Decade of Japan-ASEAN Relations", *Contemporary Southeast Asia* 10, no. 2
   (September 1988): 119–43.
2. The only exception is Masahide Shibusawa, *Japan and the Asia Pacific Region*
   (London: Croom Helm, 1983), which delineated the process of formulating
   the Fukuda Doctrine as a joint work between Japan and ASEAN.
3. See, for instance, Taketsugu Tsurutani, *Japanese Policy and East Asian Security*
   (New York: Praeger, 1981) and Donald Hellmann, "Japan and Southeast Asia",
   Asian Survey 64, no. 12 (December 1979): 1189–98.
4. Marjorie Suriyamongkal, "The Politics of Economic Cooperation in the
   Association of Southeast Asian Nations" (PhD Dissertation, University of
   Illinois, 1982), p. 276. See also Wee Nib-cheung, "How Can Japan Assist
   the Industrial Projects in ASEAN Countries", *Look Japan*, 10 July 1977,
   p. 23.
5. ASEAN, "Report of the ASEAN Economic Ministers to the ASEAN Heads of
   Government", in *Record of the Meeting of ASEAN Heads of Government* (Kuala
   Lumpur: ASEAN National Secretariat, Malaysia, 1977), pp. 23–24.
6. *Japan Times*, 16 July 1977.
7. *Straits Times*, 6 August 1977; ASEAN, "The Second ASEAN Heads of
   Government Meeting, Kuala Lumpur, 4–5 August 1977" (Jakarta: ASEAN
   Secretariat, 1977). For an in-depth discussion of Japan-ASEAN relations from
   the latter's point of view, see Japan Center for International Exchange, *Presence
   and Perceptions: The Underpinnings of ASEAN-Japan Relations* (Tokyo: Japan
   Center for International Exchange, 1986).
8. See especially Hans Indorf, "The Kuala Lumpur Summit: A Second for ASEAN",
   Southeast Asian Affairs 1978 (Singapore: Institute of Southeast Asian Studies,

1978), pp. 35–44 and Shee Poon-Kim, "A Decade of ASEAN, 1967–1977", *Asian Survey* 17, no. 8 (August 1977): 753–70 for the evaluations of ASEAN's 10th Anniversary.

9. *Far Eastern Economic Review*, 19 August 1977, p. 20.

10. Regarding early works on the Fukuda Doctrine, see especially Daoed Joesoef, "Japan and ASEAN: Policies towards Promoting Closer Cooperation", in *Japan-Indonesia Cooperation: Problems and Prospects* (Jakarta: Center for Strategic and International Studies, 1978), pp. 6–12; Toru Yano, "Toward a Reorientation of Asian Policy: The Fukuda Doctrine and Japanese-US Cooperation", in *Encounter at Shimoda: Search for a New Pacific Partner*, edited by Herbert Passin and Akira Iriye (Boulder, CO: Westview), 1979, pp. 127–45 and William Haddad, "Japan, the Fukuda Doctrine, and ASEAN", *Contemporary Southeast Asia* 2, no. 1 (June 1980): 10–29.

11. *Japan Times*, 1 February 1977.

12. Since the publication of Fukuda's memoirs, Takeo Fukuda, *Kaiko kyujunen* (Tokyo: Iwanami shoten, 1995), many works on the Fukuda Doctrine have been produced, utilizing interviews and declassified official sources. See especially Yasutomo Tanaka, "Posuto Betonamu no Tonanajia anteikaseisaku toshiteno Fukuda dokutorin", *Ajia Kenkyu* 45, no. 1 (1999): 29–60 and Hidekazu Wakatsuki, "Fukuda dokutorin: Posuto reisengaiko no yoboenshu", *Kokusaiseiji*, no. 125 (October 2002): 197–217. These studies shed new light on the process of forging the doctrine by posing three main questions. First, the existence of a "pseudo policy-making team" is rather misleading. To be sure, besides five core policymakers, many individuals were involved one way or another in the process of Fukuda's attendance at the Kuala Lumpur summit and Fukuda's official visits to six ASEAN countries after the summit. Yet, it was the unauthorized "pseudo policy-making team" that directed Fukuda's overtures in 1977. Nakae also calls it "a team" that bridged the Prime Minister's Office and the Foreign Ministry through Owada-Nishiyama's team play. Yosuke Nakae, *Ajia gaiko: Do to sei* (Tokyo: Sotensha, 2010), pp. 176–77. Second, the question of who drafted the doctrine and why there were three principles is not clarified. As explained later, since there existed many drafts or versions by various policymakers involved, it seems impossible to identify a specific author. The third is the claim that it was the Japanese media, not the Japanese government that conjured up the image of a doctrine. This claim does not hold water since one of the policymakers, Sumio Edamura, deemed it as a doctrine at the time of the announcement.

13. For the first-hand accounts of Fukuda's attempts in Southeast Asia, see Yosuke Nakae, "Nihon no tai Tonanajia gaiko", *Keidanren Geppo* (October 1977), pp. 24–27; "Nihon to ASEAN no shinjidai", *Keizai to Gaiko* (September 1977), pp. 2–15; Takehiko Nishiyama, "Fukuda sori no Tonanajia rekiho", *Gaiko Jiho*

(October 1977), pp. 3–10; Hisashi Owada, "Trilateralism: A Japanese View", *International Security* 5, no. 3 (Winter 1980/81): 14–24; Sumio Edamura, "Fukuda dokutorin no tanjo", *Gaiko Foramu* (November 2008), pp. 82–87; Sakutaro Tanino, "Japan and the United States", in *U.S.-Japan Relations: New Attitudes for a New Era* (Cambridge: Center for International Affairs, Harvard University, 1984), pp. 187–89. A former Minister of International Trade and Industry, Tanaka lucidly describes Japan-ASEAN talks at the Summit. See Tatsuo Tanaka, *Sekai ni tobu* (Tokyo: Kodansha, 1981), pp. 89–111.

14. Interview with Iichiro Hatoyama, 9 April 1985.
15. Interview with Takehiko Nishiyama, 23 October 1984 and interview with Ryozo Sunobe, former Ambassador to Indonesia, 19 March 1985.
16. The insertion of ASEAN into the communiqué was suggested by the Japanese government. Interview with Takeo Fukuda, 12 February 1985.
17. *Mainichi Shimbun*, 16 March 1977; *Asahi Shimbun*, 27 March 1977; *Straits Times*, 30 March 1977.
18. Interview with Takehiko Nishiyama, 9 April 1985.
19. Correspondence with Yosuke Nakae, 14 August 1985. See also Yosuke Nakae, "Ajia gaiko no genjo to tenbo", *Keizai Kyoryoku*, no. 130 (October 1978): 7–10.
20. *Yomiuri Shimbun*, 20 July 1977. Gaimusho (Ministry of Foreign Affairs, Japan) officials thought these commitments would serve "political purposes". See *Asahi Shimbun*, 29 July 1977. STABEX is a scheme to stabilize commodity export earnings by setting up a fund.
21. Gaimusho documents suggest that three different versions of the Fukuda Doctrine were drafted between 5 and 22 July, which represent six, five and four principles respectively. However, since the four-principle draft was not dated we can only presume it was drafted around late July. See Gaimusho, "Fukuda sori no Firipin Hinichiyukokyokai niokeru supichi an (wagakuni no Tonanajiaseisaku: Fukuda yongensoku) no hyomei", Postwar Diplomatic Records, Diplomatic Record Office (Tokyo: Ministry of Foreign Affairs) and *Tokyo Shimbun*, 6 August 1977, evening issue. The four principles are: (1) Japan is to extend positive support for regional cooperation in Southeast Asia, (2) Japan is to develop special trade and commercial relations with Southeast Asian countries, (3) Japan is to make efforts to strengthen mutual understanding and trust based on heart-to-heart communication among peoples in the region, (4) Japan is to establish good-neighbourly relations with Indochina countries.
22. Gaimusho, "Sorino Tonanajia rekiho: Wagakuni no Tonanajia seisaku no hyomei nitsuite, 5 July 1977", copies of documents obtained through Freedom of Information Act, Diplomatic Record Office (Tokyo: Ministry of Foreign Affairs, 1977). This seems to be a rough draft because the document clearly suggests a shift from the "five" principles to "six" principles.

23. Interview with Takehiko Nishiyama, 9 April 1985.
24. For Japan's Indochina policy, see especially Takehiko Nishiyama, "International Relations in Southeast Asia", mimeographed, p. 29 and Ajiakyoku, "Wagakuni no tai Tonanajia seisaku, nakanzuku do seisakuchu nishimeru tai Indoshina seisaku no ichizuke, 27 July 1977", copies of documents obtained through Freedom of Information Act, Diplomatic Record Office (Tokyo: Ministry of Foreign Affairs, 1977.
25. *Asahi Shimbun*, 17 July 1977.
26. Gaimusho "Fukuda sori no Manira niokeru supichi an (dai sanko), 22 July 1977", copies of documents obtained through Freedom of Information Act, Diplomatic Record Office (Tokyo: Ministry of Foreign Affairs, 1977). The author is grateful for Professor Paul Midford's suggestion to obtain this document.
27. As the third version of the draft indicates, there exist various interpretations of who drafted the doctrine. Nakae thought the doctrine was drafted by Nishiyama and Owada, while Kiyoaki Kikuchi, then the head of Gaimusho's Economic Cooperation section, disclosed that the doctrine was drafted by Nishiyama and himself. See Oral History Interview, "Interview with Yosuke Nakae", 22 February 1996 and "Interview with Kiyoaki Kikuchi", 15 July 1996, provided by Professor Makoto Iokibe.
28. ASEAN, "The Meeting of the ASEAN Heads of Government and the Prime Minister of Japan Kuala Lumpur, 7 August 1977" (Jakarta: ASEAN Secretariat, 1977). Since the term "special relationship" was one of the objectives Japanese policymakers tried to realize, the process of Fukuda's attendance at the summit and the process of Fukuda's visits to six ASEAN countries were mutually related. See especially Sumio Edamura, "Hatsuno Nihon ASEAN shuno kaigi", *Gaiko Foramu* (December 2008): 70–75.
29. According to Nakae, the three-principle draft was finalized just before arriving in Manila. Correspondence with Nakae, 13 August 1985.
30. *Manila Times*, 19 August 1977. Fukuda's Manila speech is annexed in Sueo Sudo, *The Fukuda Doctrine and ASEAN: New Dimensions in Japanese Foreign Policy* (Singapore: Institute of Southeast Asian Studies, 1992), pp. 241–47. Whether the press conjured up the image of the Manila speech as a doctrine or policymakers deemed it as a doctrine can be found in Sumio Edamura, "Indoneshia-Filipin to Manira supichi", *Gaiko Foramu* (January 2009), pp. 94–95.
31. See Gaimusho, "Fukuda souri no Tonana rekiho no seika to kongo no shisaku", copies of documents obtained through Freedom of Information Act, Diplomatic Record Office (Tokyo: Ministry of Foreign Affairs), for Gaimusho's overall evaluation of the Fukuda Doctrine.
32. Nakae, "Nihon to ASEAN no shinjidai", p. 10.
33. See particularly, *Sekai no Ugoki*, special issue, February 1981 and *Keizai to Gaiko*, February 1981, pp. 2–10.

34. Gaimusho, *Waga gaiko no kinkyo*, 1984, pp. 110–11. See particularly, Hideo Matsuzaki, "Future of Japan-ASEAN Relations", *Asia Pacific Community*, no. 21 (Summer 1983): 11–22 and *Sekai no Ugoki*, special issue, June 1983.

35. Gaimusho, *Waga gaiko no kinkyo*, 1986, pp. 63–64.

36. See Sunao Sonoda, *Sekai, Nihon, Ai* (Tokyo: Daisan seikei kenkyusho, 1983), pp. 137–200.

37. It should be noted here that Japan's positive approach to ASEAN induced Washington to recognize ASEAN as the critical actor in Southeast Asia for the first time. See Hidekazu Wakatsuki, *Zenhoi gaiko no jidai* (Tokyo: Nihonkeizai hyoron sha, 2005), pp. 218–19.

38. ASEAN, "Fourteenth ASEAN Ministerial Meeting and Post-Ministerial Meeting with the Dialogue Countries", in *ASEAN Documents Series, 1967–1985* (Jakarta: ASEAN Secretariat, 1985), pp. 79–80.

39. See Mana Ikegami, "Taietsu keizaienjo niokeru Nihongaiko", *Hogakuseiji Ronkyu*, 85 (June 2010): 61–90.

40. ASEAN, "Seventeenth ASEAN Ministerial Meeting", in ASEAN Secretariat, *ASEAN Documents Series, 1967–1985* (Jakarta: ASEAN Secretariat, 1985), p. 113.

41. ASEAN, "The First ASEAN-Japan Economic Ministers Meeting, Tokyo, 26–27 November 1979" (Jakarta: ASEAN Secretariat, 1979).

42. *Asahi Shimbun*, 27 November 1979.

43. ASEAN, "Joint Press Statement of the Second ASEAN-Japan Economic Ministers Meeting, Tokyo, 28 June 1985" (Jakarta: ASEAN Secretariat, 1985). See also *Sekai no Ugoki*, August 1985, pp. 9–11.

44. Takehiko Nishiyama, "Nihon-ASEAN Foramu", *Keizai to Gaiko*, May 1977, pp. 36–40. For an overview, see ASEAN Secretariat, "An overview of ASEAN" (Jakarta: ASEAN Secretariat, 1987), pp. 22–23.

45. Takehiko Nishiyama, "Nihon-ASEAN Foramu dainikai kaigo no kaisai", *Keizai to Gaiko*, December 1977, pp. 11–15.

46. *Keizai to Gaiko*, February 1980, pp. 57–61.

47. "Joint Communique of the Seventh ASEAN-Japan Forum", in *ASEAN Documents Series, 1967–1985* (Jakarta: ASEAN Secretariat, 1985), p. 303.

48. See especially Kinji Atarashi, "Japan's Economic Cooperation Policy Towards the ASEAN Countries", *International Affairs* 61, no. 1 (Winter 1984/85), pp. 109–27.

49. Eiji Sakuta, "Japan-ASEAN Economic Relations", *Journal of Japanese Trade and Industry*, September-October 1986, p. 12.

50. The bulk of Japan's investment was for the Pertamina LNG project. Japan External Trade Organization (JETRO), *Kaigaishijo hakusho* (Tokyo: JETRO, 1983), p. 12.

51. Sueo Sekiguchi, ed., *ASEAN-Japan Relations: Investment* (Singapore: Institute of Southeast Asian Studies, 1983), especially pp. 227–57.

52. See Wendy Dobson, *Japan in East Asia: Trading and Investment Strategies* (Singapore: Institute of Southeast Asian Studies, 1993).

53. See especially Masumi Ezaki, *Keizaimasatsu kaisho no taisaku* (Tokyo: Sekaiseikei bunka kenkyusho, 1983).

54. See particularly, Denis Yasutomo, *The Manner of Giving: Strategic Aid and Japanese Foreign Policy* (Lexington, MA: Lexington Books, 1986) and Anny Wong, *Japan's Comprehensive National Security Strategy and its Economic Cooperation with the ASEAN Countries* (Hong Kong: Chinese University of Hong Kong, 1991).

55. *Far Eastern Economic Review*, 12 June 1986, pp. 71–72.

56. Concerning the establishment of the Japan Foundation, see Michio Ochi, *Chichi Fukuda Takeo* (Tokyo: Sankei bizinesu, 1973) and Tadashi Ogawa, "Origin and Development of Japan's Public Diplomacy", in *Routledge Handbook of Public Diplomacy*, edited by Nancy Snow and Phillip Taylor (London: Routledge, 2009), pp. 270–81.

57. See "Background Information on the ASEAN Cultural Fund and ASEAN-Japan Cultural Cooperation", *ASEAN Digest*, January 1979, pp. 20–24.

58. Interview with Shigetami Sunada, former Minister of Education, 1 March 1985. See also Amiko Nobori, "Tonanajia niokeru Nihonimeji to Nihongaiko", in *Imeji nonakano Nihon*, edited by Yutaka Oishi and Nobuto Yamamoto (Tokyo: Keiogijukudaigaku shuppankai, 2008), pp. 135–54 for changing ASEAN's perceptions of Japan.

59. ASEAN, "All about ASEAN-COCI: Institutional Framework" (Jakarta: ASEAN Secretariat) <http://www.asean-infoculture.org>.

60. See Gaimusho, *Deta nimiru Nihon to ASEAN* (Tokyo: Ministry of Foreign Affairs, 1982), pp. 44–45.

61. *Far Eastern Economic Review*, 26 June 1986, pp. 22–25.

62. *Asahi Shimbun*, 26 June 1986, evening issue.

63. For this interpretation, see Tang Siew Mun, "The Fukuda Doctrine: Historical Relic or Enduring Wisdom?" in *Japanese Relations with ASEAN since the Fukuda Doctrine*, edited by Lee Poh Ping and Md Nasrudin Md Akhir (Kuala Lumpur: Japan Studies Program, University of Malaya, 2009), pp. 37–50.

64. *Yomiuri Shimbun*, 18 October 1986.

4

CONSOLIDATING AN ASEAN-CENTRED POLICY: The Challenge of the Intermediate Stream

In the late 1980s and first half of the 1990s, Southeast Asian international relations were preoccupied by the Cambodian conflict and the restructuring of regional order in the post–Cold War period. Having successfully resolved the much-prolonged Cambodian conflict in 1991, the Association of Southeast Asian Nations (ASEAN) emerged as a united actor to be reckoned with. Encouraged by its diplomatic success, ASEAN seized the moment to play a leading role in activating closer regional interaction, as exemplified by the establishment of the ASEAN Regional Forum (ARF), the Asia-Europe Meeting (ASEM) and other supportive organizations such as the Asia-Pacific Economic Cooperation (APEC) and the Council for Security in the Asia-Pacific (CSCAP).

Against this background, Japan also responded positively to stability in Southeast Asia. As with Fukuda's overtures, Prime Minister Noboru Takeshita attended the Third ASEAN Summit in Manila and never failed to recognize the importance of ASEAN as a partner.[1] Seizing the opportunity to officially proclaim another doctrine in 1987, Japan's ASEAN policy entered a new phase. In particular, the dawn of the post–Cold War period necessitated new initiatives from Japan. Japan's political role was required to resolve the Cambodian conflict and to offer reconstruction assistance. Japan's economic role was also needed to boost the ASEAN economies in the wake of the conflict. It was also important for Japan to further strengthen mutual understanding by promoting cultural exchanges. Following the effects of the Fukuda Doctrine, this chapter observes closely how Japan reinforced political, economic and cultural relations with ASEAN in the post–Cold War period.

ASEAN IN 1987: 20TH ANNIVERSARY

When ASEAN's third decade began on 8 August 1987, much attention was given to how ASEAN could kick off a new decade. There was a sense of déjà vu as ASEAN needed to reiterate the way it started ten years ago. The year 1987 was significant in that ASEAN deliberated on two critical issues, namely, the need to enhance tangible forms of intra-ASEAN cooperation and the need to reassess the ASEAN dialogue-partner relationships. Enhancing intra-ASEAN cooperation needed greater economic cooperation and was where ASEAN was at its weakest. The ASEAN Preferential Trading Arrangement (PTA), for instance, included a list of more than 18,000 items, but this had not made much impact because ASEAN members continued to limit its scope with substantial exclusion limits. In addition, the ASEAN industrial project scheme and the industrial joint ventures had yet to have a significant impact. The third summit, thus, was meant to be an economic summit, designed to implement effective measures to address economic woes.[2]

The inpetus to reassess the dialogue-partner relationships came from the realization that ASEAN dialogue diplomacy did not function well. Given ASEAN's priority concerns, the dialogue mechanism needed to evolve into an effective structure to coordinate and resolve pressing economic issues. As a Malaysian ambassador cogently put it, "An expanded PTA will not be a quick panacea for all ASEAN trade woes. That being the case, ASEAN will continue to look to its dialogue partners and its traditional markets. This places special importance on the dialogue relationships."[3]

ASEAN also needed another big push to sustain its regional mechanism, which was damaged by political upheavals in the Philippines as the Marcos debacle amply suggested. As a symbolic gesture, therefore, ASEAN held its third summit in Manila on 14 and 15 December 1987, producing the Manila Declaration and a joint communiqué summarizing ASEAN's major policy commitments. The joint communiqué stressed that "The Heads of Government agreed that ASEAN has grown into a viable and dynamic organization fostering the spirit of regional cooperation and solidarity and strengthening national and regional resilience. They noted that ASEAN has also developed a distinct identity and has become an effective vehicle for joint approaches to regional and international issues. They also noted that regular consultations have forged closer relations among the member states and thus promoted peace, stability and prosperity in the region", in tandem with discussing their major agenda, including political development, developments in the world economy, economic cooperation, functional cooperation, dialogue with other countries, and the machinery for ASEAN cooperation.[4]

Under the conditions of fluidity, the Third ASEAN Summit yielded limited results as opposed to the previous two summits. Nevertheless, a subtle change accrued from the summit; as one observer put it: "The summit may best represent the final achievement of consensus to move towards regional economic cooperation, rather than what was previously largely a willingness to engage in the process while avoiding the content."[5] In this respect it should be noted that, for the first time, ASEAN introduced the concept of "functional cooperation" in order to help achieve the political and economic aspirations of the peoples of ASEAN and to achieve a stronger sense of regional identity and belonging by calling for a systematic approach to the synchronization and formulation of programmes on information, education, culture and social development.

THE PROCLAMATION OF THE TAKESHITA DOCTRINE

Prime Minister Noboru Takeshita inherited from his predecessor enormous tasks that would require innovative ideas and determination to tackle them. Dwelling on Fukuda's overtures, Takeshita attended the Third ASEAN Summit in Manila. Without any doubt, the Third ASEAN Summit was an epoch-making event in Japan-ASEAN relations, for Japan stood out as the only non-ASEAN country in attendance. In a policy speech entitled "Japan and ASEAN: A New Partnership toward Peace and Prosperity", he proclaimed that:

> Ten years ago, when Prime Minister Takeo Fukuda toured the ASEAN
> countries on the occasion of the Second Meeting of the ASEAN Heads of
> Government, he expressed, here in Manila, Japan's fundamental thinking
> concerning promotion of ties based on "heart-to-heart" understanding
> with the ASEAN countries. Those ideas are still at the basis of Japanese
> policies vis-à-vis ASEAN.[6]

While enumerating three basic policies towards ASEAN — (1) to strengthen
the economic resilience of ASEAN, (2) to promote political coordination
between Japan and ASEAN, and (3) to promote cultural exchanges — the
"Takeshita Doctrine" accentuated ASEAN's fresh start to the third decade
because the main target of the Manila Declaration was strengthened
economic cooperation.

The high point of Takeshita's visit was the formalization of an ASEAN-
Japan Development Fund (AJDF) of more than $2 billion as the first phase
in its financial recycling programme, which the Japanese government
believed would stimulate the ASEAN economies by encouraging Japanese
investment in the region. The proposed fund consisted of two parts:
loans to the private sector at a low interest rate of 3 per cent per annum
for joint ventures in the region, and untied loans to ASEAN through
development institutions in each country. This fund differed from the
previous Fukuda Fund because the latter was directed only at large-scale
government projects, while the former was designed to assist small and
medium private companies in the export industry. The immediate effect
of Takeshita's proposals can be measured by the adoption of the so-called
BBC (brand-to-brand complementation) scheme, initiated and strongly
supported by Japanese private firms. Regarding the BBC scheme as one of
the most important forms of industrial cooperation, the ASEAN Economic
Ministers' Meeting issued the "Memorandum of Understanding, Brand-
to-Brand Complementation on the Automotive Industry under the Basic
Agreement on ASEAN Industrial Complementation" in October 1988.[7]

Therefore, with the Fukuda Doctrine as a road map, Prime Minister
Takeshita responded with determination to the changing needs of ASEAN.
As has been mentioned earlier, the three initiatives being implemented
or just embarked upon could boost otherwise stagnant relations between
Japan and ASEAN. A Southeast Asian scholar underscored the importance
of the summit thus: "The striking thing about the ASEAN heads of state
meeting in Manila in December 1987 is that the only non-ASEAN leader
invited to attend was the Japanese prime minister of the day, Noboru

Takeshita. This speaks volumes about the importance ASEAN attaches to its relationship with Japan. This importance is unlikely to diminish as the end of the century approaches. If anything, it is likely to increase."[8] Particularly, Japan's strategic aid to buttress the newly established Aquino regime in the Philippines was timely and well received by the ASEAN leaders. The timing seemed ripe for these initiatives to turn the tide.

REINFORCING POLITICAL RELATIONS

The overall structure of Japan-ASEAN relations is characterized by the following five main components: summits, prime ministers' visits, Foreign Ministers' Meeting, Economic Ministers' Meeting and Japan-ASEAN Forum. As Table 4.1 suggests, the main venues for political cooperation are prime ministers' visits, Foreign Ministers' Meeting and Japan-ASEAN Forum, through which Japan's positive role in regional security eventually came about.

Prime Ministers' Visits to ASEAN

In April 1989 domestic political problems worsened and forced Takeshita to resign in the midst of his preparation for the ASEAN tour. Although his resignation was made public, Takeshita decided to visit the region (Thailand, Malaysia, Singapore, Indonesia, the Philippines) in late April

TABLE 4.1
Japan-ASEAN Relations, 1987–96

	PM visit	Summit	Forum	FMM	EMM
1987		2nd	10th	9th	
1988			11th	10th	
1989	Takashita		12th	11th	
1990			13th	12th	
1991	Kaifu		14th		
1992			15th		1st
1993	Miyazawa		16th	13th	2nd
1994	Murayama		17th		3rd
1995			18th	14th	4th
1996			19th		5th

and May 1989 and made a policy speech in Jakarta, entitled "Japan and ASEAN: Thinking together and advancing together". In the speech he explained Japan's policy rationale:

> Soon after becoming Prime Minister of Japan, I have set forth an International Cooperation Initiative premised on the following three pillars. The first pillar is the strengthening of cooperation to achieve peace. Second is the expansion of Japan's official development assistance (ODA). And third is the strengthening of international cultural exchange. I believe that Southeast Asia is one of the most important areas for this International Cooperation Initiative, and I intend to promote actively the initiative in this region.[9]

Japan's diplomatic efforts to consolidate its relations with ASEAN continued after the end of the Cold War in December 1989. As the first official attempt in the post–Cold War period, Prime Minister Toshiki Kaifu visited the ASEAN countries (Brunei, Malaysia, Philippines, Singapore and Thailand) in May 1991 and made a policy speech in Singapore. Kaifu underscored the importance of Japan-ASEAN partnership in the following manner:

> I believe that Japan and ASEAN are becoming mature partners able to look seriously at what we can do for Asia-Pacific peace and prosperity and to think and act together for our shared goals. Building upon the long years of dialogue between Japan and ASEAN, we are now able to speak frankly to each other in both the economic and political spheres. Along with continuing to work to create a climate conducive to candid dialogue in all areas, I intend to make a concerted effort for greater cooperation in all fields.

While stressing that Japan would never again become a major military power, he emphasized the important role that Japan could play in the region, and stated that Japan was ready to host an international conference on the reconstruction of Cambodia when peace was restored to the war-torn country. In addressing Japan's political role, Kaifu went one step beyond his predecessors in apologizing for Japan's conduct in World War II: "I express sincere contrition for past Japanese actions which inflicted unbearable suffering and sorrow upon a great many people of the Asia-Pacific region."[10]

Immediately after the Kaifu visit, Emperor Akihito paid the very first royal visit to the region in September 1991. Visiting Thailand, Malaysia and Indonesia — the carefully selected target countries — the Emperor reiterated the phrase: "Japan is a peace-loving country and would never repeat the horrors of that most unfortunate war."[11] In at least one respect, the visit augured well since it came a few months after the May visit of Prime Minister Kaifu. By repeatedly showing sincere remorse and repentance over the country's past misdeeds, the Emperor and Empress left the impression that Japan's intention was to embark on a new era of trust and mutual cooperation with Southeast Asia.

Prime Minister Kiichi Miyazawa also visited the ASEAN region (Indonesia, Malaysia, Thailand, Brunei) in January 1993 and delivered a policy speech in Bangkok, conveying Japan's commitment to the task of forging a new order for peace and prosperity in the Asia-Pacific. He stressed that, "Japan will attach particular importance to the very process of talking with the ASEAN countries. This means that Japan will think and act together with ASEAN. I am quite confident that the wisdom and vigor of the ASEAN countries will become an important pillar which supports the future of the international community, at a time when the world is searching for a new international order." As Japan's policy initiative, Miyazawa underscored the following four points: (1) promotion of political and security dialogue among the countries of the region to strengthen Asia-Pacific peace and stability, and to think seriously about the future vision of the region's security; (2) continued efforts to enhance the openness of the Asia-Pacific economy to promote dynamic economic development in the region; (3) active efforts to tackle such tasks common to humankind as promoting democratization, and pursuing development and environmental conservation in tandem; and (4) Japan-ASEAN cooperation to build peace and prosperity in Indochina, including establishment of a forum to map out a comprehensive development strategy.[12]

In August 1994, only one year later, Prime Minister Tomiichi Murayama visited the region as the first Japanese leader of a former opposition party. Visiting Malaysia, Singapore, the Philippines, and Vietnam, Murayama repeated his apologies for Japanese wartime activities. In Singapore, Murayama for the first time laid a wreath at a memorial for victims of the Japanese occupation of Singapore. However, Prime Minister Mahathir of Malaysia told Murayama that he could not understand why Japan continued to apologize for its actions fifty years ago. Instead, Mahathir proposed that Japan should "work with us for the future".[13] In Vietnam, as the first Japanese prime minister to pay a visit after the unification of the country, Murayama and his counterpart, Vo Van Kiet, mutually agreed to promote a friendly relationship, including the adoption of a Japanese proposal for political talks between officials at the vice ministerial level. However, unlike previous visits, the coalition government headed by the Socialist Party could not announce Japan's renowned policy, including specific commitments to ASEAN.[14]

As we have seen, during the Takeshita Doctrine phase almost every prime minister of Japan visited the region. Based on the institutional networks forged during the first phase, some of the major achievements of ASEAN-Japan collaboration began to emerge (see Table 4.2). In fact, during the second phase, ASEAN-Japan relationships were strengthened in the following three areas: the Cambodian conflict, Myanmar, and the EAEC.

Foreign Ministers' Meeting

The Japan-ASEAN Foreign Ministers' Meeting has played a central role in consolidating Japan-ASEAN relations. In particular, Japan's support for the reconstruction of Cambodia and Indochina deserves special mention.

TABLE 4.2
Japanese Prime Ministers' Visits to ASEAN, 1989–94

Premier	Date	Countries visited	Results
Takeshita	April 1989	Thailand, Malaysia, Singapore, Indonesia, Philippines	(1) Takeshita Doctrine (2) Comprehensive Exchange Programme (3) ASEAN-Japan Development Fund
Kaifu	January 1991	Malaysia, Brunei, Thailand, Singapore, Philippines	(1) Matured partnership for a new age (2) Sponsoring a Cambodia Conference for Reconstruction
Miyazawa	January 1993	Indonesia, Malaysia, Thailand, Brunei	(1) Think together, act together (2) Forum for Comprehensive Development in Indochina
Murayama	August 1994	Philippines, Singapore, Malaysia, Vietnam	(1) Partnership for further advancement (2) War apology

In June 1987 Foreign Minister Tadashi Kuranari propounded the idea of a "partnership with a global perspective" between Japan and ASEAN, while keeping a low-profile posture over Cambodia, by the following four steps: (1) encouraging a dialogue between the parties concerned; (2) taking concrete measures for the smooth realization of troop withdrawal and self-determination; (3) guaranteeing the future status of Cambodia which should be free, democratic, peaceful, neutral and non-aligned as set forth in the eight-point proposal; and (4) assisting in the economic reconstruction of Indochina following the restoration of peace.[15] The repeated advocacy of these measures in resolving the Cambodian conflict underscored Japan's dilemma and illustrates the limitations on Japanese foreign policy.

In December 1987 the Japanese Foreign Ministry reportedly decided to support Sihanouk's efforts and give him all possible assistance, as exemplified by the offer of tape recorders for the Sihanouk–Hun Sen dialogue in Paris. The Foreign Ministry also expressed its readiness to invite Sihanouk to Tokyo for policy coordination. Furthermore, at the Third ASEAN Summit in Manila, Prime Minister Takeshita underscored Japan's political role in resolving the conflict by supporting Sihanouk.

A new Japanese initiative is expected to be centred on a vision of making the region's prosperity equally available to both ASEAN and Indochina and not just to serve Japan's economic interests. As former Prime Minister Nakasone convincingly put it in September 1987 at Chulalongkorn University, "It is my earnest hope that Vietnam will convert its war-time economy to a peace-time economy and give relief to its starving people. When peace prevails in this region, Vietnam can expect significant economic co-operation from the free world, including Japan; and it can be assumed that the goods for such economic co-operation will be procured in Thailand".[16]

At the eleventh meeting in July 1988, Foreign Minister Sosuke Uno announced Japan's basic policies as follows: First, in cooperation with ASEAN, Japan intended to promote the adjustment of economic structures, the strengthening of the free trade system, and to expand economic cooperation with ASEAN; Second, Japan would conduct closer dialogue and cooperation with ASEAN countries on issues that affect peace and stability of the Asia-Pacific; Third, Japan would vigorously promote two-way personal and cultural exchanges with ASEAN countries in the framework of the ASEAN-Japan Comprehensive Exchange Program (AJCEP). While simply referring to Japan's support for the peace efforts of the Cambodian problem, Uno stressed that, "Japan-ASEAN relations should be exemplary of cooperative relations among all the countries of the Asia-Pacific region and should serve as an engine for development of the region."[17]

After the resolution of the Cambodia conflict, Japan added a new element to its approach to relations with ASEAN, as Foreign Minister Yohei Kono stated at the ASEAN Post-Ministerial Conference in August 1995: "Based on the recent evolution of ASEAN, Japan regards it as particularly important at this stage that the ASEAN countries and Japan should deepen policy dialogues with both the global and regional issues on the agenda by attaching particular importance to the ASEAN Post-Ministerial Conferences, and laying great value on the vice-ministerial talks of the Japan-ASEAN Forum as well as our various bilateral talks with the ASEAN countries."[18] In a similar vein, Foreign Minister Yukihiko Ikeda expressed Japan's readiness to reconstruct its relations with ASEAN at the 29th FMM in 1996.

Japan-ASEAN Forum

Inaugurated in March 1977, the Japan-ASEAN Forum (JAF) has served as a facilitating body through extensive consultations over regional issues of mutual concern. Throughout the ninth, tenth and eleventh meetings, Japan and ASEAN discussed a wide range of subjects, such as specific trade issues and primary commodities, investment and industrial cooperation, the New Round of Multilateral Trade Negotiation, and cooperation in economics, culture, science and technology. The meeting also saw the exchange of views on how best both sides could improve ASEAN Japan Development Cooperation for their mutual benefit. In particular, at the tenth meeting it was agreed to explore the possibility of public-sector participation. In recognition of the important role that the private sector could play in the enhancement of the ASEAN-Japan Dialogue, particularly in the area of trade and investment cooperation, the meeting agreed to further explore the possibility of meaningful participation of the private sector in the ASEAN-Japan Dialogue process, including the active involvement of the ASEAN Committee in Tokyo (ACT) and the ASEAN Promotion Center (APC) in this initiative.[19]

At the eleventh meeting, furthermore, ASEAN noted that despite the various market-opening measures undertaken by Japan, ASEAN exports, in particular manufactured products to Japan, had not significantly improved. In this respect, ASEAN urged Japan to continue its efforts to improve market access for products of interest to ASEAN, particularly improvements to its GSP scheme and liberalization of its import policies, procedures and documentation. Japan explained that it would continue to strive to the best extent possible to improve market access for ASEAN products in various fields, including the generalized system of preference.[20]

The twelfth JAF held in Tokyo in September 1990 was different in that for the first time representatives of the ASEAN-Japan Economic Council participated so that the private sector's expectations and demands could be reflected. In a similar vein, the thirteenth JAF held in Tokyo in February 1993 was unprecedented in that for the first time the forum included political and security issues on the agenda. As the ASEAN chairman stated, "the inclusion of regional political and security issues on the agenda is most timely, and ASEAN intends to continue its contribution for the peace and stability of the region with Japan and other friendly countries".[21]

The fourteenth JAF was held in Bangkok in January 1995, reviewing a broad range of international, regional and bilateral issues. The private sector was also represented at the meeting for the second time since the previous meeting. The inclusion of political and security issues and the elevation of representation to the senior officials level since 1993 indicated the increased importance of the Japan-ASEAN dialogue process.[22]

Nonetheless, judging from the outcome of the dialogues, it may be concluded that the forum has neither served the original purpose, nor helped to resolve the economic problems between Japan and ASEAN. Largely because of its organizational structure, the forum has not been effective in resolving these problems. If the JAF is to discuss only economic matters between Japan and ASEAN, it is not likely to yield any significant results, simply because the representatives on both sides possess neither the authority nor the expertise to confront such issues. Economic ministers of both parties should meet more regularly, in collaboration with the JAF, or form the core of JAF itself. If the forum is to retain its original purpose, it will be necessary to institutionalize a new forum for purely economic relations between Japan and ASEAN.[23]

Japan's Security Role and the ASEAN Regional Forum

The end of the Cold War in 1989 accelerated interest in a regional approach to security cooperation in Southeast Asia. Reflecting this new environment, the director general of the Japan Defence Agency, Yozo Ishikawa, paid official visits to Thailand, Malaysia and Australia in May 1990. This was only the second time a Japanese defence minister had visited the region. Ishikawa's presence was ostensibly to conduct a fact-finding mission at the outset of the post–Cold War period. In Thailand, Prime Minister Chatichai Choonhavan proposed that the Thai and Japanese navies hold joint exercises in the South China Sea to enhance regional security in the event of a withdrawal of U.S. forces from the Philippines, and that senior Thai and Japanese military officers meet to discuss the repercussions of an American withdrawal. The proposal created fervour in Southeast Asia, leading one Thai English newspaper to immediately respond: "Without a doubt, bilateral defense cooperation among Japan and the ASEAN countries is tolerable.… But at this point, any role Japan sees for itself in defense beyond its territory is out of the question."[24] In effect, Thailand did not envisage a military buildup with Japan, but only joint training and an exchange of opinions and experience, all aimed at enhancing Japan's peacekeeping role in the region.

In Malaysia, the defence minister, Tengku Ahmad Ritaudeen, told Ishikawa that the region was concerned with the uncertainty about a possible re-emergence of Japan as a military power, given its economic strength, amid signs of a reduced United States and Soviet presence in the region.[25] Accordingly, ASEAN experts have quickly dismissed Chatichai's proposal as "premature", a unilateral action that lacked support throughout the region. Regretting the lack of consultation among member countries, Jusuf Wanandi, director of Indonesia's Center for Strategic and International Studies, who, together with other Southeast Asian experts, gathered in Bangkok for an international conference on the superpowers' relations with the region, said: "It's so sudden. It's a completely new departure for Southeast Asia's thinking about Japan's role in the region, which is mainly economic." Noordin Sopiee, director of Malaysia's Institute of Strategic and International Studies, also opined that, "Perhaps it is better if this initiative comes from countries other than Thailand which has not come under Japan's occupation. But then of course other countries are not prepared to do so."[26]

Discomfited by formidable objections, not to mention constitutional prohibition, the Japanese government quickly rejected the report that Japan was in favour of Chatichai's proposal, while explaining how Ishikawa had misled the Thai officials by his reply, "experts should be asked to consider the matter", which, in the Japanese context, usually means a polite rejection of the proposal. Despite the negative reactions, the following excerpt shows some positive aspects to the Chatichai initiative: "it is necessary to contemplate Japan's role in Southeast Asia that must mean a sharing of responsibilities for the region's peace and prosperity in the next century. This assumes the nature of Tokyo's role extending beyond mere economics and will rest on an equality of partnership that can be mutually beneficial. Beginning on a low-level basis, Tokyo will have to provide for security assistance in terms of training and the exchange of know-how. It seems unavoidable that such areas must be achieved according to the equality of the ASEAN states and which could be extended to the non-ASEAN states should they accede to free enterprise and more open and free political systems."[27]

Soon after the defence minister's visit, attention was directed towards the regional security architecture, as Canadian secretary of state for external affairs, Joe Clark, proposed a "North Pacific Cooperative Security Dialogue" in September 1990. However, ASEAN and Japan rejected the proposal because of the fact that diversified Asian countries are not ready to accept any CSCE type security institution. Instead, they came up with a new security approach, utilizing the existing framework of ASEAN-centred Post-Ministerial Conferences (PMC). The new approach is called "comprehensive security", and gained strong backing from other countries in the region, as explained by some observers: "In sharp contrast to the strong military orientation of the Western-derived concept of 'common security', 'comprehensive security', which is perhaps the most widely endorsed security concept in the region, stresses non-military means of achieving and maintaining security."[28] Well versed in the Asian security environment, Japanese leaders proposed a security forum, which was to utilize the existing security networks of PMCs.

Given the long tradition of non-security cooperation, ASEAN's decision for a new security forum deserves an explanation. Equally important, why did Japan change its Washington-centred bilateralism to join the ASEAN Regional Forum (ARF), and what kind of a security role might Japan play in resolving regional conflicts? To answer the question, we need to turn to Japanese domestic players. Judging from the cautious response to the defence minister's visit, it was apparent that it was the Ministry of Foreign Affairs rather than the Defence Agency that formulated Japan's ARF policy. As a continuation of Japan-ASEAN dialogue, or taking advantage of the institutionalization of Japan-ASEAN relations, Japanese Foreign Ministry officials had earlier been invited in their "private" capacities in June 1991 to attend the Track II meeting, ASEAN–Institute of Strategic and International Studies (ASEAN-ISIS), aimed at preparing an ASEAN-ISIS report to the 1991 ASEAN-PMC. It became clear, according to a participant, that both ASEAN and Japan had developed in tandem a number of similar security conceptions, including the idea that the PMC might be an appropriate forum for security discussions. At the 1991 PMC meeting, Japan's foreign minister Taro Nakayama stated that the annual ASEAN-centred PMC meetings should become a forum for political dialogues in the field of security as well as economic cooperation and diplomacy, and proposed that senior officials of ASEAN and its dialogue partners prepare a report on security matters.[29]

Accordingly, this Japanese initiative was hailed as a great success at home and abroad. It was the first time Japan had endorsed a multilateral security dialogue, and it was made while the United States was still officially opposed to the idea. Moreover, setting up a multilateral venue for security dialogue had another policy implication, as Sato put it: "it is important for Japan to place herself in multilateral venues, wherein the countries which are worried about the future direction of Japanese defense policy can express their concern."[30] These attempts reveal the fact that Japan wanted to utilize a multilateral security forum to complement the existing security networks, not to replace them. Accordingly, Japan envisages its role as a "political broker" rather than a regional "policeman". As such, Japan's approach to the ARF was closely linked to the concept of comprehensive security, mainly developed by the Foreign Ministry. It also meant that through interaction with the ASEAN-ISIS, Japan has come to endorse the extension of "ASEAN's model" of regional security.

Ever since Foreign Minister Nakayama's proposal, Japan had been playing an active role in promoting security dialogue. Attending the first ARF held in Bangkok in July 1994, for instance, Japanese Foreign Minister Yohei Kono stated that Japan would continue its basic security policies, which embraced an exclusively defence-oriented stance, the Three Non-Nuclear Principles, and the strengthening of a non-proliferation regime. Regarding regional security, Kono confirmed that the presence and engagement of the United States in the region is a prerequisite for regional peace and stability, yet efforts should be made to promote an increase of mutual confidence through the ARF process and to establish and improve the security environment from a long-term perspective. For this purpose,

Kono proposed concrete discussions on "Mutual Reassurance Measures" in three areas: information sharing, personnel exchanges, and cooperation towards the promotion of global activities.[31]

In early February 1995, a Philippine-China row began when Manila disclosed that the Chinese had built military-style structures on Mischief Reef, just 170 kilometres off the Philippine island of Palawan. The result was the Philippine Navy's removal of Chinese markers on Pennsylvania Reef, Jackson Atoll, Second Thomas Reef, First Thomas Shoal, and Half Moon Shoal, followed by its detention of four Chinese fishing vessels near the contested reef. Although China explained its encroachment as "providing shelters for fishermen", the incident triggered a chain reaction.

First, the Philippines approached the United States for both financial and security support in order to modernize the Philippine armed forces with special emphasis on a conventional army. As a result, the Clinton administration began to take a firmer attitude towards events in the South China Sea. Washington seemed to have realized the significance of an "American presence" in Southeast Asia. As one scholar cogently put it, "Had such cooperation survived the end of the bases relationship, it is unlikely that China would have moved on Mischief Reef."[32]

Second, the incident caused Vietnam to strengthen its relations with the Philippines as well as the United States. In particular, it should be noted that in May 1995 Vietnamese Deputy Foreign Minister Vu Khoan made an unofficial visit to the United States in order to bring attention to China's recent moves in the South China Sea. Due to Hanoi's acute anxiety, a State Department spokesman announced that "the United States is concerned that a pattern of unilateral actions and reactions in the South China Sea has increased tensions in that area".[33]

Third, many ASEAN members were compelled to reconsider their traditional policy of neutrality towards China. Indonesia was especially hard-pressed to do so because of the fact that China suddenly included Indonesia-owned Natuna Island among its claims in the South China Sea. As an Indonesian military source explained, "Before, we considered ourselves as outsiders. But now we have taken a look at the charts and we have seen the way China seems to be moving south and we are growing more concerned. What Chinese leaders say and what happens in the field is different."[34] At the same time, many Indonesian scholars had begun to advocate a joint policy by Southeast Asian countries. As Juwono Sudarsono, vice-governor of the Institute of National Defense, declared, "Southeast

Asian countries may have to prepare themselves for a possible military confrontation with China."[35]

The Japanese response was also encouraging at the second ARF held in Bandar Seri Begawan in August 1995. In fact, Foreign Minister Kono gave an avowal that Japan would like to cooperate with ASEAN in fostering a three-stage development of the ARF: by promoting confidence building, developing preventive diplomacy, and elaborating approaches to conflicts. He also stated that the territorial and jurisdictional dispute in the South China Sea could be properly taken up in the ARF. As a result, Japan was nominated as co-chair of the intersession group on confidence-building measures. Therefore, it would not be an exaggeration to say "That Japan, with its sudden burst of diplomatic activity had taken a leading role in establishing a multilateral security dialogue in the Asia-Pacific,… demonstrated by its having preempted US foreign policy for perhaps the first time since the Second World War".[36]

When China launched missiles against Taiwan in March 1996, the Clinton administration was forced into confronting China by deploying two battleships. Accordingly, ASEAN voiced concern over increasing Chinese assertiveness at the third annual ARF in August 1996. ASEAN tried in vain to resolve the issue of China's encroachment into the disputed territories within the framework of the ARF. China successfully opposed a proposal that working groups be set up within the ARF to prepare policies on specific issues in-between ministerial meetings.[37] Since the ARF was formed as a loose, informal and ad hoc multilateral forum, it is understood that such a critical issue as tensions in the South China Sea is beyond its scope. In other words, although the ARF may eventually have the power to resolve concrete security issues, it is not likely to occur any time soon.

Reflecting ASEAN's reappraisal, the third ARF in July 1996 saw some progress in the field of confidence building, such as dialogue on security perceptions, defence policy publications, enhancing high-level defence contacts, exchanges among defence staff colleges, training, and the UN register of conventional arms. Secondly, the ARF had formulated conditions for the admission of new members: (1) all new participants, who will all be sovereign states, must subscribe to, and work cooperatively to help achieve the ARF's key goals, (2) a new participant should be admitted only if it can be demonstrated that this would have an impact on the peace and security of the "geographical footprint" of key ARF activities, (3) efforts must be made to keep the number of participants to a manageable level to ensure the effectiveness of the ARF, and (4) all applications for participation should be submitted to the chairman of the ARF, who will consult all the other ARF participants at the SOM (senior official meeting) and ascertain whether a consensus exists for the admission of the new participant. Third, China's positive approach to the ARF was welcomed. However, the fact that the ARF had to take up the issue of human rights and democratization suggests the growing prominence of Western powers.[38]

REINFORCING ECONOMIC RELATIONS: CHALLENGE OF THE INTERMEDIATE STREAM

Ever since the Plaza Agreement in 1985, a new wave of Japanese foreign investment brought home the fact that ASEAN's economy and huge market were once again critical to Japan's survival. It was Japan's Ministry of International Trade and Industry (MITI) that served as a catalyst in changing the landscape of ASEAN economies.

A New Aid Plan for ASEAN in 1987

On 15 January 1987, MITI Minister Hajime Tamura proposed a new aid plan for Asian industries and a cut in the interest rate on yen loans for economic cooperation to 3 per cent. The announcement was made in his luncheon speech in Bangkok in which Tamura explained Japan's new aid policy towards ASEAN, as he said: "In envisaging the economic relationship between Japan and ASEAN as we approach the next century, I should like to propose the development of what I call a 'creative relationship of industrial interdependence'."[39] While referring to four basic directions of Japan's aid policy — (1) fostering export-oriented industries, (2) promoting direct foreign investment, (3) the need for nurturing supporting industries, and (4) creating a smooth transfer of technology — he emphasized the importance of fostering export-oriented industries, and proposed the so-called New Asia Industrial Development (NAID) Plan, intended to create a horizontal division of labour in Asia while securing Japan's economic presence and influence.

With ASEAN countries as its target, the NAID Plan had the following requirements: (1) cooperation should be extended in the selection and formulation of industrial projects that are most suitable for the recipient countries; (2) financial and technological assistance must be directed towards the development of private industries; (3) direct investments from Japanese firms must be encouraged; and (4) the Japanese market should be opened up for the import of manufactured goods from the recipient developing countries, and Japan should help them increase their exports to Japan. Although the specifics of the plan were not given by Tamura, a high expectation on the part of the ASEAN countries emerged. As one Thai official put it, "We are hopeful that Japan can overcome her credibility gap by sincerely translating all those words of wisdom and policy statements into real actions."[40]

Special mention should be made here with respect to Japanese investment in the ASEAN region. Largely because of the appreciation of the yen, many Japanese companies started to invest rather extensively in export-oriented sectors. Thailand is a case in point. In 1987, for instance, Japan registered 140 applications for investment in the first nine months. This was 4.19 times the number submitted over the same period in 1986. The value of applications by the Japanese firms during those nine months amounted to 28.5 billion baht.[41] This boded well for more balanced interdependent economic relations between Japan and ASEAN. Japan should also take bold measures to open up its market to the ASEAN countries, which would reduce the need for Japan's controversial economic aid to the region.

Finally, Prime Minister Takeshita announced a plan to establish the AJDF in December 1987 when he attended the Third ASEAN Summit meeting. Ploughing back Japan's accumulated private and public funds, the plan hoped to facilitate a major leap forward in the economic development of ASEAN's private sectors. This fund, together with the New AID Plan, had been portrayed as "the cutting edge of Japan's initiative to organize the industrial integration of East and South East Asia".[42]

Inauguration of the Economic Ministers' Meeting in 1992

A significant change in Japan-ASEAN economic relations was realized when Japan's MITI and ASEAN economic ministers (AEM) agreed to formally institutionalize an annual meeting. The MOFA's virtual monopoly of Japan-ASEAN relations was thus broken. The first meeting (AEM-MITI) was held in Manila in October 1992 and both the ASEAN economic ministers and Japan's MITI exchanged views on current global and regional issues relating to trade, investment and other areas of potential cooperation between Japan and ASEAN. They also considered various policy measures to further expand the free flow of trade and investment between the two and to contribute to the strengthening of the multilateral trading system and continued prosperity in the region. More specifically, ASEAN requested that the following measures be taken: (1) the Japan-ASEAN Experts' Group meet to review progress of implementation of the AJDF as well as the additional needs of ASEAN; (2) the institution of a programme to improve protection of intellectual property and the system for industrial standardization and quality control, which would be necessary for smoother technology transfer to ASEAN countries; (3) the establishment of a comprehensive programme for developing small and medium-sized enterprises in ASEAN; and (4) the application of MITI's Green Aid Plan to provide technical support to improve overall investment conditions of ASEAN member countries.[43]

The second meeting, held in Singapore in October 1993, saw both sides exchange views on developments in the international economic scene, namely the Uruguay Round, North American Free Trade Area, ASEAN Free Trade Area, the upgrading of ASEAN industries, and possible Japan-ASEAN cooperation with other countries. At this meeting MITI presented two future policy directions for Japan-ASEAN cooperation. The first was the policy of upgrading industries in ASEAN; the second was policy coordination for the economic reconstruction of Indochina.[44] In terms of Japan-ASEAN multilateral cooperation, the latter is quite significant because Japan and ASEAN formally discussed cooperation in Indochina for the first time. They agreed to contribute towards the process of reconstruction and structural adjustment with a view to integrating the economies of Indochina into the mainstream of the international trading system. Although there existed differences in both sides' understanding, to wit, ASEAN's request for economic assistance and MITI's preference for upgrading industries, the AEM-MITI meeting compromised on a working group on "economic cooperation" in Indochina at its third meeting in September 1994. Furthermore, at the fourth meeting a year later, the Interim Report by the working group was approved, which in turn led to policy recommendations by the working group in 1996.[45]

Thus, by the fifth meeting held in Jakarta in September 1996, both Japan and ASEAN were able to reaffirm their commitments to maintain closer economic cooperation by reviewing the progress made in the various economic cooperation activities. Among the cooperation activities discussed by both parties were: (1) a programme on cooperation in the supporting industries in ASEAN; (2) a Cambodia-Laos-Myanmar working group; (3) the ASEAN-Mekong Basin Development Cooperation Ministerial Meeting; and (4) the Common Effective Preferential Tarrif scheme for AFTA and ASEAN Industrial Cooperation Scheme. Both groups of ministers also discussed and reviewed the progress in international economic issues, such as APEC, ASEM and the World Trade Organization (WTO) ministerial conference in Singapore.[46]

Initiating Financial Cooperation with ASEAN in 1994

A new development can be detected by the first Japan-ASEAN Finance Ministers' Meeting in October 1994. This was significant in that ASEAN had not as yet held its own financial meeting. The reason behind Japan's proactive approach for financial cooperation was the fact that the APEC Finance Ministers' Meeting had just been convened a half-year before by the American initiative. It is said that the establishment of the APEC Finance Ministers' Meeting precipitated the anxiety of Japan's Ministry of Finance (MOF). Without any effective framework initiated by Asians, the United States could directly lead Asian countries in the Asia-Pacific financial framework.[47]

Thus responding to the need for an Asian financial framework, the MOF took its own initiative and turned to ASEAN. At the first meeting, held in Madrid, where the IMF annual meeting was also held, Japanese and ASEAN ministers discussed exchange rate and yen loan issues and agreed to meet twice a year at the margins of the IMF and Asian Development Bank meetings.[48] Without establishing a financial ministers' meeting, however, ASEAN could not deal with regional financial issues, and left the matter to the existing Committee on Finance and Banking. Accordingly, the Japan-ASEAN Finance Ministers' Meeting had been held on a request basis, rather than regularly. It was only after the financial crisis in 1997 that the institutionalization of the finance meeting was achieved.

Rapid Expansion of Japan's Trade, Investment and Aid

In the realm of economic relations with the ASEAN countries, Japan's policy of a triad — aid, trade and investment — had been most successful.

Perhaps it had been so successful that Japan felt obliged to address a critical problem of trade imbalance. Reflecting this, Chalmers Johnson castigated the new AID plan as "Japan's proposal for a new regional order, a new and much more prosperous version of the Greater East Asia Co-prosperity Sphere".[49] Is this really what was happening in Southeast Asia?

Table 4.3 clearly indicates that there have been two major changes in Japan's foreign economic relations. The first change is that the total volume of Japan's trade with Asia (i.e., Asian NIES and ASEAN) for the first time exceeded that of Japan-U.S. trade in the year 1990, and that the former trade volume is expanding faster than the latter. Second, Japan's aid and investment had been steadily increasing until 1990 and, accordingly, for the first time, in 1989, Japan's exports to ASEAN surpassed its imports; since then its trade surplus has been increasing rather rapidly.[50] Let us look more closely at each of these three components of Japan-ASEAN economic relations.

First, Japan-ASEAN trade relations have undergone a remarkable development. In particular, Japan's exports to the region have increased rapidly since 1993; with Japan's trade surplus soaring. Why has this occurred? Reportedly, the high growth of the ASEAN economies has been increasingly dependent on the import of Japanese capital goods, thereby eroding ASEAN's ever-favourable trade balance with Japan. As a result,

TABLE 4.3
Japan's Economic Relations with ASEAN, 1987–96 ($ million)

	Trade	Investment	ODA
1987	35,153 (9.3%)	1,524 (4.6%)	1,679 (32.0%)
1988	43,852 (9.7%)	2,713 (5.8%)	1,920 (29.9%)
1989	51,775 (10.7%)	4,684 (6.9%)	2,132 (31.5%)
1990	62,236 (11.9%)	4,082 (9.2%)	2,299 (33.1%)
1991	69,438 (12.6%)	3,696 (8.9%)	2,149 (24.2%)
1992	72,257 (12.6%)	3,867 (11.3%)	2,975 (35.1%)
1993	83,485 (13.9%)	3,040 (8.4%)	2,255 (27.7%)
1994	98,187 (14.6%)	4,957 (12.0%)	1,883 (19.5%)
1995	125,921 (16.1%)	5,475 (10.8%)	2,228 (21.1%)
1996	127,483 (16.7%)	6,382 (13.2%)	1,693 (20.3%)

Sources: MITI, *Tsusho Hakusho*, 1988–97; Ministry of Finance, *Financial Statistics of Japan*, various issues; Ministry of Foreign Affairs, *Gaiko seisho*, 1988–97.

Japanese firms in ASEAN countries have come to serve as a catalyst in forging a much broader regionalization of Japanese production. If so, are ASEAN's trade deficits bound to deteriorate indefinitely? Some argue that Japan's trade surpluses are inevitable because "Keiretsu networks are creating the exclusionary character of Japanese firms-controlled regional production networks."[51] However, other observers reached a different conclusion. Indeed, if intra-industry trade increases in Southeast Asia, as Wendy Dobson argues, behaviour of production networks will likely converge in the long term.[52]

Second, Japanese investment in ASEAN, on the other hand, decreased between 1990 and 1993, but increased almost to the level of $6 billion in 1996. This major increase was due to the following two reasons: (1) the yen appreciation pushed Japan's investment into Southeast Asia, which led to the rapid growth of Southeast Asian economies, which in turn promoted further imports and investment from Japan; (2) the government strengthened its complimentary policies towards Japanese firms. For instance, at the Japan-ASEAN Economic Ministers' Meeting, held immediately after ASEAN's Economic Ministers' Meeting in October 1992, MITI Minister Watanabe proposed a package programme designed to attract more investment and increase industrial cooperation with Japan. The proposals included a review of the implementation of the ASEAN-Japan Development Fund, improvement of intellectual property protection, establishment of a programme for developing small and medium-size enterprises in ASEAN, and application of the MITI's Green Aid Plan to provide technical support to improve the region's investment climate.[53]

To promote economies of scale and make the ASEAN market more attractive to investors, various industrial cooperation schemes were introduced in the mid-1970s and 1980s. General dissatisfaction with these schemes led ASEAN members to introduce the ASEAN Industrial Cooperation (AICO) scheme in November 1996 to accelerate the pace of industrial cooperation among private enterprises.[54] Japanese enterprises have expressed interest towards the scheme. Greater investment is anticipated in particular in the automobile and related industries should the sheme be effectively carried out.

Third, Japan's ODA to ASEAN countries reached a peak in 1992 but decreased slightly since then. MITI had been contemplating a new aid policy since 1993. Three years later it announced a policy of upgrading industrial

infrastructure in ASEAN with extensive use of yen loans. The policy
was designed to provide better assistance according to each recipient's
economic and social needs, with different targets for the following three
categories: emerging markets; semi-emerging markets; and marginalized
economies. Whilst not drastically increasing, Japan's ODA funding was
maintained as Tokyo decided to resume its aid to Vietnam, Cambodia
and Myanmar and upheld its ambitious aid promotion plan, amounting
to $70 to 75 billion for the period 1993–97.[55] At the same time, special
attention was paid to the specific conditions in each recipient nation, due
to different levels of development. Thus, cooperation to Vietnam, Indonesia
and the Philippines took the form of improving social infrastructure and
human resources through grant aid and technical cooperation, as well
as yen loans to build economic infrastructure. Thailand and Malaysia,
which had achieved substantial economic growth, were no longer grant
aid recipients. Singapore and Brunei, which enjoy very high per capita
GDP, have received technical cooperation corresponding to the level of
technology in the beneficiary nation.

These three dimensions of economic relations suggest the formation
of Japan's economic networks in Southeast Asia, which tend to retain
Japanese interest and influence in the region rather than the creation of a
new co-prosperity sphere. A critical difference is that expanded economic
networks benefit both partners rather well, thereby discouraging another
wave of anti-Japanese movements.

REINFORCING CULTURAL ASPECTS OF
JAPAN-ASEAN RELATIONS

The absence of anti-Japanese feelings and movements can also be explained
by strengthened cultural cooperation. In fact, after Fukuda's tenure, almost
every Japanese prime minister has proposed an exchange programme or
created an institution to promote cultural exchange with ASEAN countries.
These are as follows:

1. The Japan Scholarship Fund for ASEAN Youth to provide $1 million
    each year between 1981 and 1989, announced in 1979 by Prime Minister
    Ohira during a visit to Manila. After a visit to Southeast Asia in 1989,
    Prime Minister Takeshita announced provision of an additional $10
    million for the scholarship fund between 1991 and 1995.

2. The Southeast Asia Cultural Mission organized in November 1987 in preparation for Takeshita's visit to ASEAN in December 1988.
3. The ASEAN-Japan Comprehensive Exchange Program, announced in December 1987 by Takeshita, incorporating ideas proposed by the Southeast Asia Cultural Mission, including the establishment of Japan Foundation offices in ASEAN countries and the ASEAN Cultural Center, which in 1995 was transformed into the Asia Center.
4. The ASEAN Cultural Fund of 5 billion yen to promote intra-ASEAN cultural exchange, established as a follow-up to Fukuda's ASEAN speech in 1977.
5. The Southeast Asia Youth Invitation Program to promote better understanding of Japan among outstanding youth leaders of ASEAN countries through visits to Japan, established in 1979 by Ohira.[56]

Without doubt, these initiatives helped to promote exchange at the academic level as well as the citizen level. They also developed a solid group of individuals, both Japanese and Southeast Asian, who by their experience have a favourable attitude towards one another and are committed to serving the relationship in their respective capacities. In this respect, the Southeast Asian Cultural Mission deserves a special mention. Takeshita's visit to ASEAN capitals in 1989 had been well prepared by a study group of leaders from intellectual, educational, and cultural fields who had visited Southeast Asia and formulated recommendations to be announced at the time of the prime minister's official visit. Suffice it to say that some of the initiatives have had an enduring impact on exchange activities between Japan and ASEAN countries.[57]

In November 1987 a cultural mission was sent to the six ASEAN countries in order to explore ways to strengthen cultural relationships with the region, and to make recommendations to the Japanese government. On 3 December 1987 the cultural mission made three major proposals to Prime Minister Takeshita: (1) to reform the education system in Japan to suit the needs of foreign students, (2) to establish a Japan-ASEAN cultural centre, and (3) to double the Japan Foundation's annual budget. It should be pointed out that the real causes impeding Japan's cultural diplomacy have finally been addressed, and that the target of these proposals is ASEAN.[58]

Furthermore, in the era of youth and future leadership exchange, the main programmes for successor-generation leaders include the following:

(1) the Asia Leadership Fellow Program, begun in 1996 by the International House of Japan and the Japan Foundation Asia Center; (2) the Fellowship Program for Leaders of the Next Generation, begun in 1995 by the Japan Foundation Asia Center; (3) the Japan Institute of International Affairs Fellowship Program, initiated in 1989 by Foreign Minister Kuranari.[59] These programmes are designed to bring together future leaders in ASEAN, Japan, and other East Asian countries, encouraging them to work together for a period of time, thus enabling them to learn from each other and to develop collegial relations among themselves. There is the assumption in these programmes that East Asia will be more integrated in the future and that networks of young leaders will provide the joint leadership needed in the emerging regional community. In the era of academic and intellectual exchange, it is generally acknowledged that academic research, particularly policy relevant research, on Southeast Asia has not been sufficiently emphasized in Japanese universities. There are few university-wide institutes for comprehensive study in this area, and much of the academic training and research efforts have depended on the limited number of scholars with a specialty in Southeast Asia or ASEAN.[60]

Table 4.4 suggests that the total number of ASEAN students in Japan is 4,884, four times larger than in 1986. The numbers of Malaysian and Indonesian students in particular have increased remarkably. Prime Minister Takeshita's well-prepared cultural initiative improved the original approach under the Fukuda Doctrine in significant ways. The Japan Foundation, for instance, set up an ASEAN Center in 1989 and ASEAN also set up a ministerial-level meeting in 1989 with the aim of forming an ASEAN identity. The first Conference of ASEAN Ministers Responsible for Information (AMRI) agreed to enhance cooperation among the press and the electronic media of member countries, to advance the goals of ASEAN and promote the image of ASEAN. At the third Conference, the AMRI issued a declaration to strengthen regional collaboration in the field of information by adopting a framework for a plan of action.[61]

However, the closer the relations, the more difficult for Japan to avoid settling the history issue. It was due to this realization that in May 1991 Prime Minister Kaifu expressed his "sincere contrition" for the suffering Japan had caused in Asia during World War II. At the same time, he averred that in order to teach Japan's younger generations about the wrongdoings of the Japanese Imperial Army, there was an urgent necessity to "ensure that young Japanese would gain a full and accurate understanding of modern and contemporary Japanese history through their education in

TABLE 4.4
ASEAN Students Studying Abroad

Indonesia		Malaysia		Philippines		Singapore		Thailand	
US	12,820	UK	18,539	US	3,127	UK	6,787	US	12,165
Australia	2,716	US	14,015	Japan	399	Australia	5,374	UK	1,654
Germany	2,107	Australia	7,849	Australia	357	US	4,093	Australia	870
Japan	1,077	NZ	2,301	Holy See	245	Canada	973	Japan	812
UK	936	Japan	2,057	UK	213	China	304	Germany	256
Netherlands	601	Jordan	1,807	Germany	147	NZ	224	NZ	236
Canada	502	Ireland	592	Canada	124	Ireland	116	Philippines	221
Philippines	300	China	257	China	96	Japan	102	China	202
Total	22,138	Total	49,413	Total	5,107	Total	18,087	Total	17,093

Source: UNESCO Statistical Yearbook, 1998.

school and in society at large".[62] Likewise, Prime Minister Hosokawa stated that "if the Japanese government and people base their future actions on this acknowledgement of historical facts, there will be a reconciliation between Japan and its neighbors which will lead to increased confidence and cooperation between all of us. Such openness will help us put the past behind us."[63]

However, the careless statements of certain conservative leaders thwarted these sincere efforts. For instance, Justice Minister Shigeto Nagano of the Hata government stated in 1995 that "the 1937 Nanking Massacre by the Japanese army never happened and that the Nanking Massacre and the rest were a fabrication".[64] Although Prime Minister Hata forced Nagano to resign, the incident revealed not only the existence of some Japanese who will not admit that Japan did anything wrong in World War II, but also the lingering fears and suspicions of many Asian states. These factors must be taken into account if Japan is to take more active political or security roles in the region.

Recognizing the importance of history and its impact on the present, Prime Minister Murayama decided to come to grips with the issue in the form of a Diet resolution in June 1995. The resolution was the first of its kind that explicitly disclosed the Japanese Diet's view of Japanese atrocities committed during World War II. The resolution, in part, said that: "Solemnly reflecting upon many instances of colonial rule and acts of aggression in the modern history of the world, and recognizing that Japan carried out those acts in the past, inflicting pain and suffering upon the peoples of other countries especially in Asia, the members of the House [of Representatives] express a sense of deep remorse. We must transcend the differences over historical views of the past war and learn humbly the lessons of history so as to build a peaceful international society."[65] Although it failed to include such crucial terms as "apology" or "renunciation of war", the resolution could be deemed as Japan's first effort to address its tainted image as a trustworthy partner in Southeast Asia. Thus, the opinion polls in Table 4.5 can be cited as an encouraging sign.

According to the polls, Japan's aid has been regarded rather highly (Q2 and Q5) and ASEAN countries positively support Japan's PKO activities (Q3). These favourable responses could have resulted from the improved image of Japan as a peace-loving nation. The fourth question reveals the fact that, except for Thailand, history is not hindering Japan-ASEAN relations. Consequently, except for the Philippines, ASEAN tends to regard Japan as a trustworthy country in Asia (Q1).

MAJOR ISSUES FOR FORTIFYING JAPAN-ASEAN RELATIONS

Resolution of the Cambodian Conflict and Reconstruction of Indochina

The outbreak of the Cambodian conflict in December 1978 rendered a shockwave that diminished the possibility of a bridging role by Japan or of ASEAN expanding its membership. Since Hanoi's intervention, ASEAN and Japan had been mutually engaged in trying to resolve the conflict. ASEAN's efforts, especially Indonesia's mediating role, were successful in softening Hanoi's regional policies. Japan's role, on the other hand, was largely the provision of policy ideas with the help of Thailand. In fact, Thai Prime Minister Chatichai asked Japan to consider hosting peace talks on Cambodia when he visited Tokyo in early April 1990. He suggested that Tokyo could encourage contacts between Prince Sihanouk and the Phnom Penh government under Hun Sen. Citing Vietnam's withdrawal of its troops, he also called on Tokyo to resume economic aid to Hanoi. Despite expected difficulties, however, the Japanese foreign ministry accepted the proposal and took swift steps towards effecting the Tokyo meeting.[66]

TABLE 4.5
Opinion Polls on Japan's Role in Asia, 1995–96

Q1 Do you think that Japan has become a trustworthy country in Asia?

	Indonesia	Philippines	Singapore	Thailand
Yes	85%	55%	62%	79%
No	14%	43%	31%	10%

Q2 Do you think that Japan's aid contributes to your country's economy?

Yes	88%	74%	69%	71%
No	12%	24%	27%	19%

Q3 Do you support Japan's PKO participation in various places in the world?

	Indonesia	Malaysia	Thailand	Vietnam
Yes	66.9%	73.6%	73.5%	61.5%
No	8.0%	12.9%	21.2%	12.7%

Q4 Do you think what the Japanese military did in your country is still an obstacle to the relationship between your country and Japan?

Yes	11.8%	25.2%	35.3%	16.3%
No	74.1%	66.7%	60.1%	69.0%

Q5 Do you think that Japan contributes positively to the development of Asian countries?

Yes	70.2%	74.9%	84.5%	83.9%
No	15.4%	18.6%	14.4%	8.0%

Sources: For Q1–Q2, *Asahi Shimbun*, 13 August 1995.
For Q3–Q4. *Yomiuri Shimbun*, 23 May 1995.
For Q5, *Yomiuri Shimbun*, 19 September 1996.

A few months later, the Japanese government held a Tokyo Meeting on Cambodia, by inviting concerned parties (Prince Sihanouk and Son Sann from the Coalition, Hun Sen from the Phnom Penh government, Khmer Rouge representative Khieu Samphan, and Thai Deputy Prime Minister Chavalit Yongchaiyudh) to Tokyo. The major achievements were threefold: (1) the modality of the Tokyo talks, as agreed upon in preparatory meetings in Thailand, was to be a meeting between two opposing groups; (2) the different tracks of peace efforts were synchronized for the first time in Tokyo; (3) the talks detected a shift in the United States' administration's stand on its role in efforts to restore peace to Cambodia.[67]

To the Japanese the meeting was a diplomatic success. In effect the foreign ministry handled it in an adroit manner. It was the Japanese policy team headed by Hisashi Owada, deputy-minister of the Foreign Ministry, that made Japan's endeavour worthwhile. The Japanese team intended to issue a "Tokyo Declaration", a kind of binding document, in order to signify a ceasefire in the conflict, hoping that the Chinese leader, Yang Zhenya, could exert an influence on the Pol Pot faction.[68] In order to effect a comprehensive political settlement, which was strongly espoused by the United States and Thailand, the Japanese team also had to link a ceasefire in the conflict with the formation of a supreme national council to represent Cambodian sovereignty. This turned out to be the reason for the boycott by the Pol Pot faction, who previously had approved the original Thai plan for attending the Tokyo meeting.

According to Owada, in a last attempt to reach a meaningful agreement, he met with Sihanouk, Son Sann, and Chavalit in a hotel in Tokyo to discuss the joint communiqué with Khieu Samphan, who objected to the draft. Owada finally told him that the door was always open and they would be waiting for their participation later, thus resulting in the Tokyo accord, as opposed to a declaration, espoused by all parties except the Khmer Rouge.[69] In a nutshell, the Japanese team failed to accomplish the first goal but had the second agreed upon by the two warring groups in the end. Although Japan could not narrow the gap between Hun Sen and the Khmer Rouge, which had been the main cause for failure in the past conferences, it is widely accepted that Japan's efforts in the peace process marked its first independent mediation activity in a major regional conflict in the post-war period.

After the Paris agreement in October 1991, Tokyo was committed to two major policy objectives: convening an international conference on Indochina development and sending Japanese personnel to Cambodia as part of the UN peacekeeping operation (PKO). The first objective was realized in June 1992, when Tokyo held an international conference on the reconstruction of Cambodia (ICORC), with the result that fifteen countries and international organizations agreed to contribute $880 million to war-torn Cambodia and to establish an international committee as a coordinating body for the reconstruction of the country.[70] In a similar vein, after conducting much official as well as private groundwork, Japan finally decided to resume its ODA to Vietnam in November 1992. Together with its reconstruction funds, this resumption of ODA would significantly expand Japan's role in directing economic development of the Indochinese countries. Furthermore, the second ICORC meeting held in Paris in September 1993 gained momentum for the reconstruction programme, with special emphasis on agricultural rehabilitation, improvement of the transport network and funding for basic education.[71]

The second objective was rather harder to put into practice due to domestic political difficulties. Nevertheless, by adopting the United Nations PKO Cooperation Bill on 12 June 1992, Japan for the first time rid itself of a taboo regarding the deployment of armed forces overseas. This resulted in the appointment of Yasushi Akashi, a veteran Japanese diplomat, to head the United Nations Transitional Authority in Cambodia (UNTAC). In September, Japanese Self Defense Forces officials were dispatched to Cambodia to assist in the UN peace process. Japan's operation involved around 600 personnel from the Engineer Corps, who were assigned to restoring roads and bridges far from areas of danger. Despite the loss of two officials and associated pressure to withdraw earlier from Cambodia, Japan's mission was fulfilled in September 1993 with rather favourable results.[72]

Following Miyazawa's 1993 proposal of Japan's positive assistance towards Indochinese countries, the Japanese Foreign Ministry held the Forum for Comprehensive Development of Indochina (FCDI) in February 1995.[73] The purpose of the forum was to attract international attention in support of the economic recovery of Cambodia, Laos and Vietnam (CLV). In March 1996, the "Task Force for Strategies for Development of the Greater Mekong Area" was formed by private sector specialists to present a comprehensive plan aimed primarily at infrastructural development for the Greater Mekong Area, which comprises the nations on the Indochinese Peninsula. The task force published its report in August of the same year. In competition with MOFA, MITI vigorously stepped up the Working Group on Economic Cooperation in Indochina in March 1995, and agreed to provide CLV officials and specialists with opportunities for training and workshops in order to obtain the necessary knowledge and skills to become ASEAN members, and also to conduct joint research and studies for drawing up development plans in various industrial sectors.[74] The policy initiatives by MOFA and MITI were hindered by the unexpected pace of realizing the ASEAN Ten.

Myanmar

Ever since the reparation settlement in 1953, Myanmar and Japan maintained close and friendly relations. To reinforce specific ties, Japan has offered its ODA, which constitutes about 70 per cent of Myanmar's total foreign aid. Thus, Japan has come to view Myanmar as another case for its independent diplomacy by siding with ASEAN's policy of engagement over Washington's policy of isolation. For instance, Tokyo suspended its ODA to Rangoon after its leaders launched a military coup d'état and suppressed the democratic movement in September 1988. However, when Myanmar announced that it would hold elections the following year, Japan recognized the military regime, called the State Law and Order Restoration Council (SLORC), as the legitimate rulers of the newly renamed Union of Myanmar and announced plans to resume limited aid. Moreover, encouraged by SLORC's decision to temporarily release opposition leader Aung San Suu Kyi from house arrest, Tokyo also announced a first installment of $24 million in grant aid. Japan explained that this move was designed to encourage further political reforms in Myanmar. It is remarkable that Japan used ODA as a political tool to moderate the country's repressive regime. At the same time, Japan demanded economic reforms in Myanmar in return for its foreign aid. In November 1988, SLORC adopted a foreign investment law as a result of Japan's demand.[75]

In March 1995, Japan partially lifted its ODA curbs and extended humanitarian aid to Myanmar, saying that taking an extra step towards democratization in a way that is visible to Tokyo, would lead to increased aid from Japan. Japan had another reason to worry: growing Chinese influence in Myanmar would offer Beijing naval access to key shipping lanes from the Indian Ocean and a wedge position within ASEAN. In response, Myanmar relaxed some of its authoritarian controls. For instance, in July 1995 when Aung San Suu Kyi was released from house arrest, Japan responded positively by providing grants worth $17 million. Japan's Foreign Ministry reassured the United States and European Union that this move would not mean a full resumption of ODA to Myanmar, for Japan risked a contradiction of its 1992 ODA charter if it reopened full aid with no demonstrated progress from Myanmar.[76]

It should be noted that Japan's Myanmar policy began to diverge from those of the United States and the European Union, who had been pressuring ASEAN not to accept the SLORC as a new member. On this diplomatic front, Japan sided with ASEAN, claiming that Myanmar's membership in ASEAN was critical to being able to work constructively in moderating the SLORC's repressive policies, counter China's growing influence, and resist Western interference in Southeast Asian affairs. Thus, in dealings with Myanmar, Japan executed its familiar pattern: seek a bridging role, offer foreign aid incentives, and pursue a softer line towards authoritarian regimes than Washington, with a willingness to work with them in consideration of the China factor.

Multilateral Engagement: APEC, EAEC and ASEM

In January 1989 Prime Minister Bob Hawke of Australia proposed a meeting of ministers of the countries in the region. When he proposed the Asia-Pacific Economic Cooperation (APEC), ASEAN had ample reasons to be cautious. Indonesian foreign minister Ali Alatas epitomized the ASEAN view, which became known as the "Kuchin consensus": (1) APEC should not dilute the identity or limit the role of any existing regional groups, (2) APEC should be based on principles of equality, equity, and mutual benefit; (3) APEC should not be made into an inward-looking trading bloc; (4) APEC should essentially remain a forum for consultation and cooperation on economic issues, (5) APEC should strengthen the capacity of participants to promote their common interests; and (6) APEC should proceed gradually and pragmatically.[77]

Within Japan there existed nagging bureaucratic infighting between MITI and MOFA over the form Asia-Pacific Economic Cooperation should take. As suggested by the Sakamoto Report in 1988, MITI was eager to set up a ministerial forum to promote economic development in the region while MOFA feared an Asian backlash against Japan if MITI's role in promoting an intergovernmental forum became public. In essence, MOFA objected to a formal institution because of lingering animosity in East Asia to Japan's economic dominance. It was because of this infighting that Japan's approach to APEC converged with that of ASEAN. In other words, in recognizing well the position of ASEAN, MOFA's attempt to put ASEAN in the driver's seat could be highly appreciated, as one observer cogently put it: "APEC will continue to be 'nested' in ASEAN in that the sub-regional organization is playing a central role in molding the direction of APEC to be consistent with the goals of ASEAN economic cooperation."[78]

Following consultations among the countries concerned, APEC's Ministerial Meeting was held in Canberra on 6 and 7 November 1989, bringing together six ASEAN countries and six dialogue partners, including Australia, Canada, the Republic of Korea, New Zealand, the United States and Japan. On the agenda for discussion were (1) world and regional economic development, (2) global trade liberalization, (3) opportunities for regional cooperation in specific areas and (4) future steps for Asia-Pacific Economic Cooperation. As a result, agreement was reached to hold the meeting on a continuous basis as well as a Ministerial Meeting to promote the Uruguay Round. Agreement also was reached on the following principles for promoting cooperation in the region: (1) that cooperation is outward looking, (2) that diversity is respected and cooperation is expanded by stages, and (3) that participating countries stand equal and be mutually beneficial.

Without any doubt, the most telling story during the Takeshita Doctrine phase was Japan's abortive participation in the East Asian Economic Caucus (EAEC). The proposal to establish the EAEC in December 1990 was unique in that Japan for the first time was asked to clarify its political role by the Southeast Asian countries. As one scholar concluded, "A strong leadership can come only from a member economy, which stands tall in the global arena. Indonesia is much too small to play this role meaningfully. Even China cannot take on this role, despite its size, as it is still a marginal player in the international trade and investment spheres and it has a long way to go before it can get fully integrated into the global market economy. This line of reasoning would inevitably lead us to only one possibility, that is, Japan as the leader of the EAEC."[79]

Ever since Malaysian Prime Minister Mahathir asked Japan to join the EAEC, however, Japan has vacillated over its position, reflecting the substantial debate within Japan. Mahathir's original idea was to form a bloc to counter a fortress European Union and an emerging North American Free Trade Agreement (NAFTA). In response, Prime Minister Kaifu suggested that Mahathir "study the proposal more carefully" and said that he would consider it if the proposal became an ASEAN scheme. But then, when EAEC became an ASEAN scheme, Prime Minister Miyazawa cautiously rejected it, saying "the Asia-Pacific region should continue to be open in order to prevent the emergence of a fortress EC and NAFTA."[80]

Furthermore, the Foreign Ministry, reflecting a U.S.-first policy, demurred; given the fact that Washington had even asked Tokyo to reject the proposal.[81] MITI was especially vocal against the Asia-only economic grouping. Thus, at the third APEC meeting in Seoul, Japan expressed its firm support for the APEC process and emphasized the danger of "closed" regionalism (i.e., EAEC). Japan's efforts to reject EAEC escalated until early 1993, as exemplified by governmental groups as well as official white papers, including the Economic Planning Agency's White Paper on the World Economy. The only exception was Kazuo Ogura, a Foreign Ministry official, who had been openly advocating closer Japanese identification with East Asia.[82]

A significant turning point came in early 1993 when the new U.S. government under Bill Clinton began to reassess the function of the EAEC. Following Washington's reappraisal, Tokyo came to terms with the EAEC, whose function now was to accommodate APEC. Within Japan, a bipartisan committee to promote EAEC was organized in March with the participation of a few prominent political figures, such as Ryutaro Hashimoto and Hiroshi Mitsuzuka from the LDP and Tomiichi Murayama of the Socialist Party. Although the question of Japan's participation remained unsettled, MITI expressed less reluctance than before about support for the EAEC proposal. But the Foreign Ministry still remained wary of the proposal, strengthening the view that Japan would prefer others in the region to take the initiative. Understandably, Mahathir's comments on Japan's attitudes had taken on a harsh tone, as was evident when he straightforwardly stated: "We are disappointed when Japanese officials ask us to explain and explain all over again what the EAEC is all about. Even those officials who have served for years in Southeast Asia claim that they do not know about the EAEC. We are saddened by this. The only Asian country with the ability to help Asian countries refuses to do so but instead demands to know why America is not included, why Australia and New Zealand are not included? The answer is obvious. They are not East Asians."[83]

In late 1994 new developments were unravelling due to the persistent efforts of ASEAN. First, ASEAN attempted to create the EAEC in a new form, such as a special luncheon or a ministerial meeting among the East Asian countries. In fact, soon after holding an informal Foreign Ministers' Meeting in July 1994, the ASEAN Economic Ministers' Meeting in Chiang Mai decided to convene another such meeting and invite the EAEC countries. In April 1995, however, the Japanese government suddenly decided not to participate in the scheduled economic meeting in Phuket, out of apparent concern that it could be a de facto preparatory event for EAEC's inclusion, and because of the fact that the scheduled meeting left out Australia and New Zealand.[84] It was unfortunate that Japan's decision ultimately forced ASEAN to eschew the meeting in Phuket.

Second, ASEAN announced a policy of forming a high-level meeting with the European Union in October 1994, to which Japanese business groups responded positively for the first time by expressing their support for the EAEC. The Keidanren (Federation of Economic Organizations), for instance, asked the Japanese government to participate in the EAEC by citing the fact that private-level cooperation among the EAEC countries had already taken place. However, when the Keidanren sent its mission to the ASEAN countries in February 1995, its position turned somewhat negative towards EAEC, partly because of American pressure wrought through its embassy in Tokyo.[85] Nevertheless, Tokyo's positive attitude towards consolidating East Asian regionalism was induced partly by the European Union's approval of East Asian regionalism in the form of an Asia-Europe meeting.

In March 1996 ASEAN successfully convened its first top-level meeting with European leaders in Bangkok by inviting Japan, South Korea and China. The first Asia-Europe Meeting (ASEM) was heralded for its groundbreaking attempt to strengthen ties between Asia and Europe, which had been the relatively weak link in the triangular relationship between Asia, Europe and North America. The key objectives of ASEM have been stated as enhancing the mutual understanding and benefit of Asia and Europe, and contributing to the establishment of a new world order through dialogue and cooperation. To this end, the strengthening of dialogue and cooperation between these two regions on a wide range of issues was included in the chairman's statement of the March meeting. It is interesting to note that Japan, who opposed ASEM at first because of its exclusion of Australia and New Zealand, finally joined the meeting.[86]

CONCLUSION

At the end of the third decade of Japan-ASEAN relations, it seemed that the foundation of conducting the relationship was well established, as shown by Figure 4.1.[87] In particular, under the summit meeting, the Foreign Ministers' Meeting and Economic Ministers' Meeting (AEM-MITI) are both supported by coordination at the vice-ministerial and division-director levels. With the addition of the Finance Ministers' Meeting in 1994, Japan-ASEAN relations clearly became structured around three main areas: diplomatic, trade and finance, as Figure 4.1 suggests.

FIGURE 4.1
Structure of Japan-ASEAN Relations

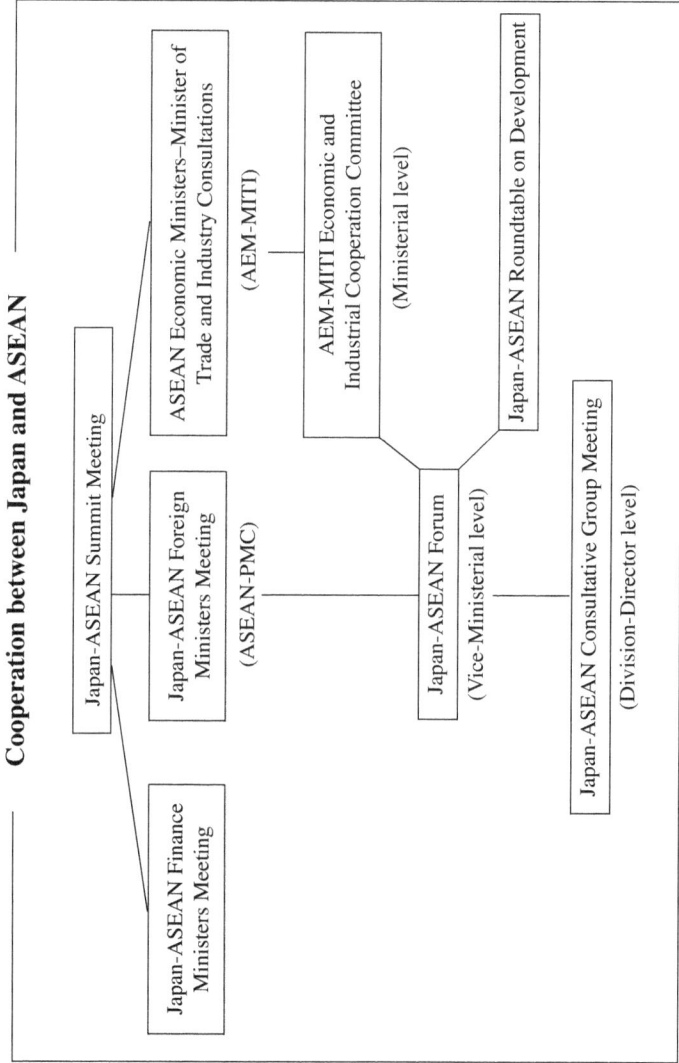

Cooperation between Japan and ASEAN

Japan-ASEAN Summit Meeting	ASEAN Economic Ministers–Minister of Trade and Industry Consultations (AEM-MITI)	
Japan-ASEAN Foreign Ministers Meeting (ASEAN-PMC)	AEM-MITI Economic and Industrial Cooperation Committee (Ministerial level)	Japan-ASEAN Roundtable on Development
Japan-ASEAN Finance Ministers Meeting	Japan-ASEAN Forum (Vice-Ministerial level)	Japan-ASEAN Consultative Group Meeting (Division-Director level)

During the Takeshita Doctrine phase, Japan-ASEAN relations became consolidated politically, economically and culturally. Politically, Japan's supportive role in resolving the Cambodian conflict and the institutionalization of the ARF should be highly regarded. Economically, Japan's contribution to the reconstruction of war-torn Cambodia was remarkable, while the New AID scheme was expected to accelerate ASEAN's economic development and Japan-ASEAN economic interdependence. Most importantly, Japan's growing economic and political involvment in Southeast Asia helped to create an integrated East Asian regional economy. It also reinforced a triangular trade structure in which Japanese exports to and investments in Southeast Asia led to a rapid expansion of Southeast Asian exports to Western markets, primarily the United States. Culturally, Japan's initiatives through the ASEAN cultural mission could serve as an eye-opening factor for ASEAN's cultural cooperation. It should be stressed that these three pillars of Japan-ASEAN relations will have a direct bearing on evolving ASEAN's regional governance.

Through mutually accommodating interaction, therefore, Japan could fortify its ASEAN-centred regional policy, thereby witnessing the realization of the Japanese Foreign Minister's institutionalized ideas. It was through this mutual interaction that ASEAN emerged as a united actor to be reckoned with. Especially during the third Indochina conflict period, the ASEAN region developed a modus operandi among its member countries. As a sub-regional organization, the countries of ASEAN have developed a rule of consensus in that individual initiatives are subjected to collective agreement as a means of strengthening ASEAN's regional resilience. It was during this time that ASEAN developed its unique style of regional cooperation, hence the ASEAN way, which has the following characteristics: (1) non-interference in the internal affairs of member countries; (2) amicable settlement of conflicts between members; (3) joint efforts towards the outside world; and (4) close consultations and consensus decision-making.[88]

The advent of the post–Cold War era in 1990 led many to consider that ASEAN lost a major underpinning force once the Cambodian conflict was over. In order to dispel this negative view, ASEAN convened another summit in January 1992. This fourth Singapore summit led to four tangible agreements, as laid out in the Singapore Declaration: (1) move to a higher plane of political and economic cooperation to secure regional peace and security; (2) seek to safeguard its collective interests in response to the formation of large and powerful economic groupings; (3) seek avenues to engage member states in new areas of cooperation in security matters; (4) forge closer relations based on friendship and cooperation with the Indochinese countries, following the settlement of the Cambodian conflict.[89]

Therefore, ever since ASEAN pledged in January 1992 to move the association "toward a higher plane", it was able to fulfill this pledge over the following five years by adopting a higher profile in the wider Asia-Pacific region, based on the ASEAN way. By introducing a new element of multilateral interaction and cooperation, ASEAN's deepening and widening efforts led to the new regionalism in Southeast Asia as a way to deal more confidently with the post–Cold War conditions. While ASEAN is actively engaged in regional activities at different levels, it maintains a unique "centripetal" principle, known as "occupying a driver seat".

Most notably, in August 1996, a meeting of NGOs was organized by the Citizens of Southeast Asia in Manila, adopting a resolution of "Toward a Southeast Asian community". This was to reappraise the ideas and recommendations concerning the region's future, as articulated in "Southeast Asia beyond the Year 2000: A Statement of Vision" which was issued in May 1994. Based on the four principles (national and regional resilience, unique in diversity, common national interests, open regionalism), the group strongly advocated the move towards a Southeast Asian community, as the resolution clearly stated: "Moved by the ideals espoused by the founding fathers of the ASEAN and expressed in the Bangkok Declaration of 1967, we reaffirm our conviction that Southeast Asia should be a community and that collectively this community should be a major political, economic, cultural and moral entity on the world stages in the twenty-first century."[90] Should there be a renewed impetus for ASEAN to become a fully-fledged community, Japan's role needs to be redefined so as to elevate Japan-ASEAN relations to a new level.

Notes

1. *Manila Times*, 16 December 1987; ASEAN, "The Third ASEAN Heads of Government Meeting, Manila, 14–15 December 1987" (Jakarta: ASEAN Secretariat, 1987).
2. For an evaluation of the 20th anniversary, see Richard Stubbs, "ASEAN at Twenty: The Search for a New Consensus", in *Regionalism in Asia: Critical Issues in Modern Politics*, edited by See Seng Tan (London: Routledge, 2009),

pp. 61–73; Ronald Parmer and Thomas Reckford, *Building ASEAN: Twenty Years of Southeast Asian Cooperation* (New York: Praeger, 1987). ASEAN's own evaluation can be found in *ASEAN, the Way Forward: The Report of the Group of Fourteen on Asean Economic Co-operation and Integration* (Kuala Lumpur: Institute of Strategic and International Studies, 1987).

3. Albert Talalla, "A Pre-Summit Evaluation", in *The Association of Southeast Asian Nations: After 20 Years*, edited by Hans Indorf (Washington, DC: Woodrow Wilson International Center for Scholars, 1988), p. 5.

4. ASEAN, "Joint Communique of the Third ASEAN Heads of Government Meeting, Manila, 14–15 December 1987" (Jakarta: ASEAN Secretariat, 1987).

5. Donald Crone, "The ASEAN Summit of 1987: Searching for New Dynamism", *Southeast Asian Affairs 1988* (Singapore: Institute of Southeast Asian Studies, 1988), p. 49. See also C.P.F. Luhulima, "The Third ASEAN Summit and Beyond", *Indonesian Quarterly* 17, no. 1 (1989): 12–28 and Michael Antolik, "The Pattern of ASEAN Summitry", *Contemporary Southeast Asia* 10, no. 4 (March 1989): 362–74 for the evaluations.

6. Noboru Takeshita, "Opening Statement", in ASEAN Secretariat, *Meeting of the ASEAN Heads of Government and Meeting of the ASEAN Heads of Government and the Prime Minister of Japan* (Jakarta: ASEAN Secretariat, 1987), pp. 86–90. For positive attitudes of Japan's Ministry of Foreign Affairs (Gaimusho), see especially Gaimusho, "Nihon/ASEAN shunokaigi wo furikaette, 13 December 1987", copies of documents obtained through Freedom of Information Act, Diplomatic Record Office (Tokyo: Ministry of Foreign Affairs, 1987).

7. ASEAN, "The 20th ASEAN Economic Ministers Meeting, Bangkok, 17–19 October 1988" (Jakarta: ASEAN Secretariat, 1988).

8. Lee Poh Ping, "ASEAN and the Japanese Role in Southeast Asia", in *ASEAN in the 1990s*, edited by Alison Broinowski (London: Macmillan, 1990), p. 162. For a general discussion of ASEAN-Japan relations, see especially James Tang, "ASEAN-Japan Relations: Literature Review and an Agenda for Further Research", in Proceedings of an Intra Universities Seminar on ASEAN-Japan Relations, Bandung, Padjadjaran University, 1990, pp. 121–35.

9. Noboru Takeshita, "Japan and ASEAN: Thinking Together, Advancing Together", *ASEAN Economic Bulletin* 6, no. 1 (July 1989): 125–33.

10. Toshiki Kaifu, "Japan and ASEAN: Seeking a Mature Partnership for the New Age", *ASEAN Economic Bulletin* 8, no. 1 (July 1991), pp. 87–94.

11. *The Nation* (Bangkok), 27 September 1991; *Jakarta Post*, 9 October 1991.

12. Kiichi Miyazawa, "New Era of the Asia-Pacific and Japan-ASEAN Cooperation", *ASEAN Economic Bulletin* 9, no. 3 (March 1993): 375–80.

13. *Yomiuri Shimbun*, 25 August 1994. See also Tomiichi Murayama, *Tenmei no 561 nichi* (Tokyo: Besuto serazu, 1996).

14. Shigeyuki Ito, *Ajia to Nihon no miraichitsujo* (Tokyo: Toshindo, 2004), chap. 10.

15. Gaimusho, *Gaiko seisho* (Tokyo: Okurasho insatsukyoku, 1988), p. 325.

16. See Yasuhiro Nakasone's speech at Chulalongkorn University, 16 September 1987; *Bangkok Post*, 17 September 1987.

17. Sosuke Uno, "Engine for Development: Japan-ASEAN Cooperation toward Peace and Stability", *Speaking of Japan*, November 1988, p. 5. Because of these positive attitudes towards ASEAN, the fear of Japan dominating the region came to the fore. See, for instance, Edward Lincoln, "Japan's Role in Asia-Pacific Cooperation: Dimensions, Prospects, and Problems", *East Asia* 8, no. 4 (December 1989), pp. 3–23.

18. ASEAN, "Foreign Minister Kono's Statement at the ASEAN Post-Ministerial Conference, Bandar Seri Begawan, August 2, 1995" (Jakarta: ASEAN Secretariat, 1995).

19. ASEAN, "Tenth ASEAN-Japan Forum, Tokyo, Japan, 21–22 September 1988" (Jakarta: ASEAN Secretariat, 1988).

20. ASEAN, "Eleventh ASEAN-Japan Forum, Manila, Philippines, 3–4 October 1989" (Jakarta: ASEAN Secretariat, 1989).

21. ASEAN, "Twelfth Meeting of the ASEAN-Japan Forum, Tokyo, September 19–20, 1990" (Jakarta: ASEAN Secretariat, 1990).

22. ASEAN, "Joint Press Statement of the 14th Meeting of the ASEAN-Japan Forum, Bangkok, Thailand, 18–19 January 1995" (Jakarta: ASEAN Secretariat, 1995).

23. *Asahi Shimbun*, 17 January 1995; *Bangkok Post*, 20 January 1995.

24. *The Nation*, 5 May 1990.

25. *Straits Times*, 11 May 1990.

26. *The Nation*, 15 May 1990. For a Southeast Asian view, see Chaiwat Khamchoo, "Japan's Role in Southeast Asian Security", *Pacific Affairs* 64, no. 1 (Spring 1991), pp. 7–22.

27. Quoted from *Asian Defence Journal*, July 1990, p. 3.

28. Paulin Kerr, Andrew Mack and Paul Evans, "The Evolving Security Discourse in the Asia Pacific", in *Pacific Cooperation: Builidng Economic and Security Regimes in the Asia Pacific Region*, edited by Andrew Mack and John Ravenhill (St. Leonards: Allen & Unwin, 1994), p. 252.

29. ASEAN "Statement by Taro Nakayama", Twenty-Fourth ASEAN Ministerial Meeting and Post-Ministerial Conference with the Dialogue Partners (Jakarta: ASEAN Secretariat, 1991), pp. 71–72. For Nakayama's attempt, see Taro Nakayama, *Ajia wa 21seiki ni dougokuka* (Tokyo: TBS Buritanika, 1997), pp. 264–66; Paul Midford, "Japan's Leadership Role in East Asian Security Multilateralism", *Pacific Review* 13, no. 3 (2001): 367–97; and Takeshi Yuzawa, *Japan's Security Policy and the ASEAN Regional Forum* (London:

Routledge, 2007), pp. 23–25. ASEAN's evaluation of the proposal can be found in Gaimusho, "PMC niokeru wagakuniteian nitaisuru sankakoku no hanno, 18 September 1993", copies of documents obtained through Freedom of Information Act, Diplomatic Record Office (Tokyo: Ministry of Foreign Affairs, 1993).

30. Yukio Sato, "Emerging Trends in Asia-Pacific Security: The Role of Japan", *Pacific Review* 8, no. 2 (1995): 267–82. In fact, the Foreign Ministry officials, including Yukio Sato, persuaded reluctant American counterparts to endorse the Nakayama proposal.

31. Gaimusho, *Gaiko seisho*, 1995, p. 35.

32. *Far Eastern Economic Review*, 3 August 1995, p. 22.

33. *Asahi Shimbun*, 14 July 1995.

34. *Far Eastern Economic Review*, 27 April 1995, p. 28; *Asahi Shimbun*, 23 April 1995.

35. *Far Eastern Economic Review*, 5 September 1996, p. 28.

36. Christopher Hughes, "Japan's Subregional Security and Defence Linkages with ASEANs, South Korea and China in the 1990s", *Pacific Review* 9, no. 2 (1996): 232. See also Michael Leifer, *The ASEAN Regional Forum*, Adelphi Paper 302 (London: Oxford University Press, 1996), pp. 23–24 for Japan's role.

37. *Far Eastern Economic Review*, 5 September 1996, p. 28.

38. *Asahi Shimbun*, 24 July 1996.

39. Hajime Tamura, "ASEAN and Japan on the Eve of the 21st Century", *ASEAN Economic Bulletin* 4, no. 1 (July 1987): 114–18.

40. *Thailand Foreign Affairs Newsletter*, May 1987, p. 16. For pros and cons of Japan's recycling policy, see *Japan Economic Journal*, 24 October 1987, pp. 1–2.

41. JETRO, "Current Trend of Japanese Investment in Thailand and Its Prospect" (Bangkok: JETRO, 1988), pp. 1–2.

42. *The Economist*, 15 July 1989, pp. 15–20. See also Hiroshi Karu, "Kanminkyoryoku niyoru kokusaikyoryoku suishin no ichihosaku", *Shakaikagaku Tokyu*, no. 117 (December 1994): 253–75 for a precise analysis on the development of AJDF.

43. ASEAN, "Meeting of the ASEAN Economic Ministers with the Minister for International Trade and Industry of Japan, Manila, 24 October 1992" (Jakarta: ASEAN Secretariat, 1992). See also MITI, *ASEAN sangyo kodoka bijon* (Tokyo: MITI, 1993).

44. ASEAN, "Meeting of the ASEAN Economic Ministers with the Minister for International Trade and Industry of Japan, Singapore, 9 October 1993" (Jakarta: ASEAN Secretariat, 1993).

45. ASEAN, "Meeting of the ASEAN Economic Ministers with the Minister for International Trade and Industry of Japan, September 1996" (Jakarta: ASEAN Secretariat, 1996).

46. *ASEAN Update*, July/October 1996, p. 5.

47. Shintaro Hamanaka, *Asian Regionalism and Japan: The Politics of Membership in Regional Diplomatic, Financial and Trade Groups* (London: Routledge, 2009), p. 109.
48. Yoichi Funabashi, *Asia Pacific Fusion: Japan's Role in APEC* (Washington, DC: Institute for International Economics, 1995), p. 214.
49. Chalmers Johnson, *Japan: Who Governs?* (New York: Norton, 1995), p. 56.
50. On Japan's trade, investment and aid, see especially Kazuo Ishii, *Nihon no Boeki 55nen* (Tokyo: JETRO, 2000); Dipak Basu and Victoria Miroshnic, *Japanese Foreign Investment 1970–1998* (New York: Sharpe, 2000); and Hirohisa Kohama, *ODA no Keizaigaku* (Tokyo: Nihon hyoronsha, 1998). For Japan's contribution to ASEAN economic development, see especially Yasutami Shimomura, "Nihon noenjo ga ASEAN no keizaihatten ni oyoboshita eikyo" in *ASEAN no Keizai hatten to Nihon*, edited by Takatoshi Ito (Tokyo: Nihon hyoron sha, 2004), pp. 54–72.
51. Walter Hatch and Kozo Yamamura, *Asia in Japan's Embrace: Building a Regional Production Alliance* (New York: Cambridge University Press, 1996).
52. Basu and Miroshnic, *Japanese Foreign Investment*, chap. 4.
53. *Japan Times*, 24 October 1992. See also Tomomitsu Oba, "Japan's Role in East Asian Investment and Finance", *Japan Review of International Affairs* 9, no. 3 (Summer 1995), pp. 246–51.
54. *ASEAN Update*, March/April 1996, p. 1.
55. Gaimusho, *Gaiko seisho*, 1993, pp. 96–97. Regarding Japan's ODA policy towards ASEAN, see especially Alan Rix, "Managing Japan's Aid: ASEAN", in *Japan's Foreign Aid: Power and Policy in a New Era*, edited by Bruce Keppel and Robert Orr (Boulder, CO: Westview Press, 1993), pp. 19–40.
56. For reliable evaluations of Japan-ASEAN cultural exchange, see especially Tadashi Yamamoto and Carolina Hernandez, "Social and Cultural Dimensions in East Asian Community Building", in *ASEAN-Japan Cooperation: A Foundation for East Asian Community* (Tokyo: Japan Center for International Exchange, 2003), pp. 171–88 and Maki Aoki, "Chiikibunkakyoryoku womeguru bunka sesshoku", in Sengo Nihon kokusaibunkakoryu kenkyukai, *Sengo Nihon no kokuksai bunka koryu* (Tokyo: Keiso shobo, 2005), pp. 179–306.
57. Sengo Nihon kokusaibunkakoryu kenkyukai, *Sengo Nihon no kokuksai bunka koryu* (Tokyo: Keiso shobo, 2005), pp. 64–66.
58. Gaimusho, *Gaiko seisho*, 1989, pp. 115–18.
59. Yamamoto and Hernandez, "Social and Cultural Dimensions", pp. 175–76.
60. Regarding problems of foreign students in Japan, see Masashi Kaneko, "Nihon no paburikku dipuromashi", in *Paburikku dipuramashi*, edited by Masashi Kaneko and Mitsuru Kitano (Tokyo: PHP kenkyusho, 2007), pp. 183–230.
61. Aoki, "Chiikibunkakyoryoku womeguru", pp. 298–300.

62. *Straits Times*, 25 May 1991.

63. *Yomiuri Shimbun*, 26 August 1993.

64. *Mainichi Shimbun*, 5 May 1994. This also explains the lack of ASEAN's support for Japan's bid to become a permanent member of the UN Security Council. *Straits Times*, 26 October 1994.

65. *Asahi Shimbun*, 10 June 1995. For a further explanation, see Yoshibumi Wakamiya, *The Postwar Conservative View of Asia* (Tokyo: LTCB International Library Foundation, 1998), chap. 1.

66. For participants' views, see Tadashi Ikeda, *Cambodia wahei enomichi* (Tokyo: Toshi shuppan, 1996); Masaharu Kohno, *Wahei kosaku* (Tokyo: Iwanami shoten, 1999); Yukio Imagawa, *Cambodia to Nihon* (Tokyo: Rengo shuppan, 2000).

67. Concerning Japan's role in resolving the Cambodian conflict and the Tokyo meeting in June 1990, see Seki Tomoda, "Japan's Search for a Political Role in Asia", *Japan Review of International Affairs* 6, no. 1 (Spring 1992): 43–60; Ronald St John, "Japan's Moment in Indochina", *Asian Survey* 35, no. 7 (July 1995): 668–81 and Kazuhide Kato, "Kambojia funso to Nihon gaiko", *Kokusaishogaku Ronshu* 13, no. 3 (2002): 35–69.

68. Hisashi Owada, *Gaiko towananika* (Tokyo: NHK Shuppan, 1996) and Kyoko Hatakeyama and Craig Freedman, *Snow on the Pine: Japan's Quest for a Leadership Role in Asia* (Singapore: World Scientific, 2010), chap. 5.

69. *Asahi Shimbun*, 6 June 1990; *The Nation*, 11 June 1990.

70. Gaimusho, "Japanese Participation in UN Peacekeeping: Cambodia" (Tokyo: Ministry of Foreign Affairs) <http://www.mofa.go.jp/policy/un/pko/pamph96/02-2.html>. For Japan's PKO to Cambodia, see especially Hugo Dobson, *Japan and United Nations Peacekeeping* (London: Routledge Curzon, 2003), chap. 5.

71. For an official view, see Masahiko Horie, "Peace Process and Japanese ODA for Cambodia", *Dokkyo International Review*, no. 10 (1977): 95–107.

72. Regarding the role of UNTAC, see especially Yasushi Akashi, *Nintai to kibo: Kambojia no 560nichi* (Tokyo: Asahi Shimbunsha, 1995).

73. Takaki Shimabayashi, "Indoshina sogokaihatsu foramu nitaisuru aratana igizuke", *Tonanajia*, no. 41 (May 2012): 70–72. See also Risako Ishii, "Posuto reisenki Indoshina niokeru Nihon no enjogaiko", *Kokusaikankeiron Kenkyu*, no. 20 (2004): 83–113 for a superb analysis on the role of MOFA and METI over the issue.

74. Gaimusho, "Indoshina sogokaihatsu foramu no mokuteki torisusume nitsuite, October 27, 1993", and "Indoshina sogokaihatsu foramu kakuryokaigi: gaiyo to seika, February 27, 1995", copies of documents obtained through Freedom of Information Act, Diplomatic Record Office (Tokyo, Ministry of Foreign Affairs, 1993 and 1995).

75. Toshihiro Kudo and Fumiharu Mieno, "Trade, Foreign Investment and

Myanmar's Economic Development during the Transition to an Open Economy", IDE Discussion Paper Series no.116, Institute of Developing Economies, August 2007, p. 15.

76. Donald Seekins, *Burma and Japan since 1940: From 'Co-Prosperity' to 'Quiet Dialogue'* (Copenhagen: NIAS Press, 2007).

77. Hadi Soesastro, "The Institutional Framework for APEC: An ASEAN Perspective", in *APEC: Challenges and Opportunities*, edited by Chia Siow Yue (Singapore: Institute of Southeast Asian Studies, 1994), p. 47.

78. Regarding the Sakamoto report, see Akiko Fukushima, "Japan's Perspective on Asian Regionalism", in *Asia's New Multilateralism*, edited by Michael Green and Bates Gill (New York: Columbia University Press, 2009), pp. 106–7.

79. Mahathir Mohamad, *A Doctor in the House* (Kuala Lumpur: MPH Group Printing, 2011), pp. 612–14.

80. *Asahi Shimbun*, 15 January 1993.

81. See James Baker, *The Politics of Diplomacy: Revolution, War and Peace, 1989–1992* (New York: Putnam's, 1995) and *Mainichi Shimbun*, 19 November 1991.

82. Kazuo Ogura, "A Call for a New Concept of Asia", *Japan Echo* 20, no. 3 (Autumn 1993): 37–44.

83. Mahathir Mohamad, "Coexistence in Asia", speech by the Prime Minister of Malaysia at the Kyushu-Asian Summit for Local Authorities in Kyushu, Japan, 21 October 1994. See also Steven Leong, "The East Asian Economic Caucus (EAEC): 'Formalized' Regionalism Being Denied", in *National Perspectives on the New Regionalism in the South*, edited by Bjorn Hettne et al. (London: Macmillan, 2000), pp. 57–107 for a Malaysian view on Japan's role.

84. *Nihon Keizai Shimbun*, 6 April 1995.

85. *Yomiuri Shimbun*, 9 April 1995.

86. Interview with Thanat Khoman, 18 April 1996.

87. Gaimusho, "Relationship between Japan and ASEAN, December 1998" (Tokyo: Ministry of Foreign Affairs, 1998).

88. Jurgen Haacke, *ASEAN's Diplomatic and Security Culture* (London: Routledge Curzon, 2003), pp. 3–7.

89. ASEAN, "Singapore Declaration of 1992" (Jakarta: ASEAN Secretariat, 1992).

90. Citizens of Southeast Asia, "Towards a Southeast Asian Community, 1996" <http://www.tripod.lycos.com>.

5

FORTIFYING A JAPAN-ASEAN STRATEGIC PARTNERSHIP: The Resurgence of the Mainstream

The end of the Cold War renewed interest in regional approaches to development and security. Apart from the obvious case of Europe with its economically integrated European Union, East Asia appears to be one of the most dynamic regions among developing countries. The Association of Southeast Asian Nations (ASEAN) has played a particular leading role in initiating closer regional interaction, as exemplified by the establishment of the ASEAN Regional Forum (ARF), Asia-Europe Meeting (ASEM) and the ASEAN Plus Three (APT). It is thus quite remarkable that these multilateral efforts are being carried out by ASEAN, whose very survival had initially seemed questionable. Even after the unprecedented financial crisis that occurred in Thailand in July 1997 and soon engulfed Northeast and Southeast Asian countries, ASEAN's regional role has been strengthened by the institutionalization of the EAS in 2005.

Beginning in 1997, Japan has also shown some notable initiatives in its foreign policy. It is notable because for the first time Japan has identified itself as part of East Asia. In particular, it was unprecedented that the Japanese government proposed the formation of an East Asian version of the International Monetary Fund in order to deal with the contagious financial crisis, despite American objections. To follow up, Japan offered the so-called Miyazawa plan and initiated the Japan-ASEAN Summit meeting, which led to the formation of a regularized APT forum.[1] The high point was the adoption of the ASEAN community and the commemorative Tokyo summit in 2003.

When a populist premier instituted his domestic and foreign policy, Japan's East Asian policy was turned around, thus adversely affecting Japan-ASEAN relations. In particular, worsening Japan-China relations caused mainly by Prime Minister Junichiro Koizumi's controversial visit to the Yasukuni Shrine, could serve as a testing ground for closer Japan-ASEAN relations in the twenty-first century. While closely following the footsteps of the Takeshita Doctrine, this chapter focuses on how Japan managed to cope with the transitional period of the late 1990s and early 2000s.

ASEAN AT THIRTY

The year 1997 was critically important for ASEAN as it celebrated its thirtieth anniversary and convened a historical meeting with China, Japan and South Korea, later known as the APT.[2] The Second Informal Summit, held in Kuala Lumpur on 15 December 1997, adopted the ASEAN Vision 2020. The document detailed four major goals: (1) a concert of Southeast Asian nations, (2) a partnership in dynamic development, (3) a community of caring societies, and (4) an outward-looking ASEAN. Moreover, ASEAN agreed to establish an ASEAN Foundation to develop fellowship and exchange programmes in the framework of human resource development, while discussing the progress of the ASEAN Mekong Basin Development Cooperation (AMBDC). It was stressed that the proposed railway link from Singapore to Kunming in China, traversing and connecting the contiguous ASEAN member countries, be implemented on a consortium basis involving all ASEAN member countries and that an early decision be made as to its implementation.[3]

The highlight of the informal summit was to convene a historical summit with three East Asian dialogue partners (Japan, China and South Korea). The first EAS, however, only agreed to regularize the summit, thus carefully issuing three ASEAN-plus-one statements. Since some countries in the region were reluctant to commit themselves to cooperation in East Asia, the APT began in quite a low-key way. No joint statement was launched and the term "ASEAN Plus Three" was rarely used in the first two meetings, much less in the agenda for the meeting.[4]

At the beginning of the fourth decade, therefore, there were still potential problems and challenges for ASEAN: (1) intra-ASEAN economic competition and rivalry, (2) coping with an enlarged and diversified ASEAN, (3) maintaining intra-ASEAN resilience against power rivalry in the region, (4) domestic challenges in individual ASEAN countries, and (5) sustaining an ASEAN identity in an age of globalization.[5]

THE ANNOUNCEMENT OF THE HASHIMOTO DOCTRINE IN 1997

In January 1997, despite the mounting problems of the hostage crisis in Peru, Prime Minister Ryutaro Hashimoto visited the ASEAN countries (Malaysia, Singapore, Vietnam and Brunei) and proposed the formation of a top-level forum between Japan and ASEAN. Furthermore, Hashimoto delivered a policy speech in Singapore entitled "Reforms for the New Era of Japan and ASEAN for a Broader and Deeper Partnership", which underscored Japan's consistent policy towards ASEAN since 1977:

> As you probably remember, in 1977 then Prime Minister Fukuda launched the so-called Fukuda Doctrine, and in 1987 then Prime Minister Takeshita proposed that Japan and ASEAN establish a new partnership. Today, I would like to deliberate with you on how Japan and ASEAN should reform their cooperative relationship in a manner suitable for a new era.[6]

Most importantly, with the Fukuda Doctrine and Takeshita Doctrine as road maps, he proposed the following three policies: to promote broader and deeper exchanges between Japan and ASEAN at all levels, to deepen mutual understanding and expand cultural cooperation so as to consolidate Japan-ASEAN friendship, and to jointly address various problems that the international community faces as a whole. ASEAN in 1997, however, was facing a critical transition. The end of its third decade was a mixed blessing for the member countries, thereby necessitating a greater stimulation for the fourth decade of the organization. In order to consolidate regional policies, ASEAN needed stronger outside assistance at the beginning of the fourth decade.

In response to this need, Hashimoto disclosed Japan's comprehensive policy at the third ASEAN-Japan summit meeting held in December 1997.

At this summit in Kuala Lumpur, Japan and ASEAN resolved to further advance their cooperation towards the twenty-first century, with a view to achieving a more profound and wide-ranging relationship by intensifying dialogues for an enhanced partnership, fostering people-to-people and cultural exchanges, promoting regional peace and stability and enhancing economic cooperation. Of note, Japan announced that in view of the East Asian economic turmoil, Japan would work with ASEAN towards stabilizing Asian currencies and financial markets, and would also assist ASEAN in achieving stable and sustained development through economic structural reform.[7]

While resolving in their Vision 2020 statement to move closer towards regional cohesion and economic integration, the hard-hit ASEAN countries, individually and collectively, turned to Japan for assistance. Thailand, for instance, sent its finance minister to Tokyo before asking for IMF assistance. For its part, Japan agreed to play a facilitating role to cope with the crisis. Collectively, Japan and ASEAN tried to set up an Asian Monetary Fund to deal with the IMF deficiency. As Thai Finance Minister Thanong explained, the scheme envisioned Japan becoming "a pillar of economic stability in the region comparable to the United States and Europe in their own continents"[8]

As such, what the Hashimoto administration attempted in 1997 would suggest a clear departure from traditional bilateralism to the new regionalism. What has drawn attention is that Hashimoto's two visits to the region symbolize Japan's gradual shift towards an independent and active role in Southeast Asia. His second visit to Kuala Lumpur in particular seems to be critical in that Hashimoto attended the first summit meeting among Northeast and Southeast Asian leaders, known as APT. Furthermore, Japan's cultural relations with ASEAN have been stressed far more than they were by Hashimoto's predecessors. For instance, the Japanese government has worked out a special programme, the "multilateral cultural exchange program" to be jointly conducted with Singapore. All in all, these major initiatives in 1997 and early 1998 strengthened Japan's diplomatic leadership, despite Hashimoto's resignation in August 1998 due to domestic problems.[9]

INVIGORATION OF TOP-LEVEL RELATIONS SINCE 1998

Since the announcement of the Hashimoto doctrine, Japan has pursued active diplomacy, consolidating top-level relations with ASEAN, especially

TABLE 5.1
Japan-ASEAN Relations, 1997–2006

	PM visit	Summit	FMM	Forum	EMM	Finance
1997	Hashimoto	3rd *	20th	15th	6th	1st
1998		4th	21st	16th		
1999		5th	22nd			2nd ***
2000	Obuchi	6th	23rd		7th	3rd
2001		7th	24th	17th	8th	4th
2002	Koizumi	8th	25th	18th	9th	5th
2003		9th **	26th	19th	10th	6th
2004		10th	27th	20th	11th	7th
2005		11th	28th	21st	12th	8th
2006			29th	22nd	13th	9th

* ASEAN officially recognizes the 1997 summit as the first summit.
** The first Commemorative Summit in Tokyo.
*** Since 1999 the Japan-ASEAN Finance Ministers' Meeting has been held as part of the APT Finance Ministers' Meeting.

in two aspects: prime ministers' visits to ASEAN and the institutionalization of summit meetings through the APT venues.

Prime Ministers' visits to ASEAN countries

In January 2000 Prime Minister Keizo Obuchi visited Laos, Cambodia and Thailand. These visits aimed to demonstrate that Japan would continue to provide support for the development and prosperity of the expanded ASEAN, to explain Japan's approach to the upcoming Group of Eight (G8) Kyushu-Okinawa Summit meeting, and to listen to the opinions of the ASEAN countries so that their views could be reflected at the summit.[10] At the meetings with national leaders, Prime Minister Obuchi laid out plans for Japan's support of the respective countries following his announcement at the November 1999 APT Summit meeting in Manila. Obuchi also disclosed Japan's intention to take the initiative in developing human resources and correcting economic disparities among ASEAN countries. Towards the Cambodian and Laotian prime ministers in particular — whose countries had just joined ASEAN and were vigorously undertaking domestic reforms — Obuchi expressed Japan's firm support. He also declared that Japan would provide every possible assistance in areas such as policy formulation and human resources development.[11]

Concerning the G8 Kyushu-Okinawa Summit, Obuchi explained to the three countries' leaders that Japan would incorporate ASEAN views and interests into the agenda. In response, Cambodian Prime Minister Hun Sen stressed the issue of economic disparities among countries in Southeast Asia and among those of the Greater Mekong Subregion, while Laotian Prime Minister Sisavath commented on the importance of developing human resources in order to cope with globalization. Prime Minister Chuan of Thailand, the country at the time holding the ASEAN chair, pointed out the importance of harmonizing the policies of such international organizations as the International Monetary Fund and the World Trade Organization, taking into consideration the situations of developing nations.[12]

In January 2002, visiting five of the ASEAN countries (the Philippines, Malaysia, Thailand, Indonesia and Singapore), Prime Minister Junichiro Koizumi explained Japan's strategy of making maximum use of the APT framework and firming up regional cooperation as a means of creating a "community that acts together and advances together", while stressing that promoting open regional cooperation in a form that is transparent to extra-regional countries would contribute to the peace and prosperity of the region.[13] In Singapore Koizumi proposed several new initiatives for cooperation, including the designation of 2003 as the Year of ASEAN-Japan Exchange, reinforced cooperation in education and human resource development, solidifying security relations, the ASEAN-Japan Comprehensive Economic partnership, and the Initiative for Development in East Asia. As he averred, "Our goal should be the creating of a community that acts together and advances together. And we should achieve this through expanding East Asia cooperation founded upon the Japan-ASEAN relationship. While recognizing our historical, cultural, ethnic and traditional diversity, I would like to see countries in the region become a group that works together in harmony."[14]

Table 5.2 summarizes the state of top-level interaction between 1997 and 2006, which indicates frequent official visits by prime ministers and accompanying commitments to ASEAN. Reflecting the close relationship, ASEAN decided to hold a commemorative summit with Japan in December 2003. The Japan-ASEAN Commemorative Summit is of historical significance, as it was the first time all ASEAN leaders met outside the region. The leaders both reflected on the relations of amity and cooperation that Japan and ASEAN had maintained for a period of more than thirty years and reaffirmed their special ties. In particular, the leaders shared

TABLE 5.2
Prime Ministers' Visits to ASEAN, 1997–2006

Premier	Date	Countries visited	Results
Hashimoto	January 1997	Thailand, Malaysia, Indonesia, Myanmar, Singapore	(1) Broader and deeper exchanges (2) Multilateral cultural cooperation (3) Promotion of joint endeavours to address global challenges
Obuchi	January 2000	Cambodia, Laos, Thailand	(1) Special assistance for individual country (2) Stress on the Obuchi plan
Koizumi	January 2002	Philippines, Malaysia, Thailand, Indonesia, Singapore	(1) Cooperation for prosperity through reforms (2) Cooperation for stability through integrated efforts (3) Cooperation for the future

the view that cooperation and partnership should be enhanced not only in the areas of the economy and security, but also in sociocultural fields. Japan reaffirmed its intention to continue to prioritize ASEAN in its various policies, and was welcomed and applauded by all ASEAN leaders. In turn, the ASEAN leaders reiterated their perception of Japan as an important partner. Most importantly, Japan and ASEAN set out the direction of their relations in the new era by issuing the "Tokyo Declaration" and "The Japan-ASEAN Plan of Action" annexed to it that synchronizes with ASEAN's three pillars of community building. Thus the leaders demonstrated their determination to go beyond fundamental principles and implement concrete measures to enhance and deepen ASEAN-Japan cooperation. Finally, Japan signed the Declaration on Accession to the Treaty of Amity and Cooperation (TAC) in Southeast Asia, demonstrating its commitment to the principle of "acting together, advancing together."[15]

Institutionalization of Summit Meetings through the APT

In addition to almost de facto top-level visits to the region, it is remarkable that a Japan-ASEAN summit meeting has become institutionalized as a result of Hashimoto's endeavour, reminding us of the fact that the Japan-ASEAN Foreign Ministers' Meeting became the Post-Ministerial Meeting in 1979. As such, Japan and ASEAN leaders have met every year since 1998 as part of the APT gatherings. In 1998, furthermore, the second ASEM and the ASEAN Summit at the end of that year moved Japan and ASEAN closer towards consolidation of regional policies.[16] The 1998 ASEM, like the previous one in 1996, was quite successful from the standpoint of policy coordination between the countries of East Asia. Likewise, the ASEAN Summit sought agreement among East Asian leaders to strengthen their unity after Prime Minister Keizo Obuchi urged more dialogues to establish a solid basis for peace and stability in the region. Specifically, Obuchi proposed the following policies: Japan would implement the $30 billion Miyazawa plan and special yen loans totaling 600 billion yen and would start local training of 10,000 people; Japan would contribute 500 billion yen to establish a "human security fund" under the United Nations to fight such threats as environmental hazards, drugs and terrorism; Japan would build a centre in Tokyo to promote intellectual dialogue between graduate students and researchers from around the world; and Japan would establish a consultative conference to discuss and make recommendations for Japan-ASEAN cooperation in the twenty-first century.[17]

The joint statement to come out of the third summit, held in Manila in November 1999, stressed the following: ASEAN noted Japan's presentation of the report of the Okuda Mission and follow-up mission that would implement the Obuchi Plan to enhance the development of human resources and human resources exchanges; ASEAN and Japan welcomed the adoption of the ASEAN-Japan Joint Action Plan of the ASEAN Economic Ministers–MITI Economic and Industrial Cooperation Committee (AMEICC) as a means to further broaden economic cooperation, particularly the development of small and medium enterprises and supporting industries, and the promotion of trade and investment; ASEAN expressed appreciation for Japan's support for the implementation of the Hanoi Plan of Action. Stressing the urgency of addressing the social impact of the economic crisis as well as the continuing need for international assistance, ASEAN expressed the hope that Japan could support ASEAN projects in the areas of social safety nets, human resource development, poverty eradication and information technology, among others. And ASEAN and Japan agreed on the need to deepen cooperation to combat transnational crime, particularly piracy. ASEAN welcomed Japan's offer to host an international conference of coastguard authorities to explore possible cooperative approaches in this area. All in all, ASEAN and Japan noted with satisfaction the fast-paced progress and dynamism that characterized the ASEAN-Japan dialogue relations, especially in the wake of the East Asian economic crisis.[18]

Strengthening regional cooperation in East Asia was the central agenda at the November 2000 APT summit in Singapore, where Prime Minister Yoshiro Mori proposed three principles to guide the promotion of East Asian cooperation towards the twenty-first century: building partnerships, open regional cooperation, and comprehensive dialogue and cooperation, including the field of political security. More specifically, Mori proposed the following cooperative policies: cooperation of Japan, China, and the Republic of Korea in the e-ASEAN Initiative, and holding of the "Joint Conference of Government Officials, Prominent Academics and Business Leaders for Information Technology (IT) Cooperation in East Asia"; a comprehensive approach towards piracy and holding of the "Asian Cooperation Conference on Combating Piracy and Armed Robbery against Ships". Prime Minister Mori welcomed the Chiang Mai Initiative on the basic principles of the swap agreement and he announced Japan's support for the ASEAN Secretariat and for cooperation in political security, especially regarding the Korean Peninsula and Indonesia.[19]

Through the fifth to ninth meetings, Prime Minister Koizumi represented Japan and actively pursued his proactive ASEAN policy with special concern for the rise of China. For instance, at the fifth summit in November 2001, Koizumi referred to Japan's efforts to strengthen economic partnerships, including the Initiatives for Japan-ASEAN Comprehensive Economic Partnership (JACEP), and stated that these efforts would lead to the energizing of economic activity and the strengthening of competitiveness in East Asia as a whole. Concerning efforts to strengthen ASEAN integration, Koizumi announced that Japan would contribute positively to the Initiative for ASEAN Integration (IAI).[20] In a similar vein, at the sixth summit in November 2002 in Phnom Penh, Koizumi proposed another initiative for development in East Asia.

Furthermore, at the 2002 ASEAN-Japan Summit, the Joint Declaration on the JACEP was finally signed. Its objectives are fivefold: to strengthen economic integration between Japan and ASEAN through the creation of a comprehensive economic partnership; to enhance the competitiveness of Japan and ASEAN in the world market through strengthened partnership and linkages; to progressively liberalize and facilitate trade in goods and services as well as create a transparent and liberal investment regime; to explore new areas and develop appropriate measures for further cooperation and economic integration; and to facilitate the more effective economic integration of the newer ASEAN members and bridge the development gap among the ASEAN members.[21] At the same time, Japan and Singapore signed an agreement for a New Age Economic Partnership (JSEPA) on 13 January 2002. This aimed to promote freer transborder flows of goods, people, services, capital and information, to reduce economic borders and to contribute to the promotion of an economic partnership in a range of areas.

When the JSEPA was signed, it was hailed as being of great strategic significance for East Asia and of offering Japan a model for future regional relationships. In terms of a regional economic agenda, Japan was quick to respond to China's 2001 overtures to ASEAN for a China-ASEAN FTA to be established by 2010. Obviously China's actions precipitated Japan's own responses and Japan-China competition has become one important driving force for greater Japanese participation in regional affairs.[22]

Similarly, at the seventh summit in October 2003 in Bali, Indonesia, the joint statement stressed that partnership between ASEAN and Japan had contributed to peace, stability and prosperity in East Asia by signing the Framework for Comprehensive Economic Partnership between ASEAN and Japan. Both Japan and ASEAN called for further development of their relations in order to enhance their cooperation at the bilateral, sub-regional and regional levels, underlining the need to ensure that the development of relations at the sub-regional level would have a positive impact on ASEAN as a whole while at the same time contribute to the efforts at narrowing the development gaps. Furthermore, they agreed to strengthen cooperation by adopting the following policies: promoting a comprehensive economic partnership through capacity-building, narrowing development gaps, engaging in sustainable development and establishing a free trade area in the future; celebrating the three decades of friendship and cooperation by observing the ASEAN-Japan Exchange Year; and engaging in security cooperation in such areas as counterterrorism, the fight against piracy and cross-border issues.[23]

The Eighth ASEAN-Japan Summit was held in Vientiane in November 2004 under the theme of "Strengthening the Dynamic and Enduring ASEAN-Japan Relations". The ASEAN leaders reiterated that Japan is one of ASEAN's oldest dialogue partners and that they highly valued the support and assistance they had received from the country over the last three decades. They called on Japan to continue its strong support for ASEAN's integration and development. ASEAN also welcomed Japan's accession to the Treaty of Amity and Cooperation in Jakarta in July 2004, which would contribute to the maintenance of peace and stability in the region. Of particular significance was the adoption of the ASEAN-Japan Joint Declaration for Cooperation on the Fight against International Terrorism. Japan welcomed the decision reached by the ASEAN leaders to convene the first East Asia Summit (EAS) in Malaysia in 2005.[24]

As a last act of his tenure, Prime Minister Koizumi stressed that Japan and ASEAN should form a strategic partnership at the ninth summit meeting in December 2005. Reflecting on Koizumi's proposal, the joint statement of the ASEAN-Japan summit — "Deepening and Broadening of ASEAN-Japan Strategic Partnership" — underscored the following: (1) supporting ASEAN community building efforts, (2) strengthening economic partnership, (3) reforming the ASEAN-Japan Center, (4) combating transnational crime and terrorism, (5) enhancing disaster management, (6) addressing infectious diseases, (7) enhancing energy cooperation, (8) promoting exchanges and people-to-people contact, (9) deepening East Asia cooperation, (10) and responding to international issues.[25] It was apparent that because of worsening Japan-China relations, Japan's ASEAN policy began to seek "strategic" dimensions in foreign policy.

MAJOR AREAS OF ENHANCED COOPERATION

Over the years ASEAN and Japan have deepened and broadened their cooperation to ensure peace, stability and prosperity in the region through various established mechanisms under the ASEAN-Japan dialogue, namely summits, ministerial meetings, senior officials meetings and expert meetings, as well as through multilateral frameworks initiated by ASEAN such as the ARF, PMC and APT processes. Focusing on ministerial meetings, we shall look at three major areas of cooperation in more detail.

Political and Security Cooperation

The first major area is political and security cooperation. Ever since the first peacekeeping operation (PKO) sent to Cambodia in 1993, Japan's political and security role has been steadily growing in Southeast Asia. Giving tacit countenance to the concept of human security, the Japanese government has come up with positive political and security policies, to wit, Japan's peace consolidation diplomacy ever since Prime Minister Obuchi's announcement in 1998 and its stipulation in the ODA Charter in 2003.[26] In this respect, Japan's accession to the TAC on 2 July 2004 increased the significance of the TAC as a code of conduct governing relations among countries and a diplomatic instrument for the promotion of peace and stability in the region. We will see first how Japan's political engagement policies towards ASEAN have worked and then look at Japan's growing role in the non-traditional security aspects of terrorism and piracy.

Initiating Japan's Peace Consolidation Diplomacy

Cambodia

In the midst of Cambodia's entry into ASEAN, Second Prime Minister Hun Sen staged a coup in July 1997. Responding to the unfortunate circumstances that saw the use of force, the members of ASEAN unanimously decided to postpone the planned invitation for Cambodia to join. Although ASEAN could not complete its long-cherished ASEAN Ten scheme at the twenty-ninth Meeting of Foreign Ministers, ASEAN immediately formed an ad hoc "troika" diplomatic team composed of the foreign ministers of Thailand, the Philippines and Indonesia, to launch an initiative to bring Cambodia back to power-sharing arrangements. The team stipulated four conditions: (1) maintain the coalition government, (2) safeguard the Constitution, (3) maintain Parliament, and (4) respect the provisions of the 1991 Paris Peace Accords. However, the initiative was immediately rejected by Hun Sen who said, "ASEAN's mediation is nothing but an interference into our domestic affairs."[27]

Responding swiftly, the Japanese government invited Hun Sen to Tokyo in November 1997 to try to reach an early settlement, resulting in a four-point proposal by the Japanese Foreign Ministry in January 1998. These points were: (1) the termination of relations between the factions of First Prime Minister Ranariddh (King Norodom Sihanouk's son) and Pol Pot, (2) an immediate truce between the forces of the government and Ranariddh, (3) early settlement of the Ranariddh trial and the provision of a royal pardon, and (4) the safe return of Ranariddh and his guaranteed participation in the coming election.[28] Following Hun Sen's endorsement of Japan's proposals in February, all four conditions were met by the end of March, thereby paving the way for the elections scheduled in July. A major obstacle to Cambodia's future was settled on 21 March when Cambodian King Norodom Sihanouk pardoned his son, which cleared the way for the prince to run in elections. Thus, Ranariddh's four-day return in March was a key step in the peace process under the terms of the Japanese peace plan.[29]

Japan's mediation continued after the election in July 1998, which resulted in Hun Sen's victory over the party of Ranariddh's FUNCINPEC. Japan's mediation with the support of ASEAN led to the establishment of a coalition government under Hun Sen's premiership. Without a doubt, what happened to Cambodia underscored the critical role played by the Japanese government. Foreign Minister Masahiko Komura described it as "scoring a victory in Japanese foreign policy that has created a foundation for the self-help mechanism in Cambodia."[30] To consolidate the Hun Sen regime, Japan convened the third Cambodian Conference in Tokyo in February 1999.[31] This provides a good example of Japan's fine-tuning of economic, political and security networking, to wit, peace consolidation diplomacy.

Myanmar

The situation in Myanmar became increasingly uncertain in the late 1990s. Japan had traditional ties with Myanmar and was engaged in various forms of dialogue with both the State Peace and Development Council and the pro-democracy forces led by Aung San Suu Kyi's National League for Democracy. Japan's policy was to promote democratization and human rights, not by isolating Myanmar, but by working patiently and persistently for improvements through ongoing dialogues with the military regime. Through various channels, including ASEAN-related forums, Japan urged the Myanmar authorities to strive for an early transition to civilian government and to improve the human rights situation in the country.[32]

Specifically, when Myanmar was admitted to ASEAN in 1997, Prime Minister Hashimoto conveyed Japan's position to the leaders of ASEAN members: "Japan does not feel international isolation is the optimal way for the improvent of [the] domestic situation in Myanmar. Rather, Japan thinks it important to give Myanmar incentives to behave in line with international norms by drawing it out as a member of the international community. From that point of view, Japan appreciates ASEAN's recent agreement to grant official membership to Myanmar. On the other hand, Japan also thinks that ASEAN membership should not provide a smokescreen for oppression in Myanmar. Accordingly, Japan hopes that ASEAN will handle the membership issue in such a manner as to contribute to the improvement of the domestic situation in Myanmar."[33]

In concrete terms, Japan's Myanmar policy has had five broad interlocking strands: first, Japan has sought to acknowledge and reward any progress made by the regime in opening up political development in the country; second, Japan has always tried to maintain pressure on the regime and to remind it of the need to show due respect for human rights and undertake meaningful political reform; third, Japan has been a vocal suporter of UN envoys seeking to promote dialogue in Myanmar and to point the way to national reconciliation and eventually democracy; fourth, Japan places no constraints on corporate investment in or trade with Myanmar; fifth, Tokyo has attempted to keep open as many channels of contact as possible into Myanmar.[34]

It is true that Japan's engagement policy with its strategic use of official development assistance (ODA) has worked to a certain extent, in that it helped improve the political situation in Myanmar while at the same time balancing Yangon's strengthening ties with China.[35] However, the recent deterioration of the situation in Myanmar suggests that Japan's role is limited due to the changes in Japan's ODA policy, Myanmar's open-door policy, strengthened economic ties with its neighbours, and China's emergence as an economic partner. This does not mean that Japan's role has totally diminished, as Akira Kudo explains: "Two extremes, that is, economic sanctions and economic cooperation without considering the governance of the recipient, promoted neither economic development nor national reconciliation. Japan can provide rich and objective knowledge to both extremes, and possibly moderate them. The role of Japan is therefore to function as an information source and to contribute to producing a moderate, constructive and consistent policy consensus on Myanmar issues in international society."[36]

Timor-Leste

Timor-Leste sits in the geopolitically important area that divides Asia and the Pacific. Recognizing a stable Timor-Leste should contribute to the peace and stability of the Asia-Pacific region. Japan has placed an emphasis on assisting Timor-Leste. From this viewpoint, Japan has been actively involved in the area of peace cooperation, based on the International Peace Cooperation Law. Japan dispatched three civilian police officers to the United Nations Mission in East Timor (UNAMET), which conducted the direct balloting in 1999 on whether the then East Timor would remain part of Indonesia. In addition, upon the request of the United Nations High Commissioner for Refugees, air transport units of the Self-Defense Forces (SDF) were dispatched and transported humanitarian relief goods to East Timor for the refugees resulting from the violence and confusion in the wake of direct balloting.[37]

The most telling story behind this is the fact that the Japanese government provided needed financial support upon request from ASEAN leaders to undertake their PKO missions in East Timor. Since then, Japan has been actively providing assistance to Timor-Leste for reconstruction and development and in humanitarian areas. In 1999 Japan hosted the First Donor's Meeting for East Timor in Tokyo. At the meeting Japan pledged assistance that totaled $130 million for three years, with particular emphasis on infrastructure, agriculture and human resources development. Japan has been supporting Japanese non-governmental organizations that are active in Timor-Leste, with financial assistance totaling $1.46 million under the grass-roots grant aid scheme.[38]

Under an operation based on the International Peace Cooperation Law, Japan dispatched 680 Ground SDF personnel in Engineer Units and ten PKF headquarters personnel to the United Nations Transitional Administration in East Timor (UNTAET). Those dispatched carried out such logistic-support operations for the UNTAET as the maintenance and repair of roads and bridges. Such operations were implemented to provide assistance for the economic activities and daily lives of the people of Timor-Leste. This deployment of SDF personnel, the largest ever to a UN peacekeeping operation, was an epoch-making initiative.

Under the transitional rule of the UNTAET, the representatives of a Constituent Assembly were elected in August 2001. Timor-Leste's administrative structure began to materialize, including the establishment of the first administration under the management of the people of Timor-Leste. The Constitution of Timor-Leste was finalized in March 2002 and the presidential election was conducted on 14 April. Eventually, Timor-Leste became formally independent on 20 May. Having gone through various conflicts and confrontations, Timor-Leste is now focusing on reconciliation among its citizens, and reconstruction and development of the country. Japan sees such efforts as an important initiative for conflict resolution and nation building in the international community. As Timor-Leste faces many challenges, Japan as an Asian nation will continue to actively support Timor-Leste.[39]

Aceh

Given the prolonged armed conflicts that had been a source of instability in Indonesia, Japan began using its ODA for peace-consolidation efforts in Aceh in December 2002. On 9 December 2002 the Indonesian government and the Free Aceh Movement (GAM) reached an agreement for the cessation of hostilities. This was preceded by the preparatory conference on peace and reconstruction in Aceh, held in Tokyo on 3 December 2002, to indicate the international community's encouragement for the signing of a peace agreement, and to clarify Japan's stance regarding reconstruction and development assistance. Japan expressed its strong hope for a peaceful resolution in Aceh and its willingness to actively support reconstruction and development in the region once peace was achieved. Furthermore, at the Twelfth Consultative Group Meeting on Indonesia in January 2003, Japan announced that it would provide over $6.2 million to facilitate and support the peace process in Aceh. Despite challenging problems, the Aceh peace process began in earnest and Japan sought to consolidate peace in the region in collaboration with the Indonesian government, other donor countries, and multilateral organizations.[40]

Whilst the negotiations did not proceed easily, the next two years saw important changes on both sides that paved the way for the ceasefire agreement. The government's military offensive took a major toll on GAM and gave rise to battle fatigue. Similarly, many GAM leaders began to feel their existing strategy of armed struggle for independence had reached an impasse. Most importantly, in late 2004, significant political change brought new elements to Indonesian politics, exemplified by the advent of President Susilo Yudhoyono, who was personally committed to negotiations as a means of ending conflict. Early steps towards the ceasefire agreement came in late 2004, and were accelerated by the impact of the devastating Indian Ocean tsunami of 26 December which caused great loss of life in Aceh and opened the province to a substantial international humanitarian presence. An agreement became possible after GAM announced in February 2005 that it was willing to set aside its goal of independence and accept a solution based on "self-government" for Aceh within the Indonesian state.

Although the government of Finland finalized the Helsinki agreement, Japan made three significant contributions to this process. First, given the lack of funds and manpower, Japan was willing to provide substantial ODA to support peace initiatives in Aceh. Second, Japan compensated for the negotiating parties' lack of diplomatic clout by bringing together twenty countries and international organizations to discuss substantial foreign aid for peace building at a Tokyo Conference, just six days before the Cessation of the Hostility Agreement was signed. Third, Japan subsequently dispatched 1,000 Self-Defense officials to take part in relief efforts in the aftermath of the tsunami.[41]

Mindanao

Japan also began using ODA to support the consolidation of peace in Mindanao, the Philippines in 2002. Mindanao had been affected for many years by conflicts involving various anti-government groups. This has exacerbated poverty in the region, turning it into a hotbed of terrorism. The situation has become a barrier to the overall economic development of the Philippines, in part causing the deterioration of the country's image as a target for investment. It has also become a serious issue affecting stability and development in the ASEAN region. Under this precarious situation, the Philippine government began to negotiate a final peace settlement with the Moro Islamic Liberation Front (MILF). Terrorist acts, localized conflicts and kidnappings have continued during this process. Seizing the opportunity, Japan decided to provide ongoing support based on medium- and long-term perspectives under the Support Package for Peace and Stability in Mindanao, designed to contribute to poverty eradication, peace negotiations, and peace consolidation. It was announced by Prime Minister Koizumi during a visit to Japan by Philippine President Gloria Macapagal-Arroyo in December 2002.[42]

Following the ceasefire in July 2003, the International Monitoring Team (IMT) — established in October 2004 and consisting of Malaysia, Brunei, and Libya — asked Japan to dispatch an expert who could play a leading role in "socio-economic monitoring", which is one of the IMT's two important pillars, the other being "ceasefire monitoring". Owing to the IMT's presence, the peace and order situation in the conflict-affected areas has dramatically improved. Under these circumstances, the GRP and the MILF formally invited Japan to dispatch its PKO to the Autonomous Region in Muslim Mindanao (ARMM).

Japan followed up with policies to support the resolution of the conflict. First, Japan developed its "Support Package for Peace and Stability in Mindanao" in 2002, which specified three core areas: (1) support for policy formulation and implementation (targeted at the ARMM government), (2) support for improvement of basic human needs, (3) support which contributes directly towards peace-building and the fight against terrorism. Second, the Japanese government pledged to support the peace process in 2006 through a socio-economic development plan for the Bangsamoro people. Specifically, it launched the project called the Japan-Bangsamoro Initiatives for Reconstruction and Development on 7 December of the same year. This umbrella of initiatives includes the Grant Assistance for Grassroots and Human Security Projects, Japanese ODA loan projects, technical cooperation projects, a development study, and grant aid projects. Third, the Mindanao Taskforce, which is spearheaded by the Embassy of Japan, Japan International Cooperation Agency (JICA), and Japan Bank for International Cooperation (JBIC), is currently developing the policy paper for Mindanao's reconstruction.

Japan's contributions were significant in three ways. First, although the ARMM was formerly the main focus, the later scope of support was broader and aimed at other regions. Second, the primary approach of the Japanese support programme to the peace process between the Philippines government and the MILF was through socio-economic development. As such, Japan adopted a different approach from other donors who used development assistance itself as a tool for leverage, mainly through the MTF. Third, although Japan usually provided development assistance after a peace agreement had been signed by parties to the conflict, in the case of Mindanao, it provided the assistance before the peace agreement. This is based on the recognition that socio-economic projects may provide an incentive for the involved parties to conclude the peace agreement.[43]

Japan's Support for ASEAN Security Issues: Terrorism and Piracy

In view of the fast-changing regional and international security environment, particularly exemplified by the emerging "Second Front" of transnational terrorism, ASEAN and Japan have enhanced closer cooperation in maintaining peace and stability in the region and in addressing issues on counterterrorism, anti-piracy and combating other transnational crimes. For instance, Japan attended the First APT Ministerial Meeting on Transnational Crime held on 10 January 2004 in Bangkok, which endorsed in principle the concept plan to implement cooperation in eight areas, namely terrorism, drug trafficking, trafficking in persons, sea piracy, arms smuggling, money laundering, international economic crime and cybercrime. The first annual ASEAN-Japan Consultation on 29 September 2004 in Bandar Seri Begawan exchanged views on ways and means for future ASEAN-Japan cooperation.

Terrorism

Following the Tokyo Declaration for the Dynamic and Enduring ASEAN-Japan Partnership, Japan and ASEAN jointly worked on the draft "Joint Declaration for Cooperation on the Fight Against International Terrorism" issued at the ASEAN-Japan Summit in November 2004, in which ten areas of cooperation were specified: (1) to strengthen exchange of information and law enforcement cooperation on the activities of terrorists and terrorist organisations; (2) to ensure the early conclusion and implementation of all relevant counterterrorism conventions and protocols; (3) to strengthen measures to prevent the financing of terrorists and the use of alternative means of remittance such as illegal money transfer; (4) to implement appropriate measures so that terrorists will not use charitable organizations and groups to cover their activities; (5) to strengthen immigration controls to prevent the movement of terrorists and provide assistance to address the challenges of border and immigration control; (6) to develop cooperation to enhance national transport security, including aviation security, maritime security and container security; (7) to strengthen capacity-building efforts through training and education; (8) to develop cooperative projects with the Southeast Asia Regional Centre for Counter-Terrorism in Malaysia and explore cooperation with the International Law Enforcement Academy in Thailand and the Jakarta Center for Law Enforcement Cooperation in Indonesia; (9) to develop multilateral cooperation on combating terrorism in the international fora; (10) to support development projects that aim at reducing poverty and socio-economic disparity and injustice, as well as elevating standards of living, in particular of underprivileged groups and people in underdeveloped areas.[44]

The ASEAN-Japan Counter-Terrorism Dialogue was held in Tokyo in June 2006. Underscoring the fact that terrorism constitutes a serious threat to the peace, security and economic prosperity of ASEAN and Japan, and that countering terrorism requires a comprehensive approach that embraces action on many fronts, including issues of addressing the root causes of terrorism, enforcement and its follow-up measures, both ASEAN and Japan determined to prevent, suppress and eliminate all forms of international terrorism in accordance with the Charter of the United Nations, international law and all the relevant United Nations resolutions or declarations on international terrorism. Specifically, they identified the following areas of cooperation in combating terrorism: (1) transport security, (2) border control and immigration, (3) law enforcement, (4) maritime security, (5) public involvement in countering terrorism, and (6) capacity-building on legal affairs. Discussing the modality of cooperation, Japan made a presentation on its concept for an assistance scheme for counterterrorism measures, including technical assistance, grant aid and security enhancement.[45]

Japan's support for counterterrorism in Southeast Asia places greater emphasis on civilian law enforcement efforts due to its domestic and region-specific historical constraints. According to Fouse and Sato, this approach helps make Japan's assistance more acceptable to Southeast Asian coutries.[46] Japan's aid is highly appreciated by Southeast Asia's least counterterrorism-capable states, such as the Philippines and Indonesia.

Piracy

Japan has a long history of cooperation with the littoral states of the Strait of Malacca in the area of navigation safety, surveying the strait and providing equipment and training to the Southeast Asian coastal patrol authorities.[47] In April 2000, Japan hosted the "Regional Conference on Combating Piracy and Armed Robbery against Ships" with the participation of ASEAN, India, Sri Lanka, Bangladesh, the Republic of Korea, China and Hong Kong. At this inaugural conference, the participating countries agreed to strengthen regional cooperation in order to tackle piracy and armed robbery against ships, which were becoming more brutal and organized.[48] Soon after the conference, Japan dispatched the "Mission for Combating Piracy and Armed Robbery against Ships" to the Philippines, Malaysia, Singapore and Indonesia in September 2000, in order to consult with the coast countries about more specific measures of assistance and cooperation. Furthermore,

Japan hosted another conference on combating piracy in Tokyo in October 2001 in order to discuss medium- and long-term visions concerning a regional cooperation framework. At this conference all the participants shared the view that in light of the current situation — with the number of piratical cases still increasing despite the various efforts made — it was necessary to explore a new approach and to consider developing a regional cooperation agreement.

Specific measures of cooperation and support were as follows: first, the Japan Coast Guard sent a patrol vessel to Malaysia (November 2000) and the Philippines (October 2001) to conduct combined exercises and exchange views; second, the Japan Coast Guard Academy accepted students from five countries (Thailand, Indonesia, the Philippines, Malaysia and Vietnam) from April 2001; third, JICA hosted the "Maritime Law enforcement Seminar", in cooperation with the Japan Coast Guard (October 2001, in Kitakyushu, Japan); fourth, the MLIT (Ministry of Land, Infrastructure and Transport) cooperated with expert members of ASEAN countries to reinforce effective self-protection measures on ships; fifth, the MLIT established an international emergency information network and compiled and distributed a list of emergency contact points of coastal/port authorities.[49]

Japan's anti-piracy efforts have also encouraged litoral states to form a joint patrol unit, called "MALSINDO" and promoted multilateral institution building in the region. Established in November 2004, the Regional Cooperation Agreement on Combating Piracy and Armed Robbery against Ships in Asia (ReCAAP) comprises eight ASEAN members, China, Japan, South Korea, Bangladesh, India and Sri Lanka. The fourteen members agreed to establishing an Information Sharing Center (ISC) and a secretariat in Singapore. The ISC is tasked with the collection, analysis and dissemination of reports of incidents of piracy in the region.[50] Despite the absence of Indonesia and Malaysia, ReCAAP activities have been higly evaluated and it is likely to be a model for other regional organizations.

Japan has financed efforts of the International Maritime Organization (IMO) to track and study piracy incidents. At a meeting of the IMO in September 2006, Japan proposed voluntary cost sharing for safety, security and environmental protection of the Malacca and Singapore Straits among the three littoral states, user states, the shipping industry and other stakeholders. Japan's offer of three patrol ships to Indonesia in 2006 was a symbolic event in this respect. Overall, Japan's maritime security assistance to Southeast Asia has been favourably received. Despite some shortcomings in its assistance programmes and a heavy focus on the Strait of Malacca, Japan's capacity-building assistance in the region meshes well with the broader maritime security priorities of the Southeast Asian governments and Japan's principal allies in the region, the United States and Australia.[51]

Economic Cooperation and the Financial Crisis

The second area is economic cooperation, in which traditionally Japan's role has been regarded as predominant. For instance, statistics of trade, investment and aid amply suggest a leading role for Japan in the region, although recent development underscores a significant change. Notwithstanding this traditional relationship, there are additional elements of Japan-ASEAN economic relations in terms of METI's Nikai Initiative, the Indochina subregion development and financial cooperation.

Slow Developments of Trade, Investment, ODA

Japan's total trade with ASEAN increased 72 per cent, from $120 billion to $165 billion between 1997 and 2006. However, ASEAN's share of Japan's total trade steadily declined from 15.8 per cent to 13.4 per cent. The relative importance of Japan as a trading partner for ASEAN can also be found in the statistics from the ASEAN Secretariat. The most important export markets for ASEAN between 1997 and 2006, in order, were ASEAN, the United States, the European Union and Japan. Japan's market share of total ASEAN exports maintained fourth place throughout the period, although Japan's share slightly declined from 15 per cent in 1997 to 10.4 per cent in 2006. In contrast to the export market, the most important origin of imports for ASEAN was Japan. Japan's market share of total ASEAN imports, however, declined from 24 per cent in 1997 to 12.1 per cent in 2006.[52]

Fluctuating the most has been the inflow of foreign direct investment (FDI). The total amount of Japan's FDI to ASEAN countries between 1997 and 2006 was $36.6 billion (see Table 5.3). The annual FDI inflow to ASEAN reached a peak ($7.7 billion) at the time of the Asian economic crisis in 1997, after which it dropped sharply to $0.2 billion in 2000. This drop can be explained by the economic downturn of ASEAN after the crisis, a resultant loss of the attractiveness of ASEAN markets, and the switching

TABLE 5.3
Japan's Economic Relations with ASEAN, 1997–2006 ($ million)

	Trade	Investment	ODA
1997	120,689 (15.8%)	7,780 (29.8%)	1,354 (14.4%)
1998	85,994 (12.8%)	4,454 (18.0%)	2,356 (22.1%)
1999	88,873 (12.1%)	1,032 (4.6%)	3,920 (32.2%)
2000	127,773 (14.7%)	207 (0.6%)	3,126 (23.1%)
2001	111,294 (14.7%)	4,013 (10.4%)	2,108 (21.4%)
2002	109,097 (14.4%)	4,256 (13.1%)	1,747 (20.9%)
2003	119,715 (14.0%)	432 (1.4%)	1,488 (16.7%)
2004	143,096 (14.0%)	2,800 (9.0%)	897 (10.0%)
2005	153,949 (13.7%)	5,002 (11.0%)	1,968 (14.9%)
2006	165,444 (13.4%)	6,923 (13.8%)	703 (6.2%)

Sources: METI, *Tsusho Hakusho*, 1998–2007; JETRO, *Nihon no toshi*, 1998–2007; Ministry of Foreign
   Affairs, *Japan's ODA*, 1998–2007.

of world investment flow possibly from ASEAN to China. This contrasting
phenomenon certainly reflects the prolonged economic recession in Japan
as well as the surge of the Chinese economy in recent years. The dominance
of FDI inflows from Japan to ASEAN was especially significant and had
contributed to the industrialization of ASEAN countries.

It should be emphasized that Japan's ODA on a government level
also played a significant role in facilitating and expanding trade and
investment activities between the two. Japan had been the leading donor
country between 1997 and 2006. Japan's bilateral ODA to ASEAN countries
amounted to $1.9 billion or 14.9 per cent of Japan's total ODA worldwide
in 2005, although its value declined substantially in 2006.[53] The bulk of
Japan's ODA to ASEAN takes the form of government loans. The rest are
more or less equally divided between grants-in-aid and technical assistance.
Most government loans were distributed to Indonesia, the Philippines, and
Thailand, which received 60 per cent of Japan's total government loans to
ASEAN, whereas the newer members of Cambodia, Laos, Myanmar and
Vietnam (CLMV) received only 26 per cent during 1997–2006. However,
for grants-in-aid and technical assistance, where there is no repayment
obligation, CLMV countries received around 61 per cent of the total to
ASEAN for each category during the same period.

Indochina Subregion Development

Years of turmoil in Vietnam, Cambodia, and Laos have come to an end. These three countries, together with Thailand, Myanmar, and China's Yunnan Province, are today regarded as a single economic zone formed around the Mekong River. The Mekong River originates in Tibet and flows through Yunnan Province in China, Myanmar, Thailand, Laos, Cambodia, Vietnam and into the South China Sea. It is the main artery for Indochina. The extensive area is blessed with natural and human resources and is spurring great expectations due to its huge potential for economic growth. However, apart from Thailand, all of these nations are under centralized economies that have been ravaged by internal conflicts and suffered setbacks in economic development. For efficient and effective development of the Mekong River Basin, development must take the form of a comprehensive approach with attention to balanced development of the entire region, rather than through independent development pursued by each country. Of particular importance is development with attention paid to achieve regional balance, including development of road and railway infrastructure and preservation of the environment to ensure sustainable development.

Japan's main focus has been on CLV (Cambodia, Laos and Vietnam) countries. Since hosting the "Ministerial Meeting of the Forum for Comprehensive Development of Indochina" in Tokyo in February 1995, the Ministry of Foreign Affairs (MOFA) has conducted a number of major projects, including the following: a Forum for Comprehensive Development of Indochina, a Task Force for Strategies for Development of the Greater Mekong Area, a Seminar held in Indochina, and Japan's cooperation in the Initiative for ASEAN Integration.[54] In order to further contribute to the development of Indochina, MOFA has extended bilateral assistance to the new members of ASEAN. Of note, Japan actively cooperated with ASEAN in efforts to promote the IAI by assisting new member countries. Following Vietnam's entry into ASEAN, however, MOFA changed its orientation from Indochina to the Mekong region by incorporating ASEAN's Mekong development initiative and the Asian Development Bank's Greater Mekong Subregion (GMS) initiative.

As for cooperation with the ASEAN Secretariat, a number of projects are under consideration or are being carried out in cooperation with the ASEAN Secretariat to assist CLMV (Cambodia, Laos, Myanmar and

Vietnam) countries by utilizing the Japan-ASEAN General Exchange Fund (JAGEF). These include (1) the provision of IT equipment to Ministries of Foreign Affairs of the CLMV, (2) the attachment programme at the ASEAN Secretariat for Junior Diplomats of the CLMV, (3) the capacity-building workshop for Ministry of Foreign Affairs personnel of the CLMV, (4) the Human Resources Development Workshop for non–Ministry of Foreign Affairs personnel of the CLMV, (5) the workshop to formulate a workplan for the integration of CLMV into ASEAN.[55]

While recognizing MOFA's inclination towards the GMS, METI, on its part, came up with ASEAN-METI Economic and Industrial Cooperation (AMEICC) in November 1998. AMEICC's main function is to help the CLMV countries tackle divisive ASEAN issues and to enhance the competitiveness of ASEAN economies by promoting regional integration and upgrading major industries, not just for new members of ASEAN, but also for the original members hit by the financial crisis. In addition, MOFA initiated a ministerial meeting and summit meeting with the CLV countries in November 2004.[56]

Immediately after ASEAN formed a task force on the Initiative for ASEAN Integration in February 2001, the Japanese government offered its assistance through the Japan General Exchange Fund. Japan dispatched a joint mission with the Asian Development Bank (ADB) to the countries concerned (CLMV and Thailand) in July 2001. Based on the findings of the mission, Japan put priority on the East-West Corridor project (Maulamyaing-Mukdahan-Da Nang) and the 2nd East-West Corridor project (Ho Chi Minh City-Phnom Penh-Bangkok). In a similar vein, Japan extends its assistance programme to CLMV countries with other ASEAN member countries (Singapore, Thailand and the Philippines). For instance, there is a joint programme for building human resources of developing countries, the cost of which is borne by Japan and Singapore on a 50:50 basis. It is called the "Japan-Singapore Partnership Program for the 21st Century." Every year nearly twenty training courses are offered, accepting trainees from neighbouring countries.[57]

The Financial Crisis and Japan-ASEAN Financial Cooperation

In the middle of 1997 Thailand suddenly devalued its currency and announced its policy of adopting a floating exchange system, caused by the mass selling of the baht by currency speculators, thereby triggering the financial crisis in East Asia. Soon after the 2 July devaluation of the baht, the Japanese Finance Ministry began a discussion with key Asian countries over a possible rescue plan due to the shared fear that the Thai currency crisis might trigger a chain reaction in neighbouring economies. The resulting Tokyo meeting was significant simply because Japan led the pack of neighbouring countries providing Thailand with a $16.7 billion bailout fund.

In dealing with the Asian financial crisis, there were two policy initiatives by the Japanese government, i.e., the Asian Monetary Fund proposal and the new Miyazawa plan, which culminated in the adoption of the Chiang Mai Initiative in 2000.[58] Led by a policy entrepreneur Eisuke Sakakibara of the Finance Ministry, Japan and ASEAN proposed setting up an "Asian Monetary Fund (AMF)". The idea was to establish a $100 billion Asian bailout fund.[59] Like Mahathir's proposed East Asian Economic Caucus, the rationale was the exigency to deal with regional economic problems locally, because international organizations — such as the IMF or the World Bank — have serious deficiencies in handling regional crises. Besides, as many Asian leaders contend, the IMF's offers of financial assistance come with strict conditions, a sine qua non for domestic adjustment policies.

However, the United States strongly opposed the proposal that could directly challenge the function of the IMF.[60] In particular, U.S. officials worried that an independent regional fund for international bailouts would not carry the stringent austerity conditions. Due to American opposition, representatives from Asia-Pacific countries decided to seek a looser arrangement involving a regional commitment to pool resources at a time of crisis, rather than setting up a permanent fund at the financial meeting in Manila. The resulting agreement included four areas of cooperation: first, a mechanism for regional economic surveillance to complement the IMF's global role; second, enhanced economic and technical cooperation in strengthening domestic financial systems and regulatory mechanisms; third, measures to bolster the IMF's ability to respond to financial crises; and fourth, a cooperative financing arrangement that would supplement IMF resources.[61] This compromise was far from sufficient to resolve the crisis. Suffice it to say that APEC leaders, who met in November during the height of the crisis, could not reach any agreement that would alleviate the financial crisis, except for reiterating some preventive policies along the lines of the IMF. The AMF proposal died early on, but many East Asian leaders hoped for an alternative solution, as one observer noted, "the desire to stabilize regional finance under Japanese leadership even in competition with the United States, died hard among Japanese policymakers, and expectation of an active Japanese role lingered among some Asian leaders from 1997 to 2000".[62]

In a joint search for a solution, a positive step was made at the Financial Ministers' meeting between ASEAN and Japan on 1 December 1997, when all the leaders agreed to form a group and to meet annually.[63] This agreement seemed to herald the dawn of "East Asianness" in the minds of policy entrepreneurs. The Second ASEAN Finance Ministers' Meeting, held in Jakarta in February 1998, saw agreement to immediately establish a policy surveillance mechanism, with its secretariat based at the Asian Development Bank, to promote the use of ASEAN currencies in intra-regional trade. This was planned to initially be on a voluntary basis and to evolve into a multilateral arrangement. Japan's pledge to stimulate domestic demand was welcomed and it was called on to take the lead in bringing the region out of the crisis.[64]

Upon assuming the premiership, Prime Minister Keizo Obuchi appointed former prime minister Miyazawa as finance minister with the mission of invigorating Japanese and Asian economies. Although Japan had already committed more than $40 billion bilaterally as part of rescue packages for Thailand, Indonesia and the Republic of Korea, Miyazawa soon disclosed a $30 billion aid package for ailing Asian economies when he met with finance ministers and central bank governors from the five original ASEAN members in October 1998. The joint statement issued after the meeting stipulated that "to overcome the current economic difficulties, while avoiding the risk of falling into deflationary spiral, they agreed that it is imperative for the Asian economies to take stimulus measures to put their economy on the path of recovery and sustainable growth".[65] This was significant not only because Miyazawa's new policy "package" was presented as a form of recovery assistance, but also because it laid an important foundation for subsequent developments in East Asian financial cooperation.[66]

One of the most important developments in regional financial cooperation was the inauguration of the APT Finance and Central Bank Deputies in March 1999. That initial meeting was followed by a meeting of the Finance Ministers of ASEAN, China, Japan and the Republic of

Korea in Chiang Mai in May, to discuss further measures and plans to carry out the APT Leaders' Joint Statement on East Asia Cooperation, issued in Manila in November 1999. Through these meetings came several proposals for a regional support mechanism that would include setting up a network of East Asian training and research institutes and establishing a regional financing arrangement to supplement existing international facilities. Besides setting up the vision group, the central task of APT has been to establish a surveillance mechanism to anticipate and head off future financial crises.

Top-level discussion also took place regarding common currency baskets and joint intervention arrangements — to replace both the discredited dollar pegs of the past and the costly free floats imposed by the crisis. Most dramatically, the APT finance ministers met in Chiang Mai in May 2000 to discuss a regional support mechanism that could promote further regional financial stability. They agreed to establish a regional financing arrangement called the "Chiang Mai Initiative".[67] This had two components: an expanded ASEAN Swap Arrangement (ASA) and a network of bilateral swap arrangements among ASEAN countries, China, Japan and the Republic of Korea. To help countries meet temporary liquidity problems, ASEAN agreed to expand the ASA. The ASEAN central banks agreed on the principles governing the expanded facility and aimed to conclude the agreement before the ASEAN Summit in November 2000. Besides the expanded ASA, a network of bilateral swap arrangements and repurchase agreements among ASEAN countries, China, Japan and the Republic of Korea was also being negotiated to provide temporary financing for members undergoing difficulties with balance of payments. A working group of the APT finance and central bank deputies was formed to finalize the basic framework and principles of the bilateral swap arrangements and repurchase agreements before the APT Summit in November 2000.

In order to create viable surveillance mechanisms in East Asia, Japan's Ministry of Finance established the Japan-ASEAN Financial Technical Assistance Fund (JAFTAF) under the ASEAN Secretariat in September 2001. APT also recognized the importance of capacity building efforts for further development of the technical assistance initially provided by JAFTAF. In 2001 APT countries established the Financial Technical Assistance Fund (FTAF). FTAF has supported a number of projects and research activities in the region, including "Monitoring of Short Term Capital Flows" and "Promoting Research on an Appropriate Financial Support Mechanism".[68]

JAFTAF also provided assistance by strengthening participating members' monitoring systems and capacity in generating and compiling more accurate and timely data, to enhance the effectiveness of the economic review and policy dialogue process.

METI's "Nikai Initiative" in 2006

Since APEC's trade liberalization scheme was abandoned in 1998 — due mainly to objection from Japan — METI had to wait for eight years before it could overcome its predicament. Particlarly with the rise of China, METI officials were compelled to seek an alternative trade policy in order to protect Japan's vested interests in the region.[69] In April 2006 METI came up with a global economic strategy that included three policies to deal with the rapid developments of globalization. These were joint development in Asia, taking advantage of "soft power", and a contribution to global values. Among the three, the first policy was stressed because of the recognition that economic activities in Japan are deeply embedded in the dense manufacturing network in East Asia. In order to ensure a foundation for long-term growth in Japan, it is necessary to strengthen the growth mechanism through which growth in Asia as a whole drives continuing growth in Japan. For this it is necessary to create "a Free and Open Economic Area" in Asia where free trade and business activities are governed by the rule of law. In order to further develop economic integration in East Asia, METI stressed two proposals: the vision of a Comprehensive Economic Partnership in East Asia (CEPEA); and the establishment of an international organization in East Asia to serve as a policy forum and think tank that operates like the Organization for Economic Cooperation and Development.[70]

At the thirteenth AEM-METI meeting, held in Kuala Lumpur in August 2006, METI Minister, Toshihiro Nikai, announced a proposal for an East Asian economic partnership agreement, called the "Comprehensive Economic Partnership for East Asia, CEPEA", consisting of the current members of the EAS, and promised up to $100 million to kick-start efforts to establish such a free trade bloc. The Nikai initiative also included the creation of an institution to be named the East Asia Economic Research Institute for ASEAN and East Asia (ERIA), to study the pros and cons of the proposed CEPEA. Its aim is to create a multi-regional organization of East Asian, Indian Ocean and Southeast Asian countries, for greater economic partnership. The approximate population of these areas combined is currently three billion with an economic capacity in the region of nine trillion dollars, more than 20 per cent of world economic output. If it functions effectively, the market would become wider and more attractive, not only to the Oceanic countries but also to ASEAN members more than ever before.[71]

At the thirteenth AEM-METI meeting, ASEAN basically agreed with these two proposals, but asked for further clarification. To the first proposal, ASEAN ministers reiterated the need to expeditiously conclude the AJCEP as the basis for such expanded regional integration. To the second proposal, ASEAN simply requested Japan to discuss this proposal further with the ASEAN Secretariat.[72]

Cultural Cooperation through the Multilateral Cultural Mission

The third area is cultural cooperation, which has been stressed since the announcement of "heart-to-heart understanding" of the Fukuda Doctrine. Following the footsteps of Fukuda and Takeshita, Hashimoto also emphasized the importance of cultural exchange cooperation by sending the Multilateral Cultural Mission to ASEAN in 1997.[73] On 4–6 November 1997, the Multinational Cultural Mission met in Singapore and agreed on Part I of the Action Agenda, comprising the objectives, general policy orientations and priority areas. The mission held its Concluding Meeting in Japan on 14–17 April 1998 and adopted Part II of the Action Agenda, consisting of specific proposals to be implemented to further cultural exchange and cooperation among the ASEAN countries and Japan.[74] This attempt was regarded by the Japanese as "epoch-making" for Japan-ASEAN relations.

As such, ASEAN and Japan have placed emphasis on people-to-people and cultural exchanges, particularly among youths and intellectuals, with a view to fostering a sense of togetherness, mutual trust, respect and understanding of each other's traditions and values. Japan provides its support to the Ship for Southeast Asian Youth Program and the ASEAN-Japan Youth Friendship Program. The programmes also include an exchange of academics, researchers and students. As one observer put it, "the ASEAN-Japan relationship, through concerted efforts at exchange and collaboration, goes a long way toward setting the stage for broader regional community building".[75] The implications for policy of various academic interactions is significant, as demonstrated by the Japan-ASEAN

Dialogue sponsored by the Global Forum of Japan and ASEAN Institutes of Strategic and International Studies.

In the area of people-to-people exchange, steady progress has been made. Since December 2003, Japan had brought over some 6,500 ASEAN youths, more than half the 10,000 it had pledged to invite by 2008. As part of the effort to promote Asia-Africa cooperation, the "Asia Young Volunteers" programme was initiated with the help of Japan's contribution of $650,000 to the United Nations Volunteers in 2006.[76]

The advancement of cultural exchange programmes, however, does not necessarily suggest a commendable level of mutual understanding between Japan and ASEAN. The number of ASEAN students in Japan, for instance, is not at a satisfactory level (see Table 5.4) compared with the number of Chinese students in Japan (approximately 80,000 in 2007).

CHALLENGING ISSUES FOR EAST ASIAN REGIONALISM: MAINSTREAM'S RESURGENCE

The above analysis suggests that challenges to promoting new regionalism in East Asia emerged.[77] Here we examine three such major challenges for Japan and ASEAN.

TABLE 5.4
ASEAN Students in Japan, 1997–2006

	ASEAN	Total
1997	4,872 (*)	51,047
1998	5,141 (*)	51,298
1999	5,387 (*)	55,755
2000	6,422 (10.0%)	64,011
2001	6,878 (8.7%)	78,812
2002	7,403 (7.7%)	85,550
2003	8,096 (7.4%)	109,508
2004	8,488 (7.2%)	117,302
2005	8,962 (7.4%)	121,812
2006	9,518 (8.1%)	117,927

Notes: (*) includes only Indonesia, Malaysia, the Philippines, Thailand and Vietnam.
Source: Monbukagakusho, *Monbukagaku hakusho*, various issues.

Japan-ASEAN Strategic Partnership and the Rise of China

ASEAN's apparent response to the financial crisis was to forge a new regionalism in East Asia while retaining ASEAN's position in the driver's seat. Accordingly, the APT framework emerged from an increasing drive among the East Asian countries to learn from the currency and financial crisis and strengthen regional cooperation. Now that neither ASEAN nor APEC could deal with the financial crisis, Asian leaders turned to East Asian cooperation instead. Specifically, ASEAN-Japan relations have come to be seen in a common strategic perspective, as Singapore Deputy Prime Minister Lee Hsien Loong explained: "In 1977, ASEAN was in a precarious position not long after the fall of Indochina. Japan's support to ASEAN at a time of need was deeply appreciated. Now ASEAN is again going through a difficult period. Japan's assistance to the crisis economies has not only assisted the countries with their economic problems, but also produced positive political impact by helping to stabilize the region. This has earned Japan goodwill and respect as a long-term player with an enlightened understanding of its own interests."[78] At the third APT meeting in 1999, furthermore, APT leaders adopted the "Joint Statement on East Asia Cooperation", in which the thirteen leaders resolved to promote cooperation in a wide range of areas encompassing monetary and financial cooperation, social and human resources development, scientific and technical development, the cultural and information area, development cooperation, political-security, and transnational issues."[79]

When China started its relations with ASEAN as a dialogue partner in 1996 and agreed to a free trade arrangement in 2001, the rise of China had become a reality as its mushrooming increase of trade with ASEAN amply shows. Table 5.5 suggests the fact that China is catching up rapidly with Japan, so far the single most important economic partner of ASEAN.[80] The so-called rise of China, however, bifurcated dominant arguments for economic benefits and security concerns, thus implying a dual edge for ASEAN. Nevertheless, regardless of Beijing's intentions, ASEAN has come to grips with an intricate dilemma of having to balance economic gains from cooperating with China, against security gains from counterbalancing or "hedging" against China.[81]

Against this background, Japan began to formulate its strategic relationship with ASEAN in 2003. At the summit meeting with Japan, ASEAN commended Japan's commitment to enhance its support for the

TABLE 5.5
ASEAN Trade with Japan and China, 1997–2006 (US$ million)

	Japan		China	
	1997	2006	1997	2006
Export	42,009 (12.3)	81,284 (10.8)	9,168 (2.7)	65,010 (8.7)
Import	71,264 (20.0)	80,495 (12.3)	13,483 (3.8)	74,950 (11.5)
Total	113,273 (16.2)	161,780 (11.5)	22,651 (3.2)	139,961 (10.0)

Note: Figures in parentheses are percentages in ASEAN's total trade.
Source: *ASEAN Statistical Yearbook*, 2007.

IAI and other subregional development endeavours, such as the Brunei, Indonesia, Malaysia, Philippines, East Asian Growth Area (BIMP-EAGA) and the Ayeyawady–Chao Phraya–Mekong Economic Cooperation Strategy (ACMECS), while reiterating its determination to conclude a satisfactory and mutually beneficial AJCEP by April 2007. The ASEAN leaders expected the AJCEP to be more than a compendium of Japan's bilateral Economic Partnership Agreements with individual ASEAN countries. As the statement suggests, it has gained momentum towards the strategic partnership: "We welcomed Japan's recognition of its support for ASEAN as being in its national interest. We shared Japan's sentiment that the ASEAN-Japan strategic partnership is important to the stability and prosperity of the region."[82]

Furthermore, at the Ninth ASEAN-Japan Summit held in Kuala Lumpur in December 2005, both Japan and ASEAN agreed to deepen and broaden the ASEAN-Japan Strategic Partnership. As its joint statement stressed: "Based upon the achievements for the past 30 years, ASEAN and Japan are now closely working together on equal footing to address common challenges and opportunities. Japan fully supports ASEAN's increasingly active contributions to regional cooperation in East Asia, particularly through its role as the driving force as well as its dynamic initiative to further advance ASEAN integration. In recognition of this, we reaffirmed our determination to deepen and broaden the strategic partnership between ASEAN and Japan."[83] It is indeed significant for Japan and ASEAN to reconfirm their strategic partnership by (1) supporting ASEAN community building efforts, (2) strengthening economic partnership, (3) reforming the ASEAN-Japan Centre, (4) combating transnational crime and terrorism,

(5) enhancing disaster management, (6) addressing infectious diseases, (7) enhancing energy cooperation, (8) promoting exchanges and people-to-people contact, (9) deepening East Asia cooperation, (10) and responding to international issues.

It is interesting to note here that the strategic partnership reflects on bilateral relations as well. On the occasion of the state visit of the Indonesian president to Japan in November 2006, for instance, Prime Minister Shinzo Abe and President Yudhoyono held a summit meeting in which the two leaders underlined that the strategic partnership between Indonesia and Japan would be a significant means to deepen and expand mutually beneficial bilateral ties and cooperation. The partnership should also address new non-traditional security threats such as the danger of infectious diseases, including avian influenza; terrorism; natural disasters and transnational crimes. As the statement succinctly put it, "The two leaders reconfirmed that Japan and Indonesia share such basic values as freedom, democracy, human rights and rule of law and also shared commitment to stability and development of the Asia Pacific region. They also affirmed that they would strengthen the strategic relationship in addressing political and security issues, as well as reinforced the long-standing economic relations. Both leaders emphasized the importance of holding summit meetings between them as frequently as possible and agreed to intensify high-level consultations taking advantage of opportunities at regional and multilateral meetings."[84]

Should this be the case, the Japan-ASEAN strategic partnership could play a central role in promoting a new regionalism in East Asia. As a Japanese diplomat put it, "I believe the Japan-ASEAN relationship should be the engine for the creation of the EAC (East Asian Community) because we have accumulated, for more than thirty years, a solid foundation of regional cooperation. We should promote East Asia cooperation, utilizing the Japan-ASEAN cooperation model."[85]

Towards a development regime

As part of the Koizumi Initiative, moreover, Prime Minister Koizumi proposed a comprehensive plan to elevate the existing ASEAN-Japan economic relations into a development regime at the commemorative meeting in December 2003. Two documents are worthwhile mentioning here. The first is the "Tokyo Declaration for the Dynamic and Enduring

Japan-ASEAN Partnership in the New Millennium", in which both parties adopted the following principles and values: first, Japan and ASEAN will further deepen and broaden their relationship; second, Japan and ASEAN will enhance their cooperation through closer consultation; third, Japan and ASEAN will contribute to the creation of an East Asia region; fourth, Japan and ASEAN will forge common visions and principles, including respect for the rule of law and justice, pursuit of openness, promotion and protection of human rights and fundamental freedoms of all peoples; fifth, Japan will give high priority to ASEAN's economic development and integration efforts as it strives to realize the ASEAN Community; sixth, Japan and ASEAN will collectively promote the development of regional and trans-regional frameworks; and seventh, Japan and ASEAN will address regional and global issues, keeping in mind their special relationship based on equality, mutual respect and mutual benefit.[86]

The other is the "Action Plan" which specified common strategies for joint action in the following areas: (1) reinforcing comprehensive economic partnership and monetary and financial cooperation, (2) consolidating the foundation for economic development and prosperity, (3) strengthening political and security cooperation and partnership, (4) facilitating and promoting exchange of people and human resource development, (5) enhancing cooperation in culture and public relations, (6) deepening East Asia cooperation for an East Asian community, and (7) cooperation in addressing global issues. With these two documents, Japan has clarified its commitments and defined the future direction of ASEAN-Japan relations. That is, Japan has committed itself to further pushing ahead with CEP and stressed the importance of creating an East Asian community.[87] Without any doubt, the holding of the very first commemorative summit was meant to be a timely joint endeavour, realizing ASEAN's community building and Japan's aspiration for maintaining its regional role.

Have Japan's initiatives and commitments produced tangible results so far, or have they merely been lip service? At the Ninth ASEAN-Japan Summit Meeting held in Kuala Lumpur on 13 December 2005, ASEAN and Japan reaffirmed their commitment to deepen and broaden the ASEAN-Japan strategic partnership. Since then, various projects and measures have been implemented as illustrated in the Executive Report on Progress of Implementation of the ASEAN-Japan Plan of Action.[88] The following are salient points from the report. First, on political and security cooperation, Japan has made vigorous efforts in areas such as counterterrorism, transnational crime, maritime security, piracy, non-proliferation and drug control through capacity-building, training and information exchange. Japan informed ASEAN of its newly established grant-aid scheme for cooperation on counterterrorism and security enhancement in 2006. In June 2006 Japan hosted the First ASEAN-Japan Counter-Terrorism Dialogue in Tokyo.

Second, on the economic front, progress has been made in reforming the centre based on the recommendations of the Eminent Persons' Committee. Development cooperation has also substantially progressed in various sectors and areas. The Japan-ASEAN Integration Fund, to which Japan has contributed $70 million, was established in March 2006 to support ASEAN's effort to establish the ASEAN Community by 2020. Efforts to reduce the development gap in ASEAN have continued under the Initiative for ASEAN Integration, for which Japan has extended assistance to twenty-four projects worth over $4 million in the area of human resource development. Concerning development of the Mekong region and the Human Resource Development Total Plan, cooperation marked a new high with the realization of Japan's commitment to extend assistance of $1.5 billion within three years since December 2003.

Third, East Asian cooperation has continued to expand in various areas. For instance, ASEAN agreed to a proposal for a Track II study on a possible Comprehensive Economic Partnership in East Asia. ASEAN also agreed to Japan's proposal to establish an Economic Research Institute for ASEAN and East Asia, and asked Japan to discuss this proposal further with the ASEAN Secretariat. Working closely with the ADB, Japan's pursuit of a regional development regime could bring favourable results to East Asia.

ASEAN Plus Three versus the East Asia Summit

It is well known that the APT framework emerged from an increasing drive among the East Asian countries to learn from the currency and financial crisis and strengthen regional cooperation.[89] The first APT summit took place in December 1997, with leaders agreeing at the second summit in December 1998 to regularize the event. Since some countries in the region were reluctant to commit themselves to cooperation in East Asia, the APT began in quite a low-key way. China's cautious approach is a case in point. In fact, in opposing Japan's proposal for the Asian Monetary Fund,

China remained critical in forging its regional policies. Accordingly, no joint statement was launched. Moreover, the term "ASEAN Plus Three" was cautiously and rarely used in the first two meetings, much less in the agenda for the meeting. It was only after the APT meeting of finance ministers in March 1999 that the term "ASEAN Plus Three" was widely used. Let us see more closely how this process has been evolving.

At the third meeting in 1999, the Plus Three leaders adopted the "Joint Statement on East Asia Cooperation", in which leaders resolved to promote cooperation in a wide range of areas encompassing monetary and financial cooperation, social and human resource development, scientific and technical development, the cultural and information area, development cooperation, political security and transnational issues.[90] Given the importance of steadily implementing the joint statement in the future, it was decided that the first APT Foreign Ministers' Meeting would be held on the occasion of the ASEAN PMC in Bangkok in July 2000. At this summit, the first dialogue among the leaders of Japan, China and South Korea took place as a breakfast meeting.

The momentum towards East Asian regionalism picked up at the November 2000 APT summit in Singapore, where ASEAN proposed an East Asia Summit and an East Asian Free Trade and Investment Area. It was decided that the East Asian Study Group (EASG) advocated by South Korean President Kim Dae Jung would consider these proposals from a medium-to-long term perspective. Prime Minister Goh Chok Tong of Singapore summarized the discussions, commenting that it is conceivable that the "APT Summit Meeting" — in which the member countries discuss how Japan, China, and the Republic of Korea should cooperate with ASEAN — will evolve into an "East Asia Summit", in order to advance cooperation in the East Asia region. Prime Minister Goh said that he would have the EASG consider the possibility of an "East Asia Summit" as well as the possibility of a free trade and investment area in East Asia.[91]

The November 2001 APT summit in Brunei was intended to form a closer East Asian partnership, whereby leaders could exchange views on terrorism and the progress of APT cooperation in particular. Accordingly, the main discussions of the fifth summit were as follows: (1) the nuclear problem in the Korean peninsula, (2) strengthening of economic cooperation, (3) the report of the East Asia Study Group, (4) the Initiative for Development in East Asia (IDEA), and (5) cooperation for transnational issues. China proposed the holding of a ministerial meeting on transnational crime and many leaders expressed their support. Many leaders declared their antiterrorism intentions. An EAVG report was also submitted to the summit. This contained significant proposals, including an East Asia Free Trade Agreement (EAFTA) and an EAS.[92] It should be noted here that the EAS was originally meant to be an alternative to ASEAN leadership, which was deemed to be too slow and informal.

Furthermore, at the sixth summit in November 2002 in Phnom Penh, the APT process had expanded to include regional political and security issues such as the fight against terrorism and transnational crime. The leaders expressed willingness to explore the phased evolution of the APT summit into an East Asia summit.[93] In addition to supporting ASEAN initiatives, the three countries have been helping integration through their own efforts, notably Japan's Initiative for Development in East Asia (IDEA), the East Asia Vision Group and the East Asia Study Group initiated by the Republic of Korea and the Framework Agreement on ASEAN-China Economic Cooperation. The final report of the study group was submitted to the summit and twenty-six specific measures were recommended. The thirteen leaders tasked their economic ministers to study and formulate options on the gradual formation of an East Asia Free Trade Area and report the results to them at the next summit.[94]

Following suit, the seventh summit was held in October 2003 in Bali, where thirteen leaders discussed several important issues, such as the nuclear question on the Korean Peninsula, the future of East Asian cooperation, poverty alleviation, human resources development and the development of infrastructures for ASEAN Integration. They also endorsed the Implementation Strategy of the Short-Term Measures of the Final Report of the East Asia Study Group, while discussing the progress of the Initiative for Development in East Asia in the framework of APT cooperation.[95] It was agreed to ensure that the measures would be implemented effectively, efficiently and systematically.

Having adopted the Bali Concord II on 7 October 2003, ASEAN agreed unanimously to strengthen its political, economic and cultural foundations on which the development of the APT hinges. Indeed, it is remarkable that ASEAN members promised to live at peace with each other and with the world at large "in a just, democratic and harmonious environment". ASEAN leaders also pledged to achieve an ASEAN Community by the year 2020 which would rest on the three pillars of an ASEAN security community, an ASEAN economic community, and an ASEAN social-cultural community embodied in the Bali Concord II.[96] Moreover, ASEAN and the Plus Three countries agreed with establishing an APT Unit within the ASEAN Secretariat in December 2003.

As proposed by the EAVG, the establishment of an East Asian community was discussed intensively at the APT Foreign Ministers' Meeting in Jakarta in July and the thirteen leaders agreed to convene a summit meeting in 2005 at the Eighth ASEAN Summit in November 2004. This decision was critical, as the joint statement avers: "We agreed that the establishment of an East Asian Community is a long-term objective. We reaffirmed the role of the ASEAN+3 process as the main vehicle for the eventual establishment of an East Asian Community. China, Japan, and the Republic of Korea reiterated their support for ASEAN's role as the major driving force in East Asia cooperation. In addition, to mark the 10th Anniversary of the ASEAN+3 cooperation in 2007, we agreed to consider the idea of issuing the 2nd Joint Statement on East Asia cooperation as well as a work plan to consolidate the existing and future cooperation."[97]

When the APT decided to hold its first meeting of the EAS in November 2004, several concerns emerged among the members. First, it was not clear who would be leading the summit, Japan, China or ASEAN. Given the marginal role of China in financial cooperation, it is apparent that APT is not China-centred. Yet, China's free trade initiative with ASEAN has become complicated due to Sino-Japanese antagonism, as shown by Koizumi's repeated visits to the Yasukuni Shrine. Second, it was not clear what role the summit could play in East Asian regionalism, as opposed to the APT. Third, who would participate in the summit was not clear, although ASEAN made it clear that ASEAN would play a central role.

Concerning membership, APT members were debating whether or not non–East Asian countries should be admitted to the EAS. China and Malaysia wanted the membership confined to those of the APT, while Japan, Indonesia and Singapore advocated the inclusion of Australia, New Zealand and India. Indonesia in particular did not want the East Asian Community to happen too soon, as that might undermine the importance of ASEAN's community-building efforts, besides the problem of duplication of both an APT summit and the EAS. After heated debate, a consensus was reached at the APT Foreign Ministers' Informal Meeting in April 2005 that the EAS would accept the participation of countries other than APT members. The decision was apparently influenced by the politics of institutional balancing. In July ASEAN came up with the three conditions for admission to the EAS: full dialogue partner with ASEAN, engaged substantially in the region, and signatories to the TAC.[98]

The Japanese Foreign Ministry floated the so-called "Issue Paper" in June 2004. In the paper Japan proposed a three-step approach: (1) promotion of functional cooperation on wide-ranging issues, (2) introduction of region-wide institutional arrangements such as an EAS, and (3) creation of a "sense of community". At the same time three points were raised to clarify the modality of the EAS: (1) the fundamental objective of the EAS, (2) the difference between the EAS and the APT Summit, (3) the organization of the EAS.[99] It was obvious that by laying out these agendas that the Japanese government intended to have a summit that would be open and inclusive.

The sixteen participants in the first EAS duly met on 14 December 2005. The meeting was relatively short and few specific decisions were made; the emphasis was on developing communication among the members. The main issues discussed during the summit included the need for de-nuclearization of the Korean peninsula, terrorism, avian flu, sustainable development, the need for progress in the Doha round of World Trade Organization negotiations and the role which the EAS should play as a complement to the APT in the process of community building in the region. At the end of the meeting the Kuala Lumpur Declaration on East Asia Summit was signed, which indicated that the EAS would be a forum for dialogue on broad strategic, political and economic issues of common interest and concern, with the aim of promoting peace, stability and economic prosperity in East Asia.[100]

Two major problems are the division of labour between the EAS and the APT and the concept of the East Asian Community. Questions remain as to exactly what geographical area is covered by East Asia and how far regional integration is to be taken. The problem of participation by Russia and the United States in particular is a critical matter that cannot be avoided. Not only is there dissent between those in ASEAN who want restricted participation (Malaysia, the Philippines, Thailand, Myanmar and Laos) and those who want expanded participation (Indonesia, Singapore and Vietnam), but a shadow has also been cast by the leadership struggle between China, which seeks a dominant role in the region and wishes to exclude countries from outside the region, and Japan, which seeks to maintain balance by accepting countries from outside the region.

MAJOR TASKS AHEAD

The discussion above suggests three emerging issues that need to be tackled. The first is related to the membership of the EAS, which to a large extent was affected by Japan's EAEC Syndrome. As discussed earlier, both China and Japan have embarked on attempts for regional economic leadership. China's political and economic influence is fast rising within East Asia at a time when that of Japan is noticeably declining, which has expedited changes in regional economic and industrial structures. At the same time, China is intensifying economic cooperation with ASEAN. China's commitment to form an FTA with ASEAN strongly reflects its political and economic intention to gain regional leadership. In turn, this forces Japan into a new strategy for Asia, focusing on a comprehensive economic partnership to act as leverage to counter China's influence. ASEAN is thus in a good position to use this rivalry between China and Japan to their advantage.

Prime Minister Koizumi's attitudes towards China, however, almost jeopardized Japan's constructive role in promoting East Asian regionalism. In fact, worsening China-Japan relations due to Koizumi's visit to the Yasukuni Shrine ultimately prevented Japan from serving in a go-between capacity. Understandably, no ASEAN countries supported Japan's bid to obtain a permanent seat on the UN Security Council.[101]

As for the second issue, the controversy over the modality of the EAS needs to be resolved amicably. Although ASEAN set up three qualifications for admission to the summit — (1) dialogue partner with ASEAN, (2) engaged economically in East Asia, (3) signatory to the ASEAN Treaty of Amity and Cooperation — the so-called "plus 3 vs. plus 6" rivalry could serve as a stumbling block for the new regionalism attempts, as a Southeast Asian scholar convincingly put it: "if Japan is clouded with relative gains considerations vis-à-vis China, it might well play the spoiler role and slow down the pace of progress".[102]

The third issue is ASEAN's expectations for Japan's role in East Asia. Should ASEAN and Japan constitute a core of promoting a new regionalism in East Asia, their mutual perceptions of each other need to be congenial. It is quite remarkable to witness the emerging perception of ASEAN leading community building in East Asia with strong support from Japan.[103] Further evidence can be obtained from an opinion poll conducted by a major Japanese newspaper (see Table 5.6). It amply suggests that while ASEAN relations with Japan and the evaluation of Japan's aid had improved

TABLE 5.6
Opinion Poll on Japan, 2006

Q1 Do you think that Japan has become a trustworthy country in Asia?				
	Indonesia	Malaysia	Thailand	Vietnam
Yes	88%	77%	92%	75%
No	10%	18%	5%	13%
Q2 Do you think that your country's relations with Japan are good at present?				
Yes	96%	90%	95%	92%
No	2%	4%	3%	3%
Q3 Do you think that Japan will be a military power?				
Yes	39%	37%	42%	38%
No	48%	36%	44%	23%
Q4 Do you think what the Japanese military did in your country is still an obstacle to the relationship between your country and Japan?				
Yes	33%	22%	43%	10%
No	62%	65%	49%	72%
Q5 Do you think that Japan contributes positively to the development of Asian countries?				
Yes	88%	87%	91%	89%
No	8%	10%	5%	3%

Source: Yomiuri Shimbun, 10 September 2006.

(Q2 and Q5), ASEAN still has concerns related to Japan's military power (Q3) as well as lingering memories of World War II (Q4).

CONCLUSION

With the Hashimoto Doctrine as a turning point in ASEAN-Japan relations, it is possible to witness the beginning of Japan's dynamic diplomacy in close collaboration with ASEAN. In tandem with Hashimoto's principle of regional peaceful coexistence, Japan has sought to strengthen top-level dialogue with ASEAN politically and economically. Thus, contrary to the traditional reactive nature of Japan's foreign policy, it can be concluded that its policy was assertive and dynamic during the past decade. Compounded by the rise of China, Japanese attitudes towards ASEAN have become strategic, particularly since the Tokyo summit in 2003. The advent of the strategic partnership is a noteworthy example. Japan's political and security role retains a low profile, yet contributes significantly to stability in Southeast Asia.[104]

Paradoxically, the 1997 financial crisis created new possibilities for ASEAN as a regional political and economic actor. For instance, the crisis led to the formation of the APT; and because of the APT framework ASEAN has been able to enhance its political leverage vis-à-vis Japan and China, profiting politically and economically from their rivalry. ASEAN members can be comfortable with the Northeast Asian giants vying for influence in Southeast Asia, and each struggling to accommodate their Southeast Asian neighbours as best they can.

Through mutually supportive interaction, Japan and ASEAN further learned from each other and came to share values. Politically significant results have been the regularization of top-level meetings and joint efforts towards East Asian regionalism. In particular, beginning with the Cambodian debacle in 1997, Japan's political role has been expanded as shown in its peace consolidation diplomacy with regard to Aceh, Myanmar, Timor-Leste, Mindanao and the Malacca Strait. Economically, Japan and ASEAN put firm support behind the Chiang Mai initiative to deal with the financial crisis and the development of the Mekong subregion. Culturally, through the multilateral cultural mission, Japan and ASEAN were able to strengthen their basic framework, incorporating interaction at the people-to-people level. This attests to the fact that MOFA's institutionalized ideas were upgraded at critical junctures in 1987 and 1997 and have persisted at the core of Japan-ASEAN relations, although METI's open regionalism and MOFA's Asia-first orientation have come to surface as rival ideas.

The most significant development was the birth of a new regionalism in East Asia, which was long regarded as an arid region. East Asian regionalism could not have been realized without the vibrant Japan-ASEAN partnership, constituted by Japan as an ideational facilitator and ASEAN as the driver. This unique experience of a successful new regionalism in East Asia could illuminate the possibility of regional governance by developing countries.

Notes

1. This chapter is largely based on Sueo Sudo, "Japan's ASEAN Policy: Reactive or Proactive in the Face of a Rising China in East Asia?" *Asian Perspective* 33, no. 1 (2009): 137–58.

2. On ASEAN's 30ᵗʰ anniversary, see Hussin Mutalib, "At Thirty, ASEAN Looks to Challenges in the New Millennium", *Contemporary Southeast Asia* 19, no. 1 (June 1997): 74–85; Jorn Dosch and Manfred Mols, "Thirty Years of ASEAN: Achievements and Challenges", *Pacific Review* 11, no. 2 (1998): 167–82; Kusuma Sumitwongse, "Thirty Years of ASEAN: Achievements through Political Cooperation", *Pacific Review* 11, no. 2 (1998): 183–94.

3. ASEAN, "Press Statement of the 2nd ASEAN Informal Meeting of Heads of State/Government of the Member States of ASEAN, Kuala Lumpur, Malaysia, 15 December 1997" (Jakarta: ASEAN Secretariat 1997).

4. *New Straits Times*, 16 December 1997; *Nihon Keizai Shimbun*, 17 December 1997.

5. Mutalib, "At Thirty", pp. 81–84.

6. Ryutaro Hashimoto, *Reforms for the New Era of Japan and ASEAN: For a Broader and Deeper Partnership* (Singapore: Institute of Southeast Asian Studies, 1997). It should be noted that Gaimusho (Ministry of Foreign Affairs, Japan) deemed the speech as a doctrine for the first time. See *Gaiko seisho*, 1998, vol. 1, p. 112.

7. ASEAN, "Joint Statement of the Meeting of Heads of State/Government of the Member States of ASEAN and the Prime Ministers of Japan, Kuala Lumpur, 16 December 1997" (Jakarta: ASEAN Secretariat, 1997). See also Gaimusho, "ASEAN tono shunoukaigi: gaiyo to hyoka, December 1997", copies of documents obtained through Freedom of Information Act, Diplomatic Record Office (Tokyo: Ministry of Foreign Affairs, 1997), for Gaimusho's evaluation of the Hashimoto Doctrine.

8. *Bangkok Post*, 20 September 1997.

9. Sueo Sudo, *Evolution of ASEAN-Japan Relations* (Singapore: Institute of Southeast Asian Studies, 2005), pp. 36–37.

10. *Mainichi Shimbun*, 11 January 2000.

11. *Asahi Shimbun*, 13 January 2000.

12. Gaimusho, "Overview and Evaluation of Prime Minister Keizo Obuchi's Visit to Cambodia, Laos, and Thailand, January 2000" (Tokyo: Ministry of Foreign Affairs, 2000).

13. *Yomiuri Shimbun*, 15 January 2002.

14. Junichiro Koizumi, *Japan and ASEAN in East Asia: A Sincere and Open Partnership* (Singapore: Institute of Southeast Asian Studies, 2002).

15. Gaimusho, "ASEAN-Japan Commemorative Summit (Evaluation), December 2003" (Tokyo: Ministry of Foreign Affairs, 2003).

16. Julie Gilson, "Japan's Role in the Asia-Europe Meeting", *Asian Survey* 39, no. 5 (September/October 1999): 736–52.

17. Gaimusho, "Prime Minister Obuchi's Four Initiatives for Japan-ASEAN Cooperation toward the 21ˢᵗ Century, December 1998" (Tokyo: Ministry of Foreign Affairs, 1998). It should be noted here that the Obuchi initiatives were to upgrade Japan's assistance required by the ASEAN Vision 2020.

18. ASEAN, "Press Release of the Chairman on the ASEAN+1 Summit Meetings between the Heads of State/Government of ASEAN and China, Japan and the Republic of Korea, Manila, 28 November 1999" (Jakarta: ASEAN Secretariat, 1999).

19. Gaimusho, "Summary of the ASEAN+1 (Japan) Summit Meeting, 25 November 2000" (Tokyo: Ministry of Foreign Affairs, 2000).

20. ASEAN, "Press Statement by the Chairman of the 7th ASEAN Summit and the Three ASEAN+1 Summits, Brunei Darussalam, 6 November 2001" (Jakarta: ASEAN Secretariat, 2001). ASEAN adopted the IAI in February 2001 in order to realize an economic integration by resolving a growing development gap.

21. Gaimusho, "Joint Declaration of the Leaders of Japan and ASEAN on the Comprehensive Economic Partnership" (Tokyo: Ministry of Foreign Affairs, 5 November 2002) <http://www.mofa.go.jp/region/asia-paci/asean/pmv0211/joint.html>.

22. For Japan-China leadership competition, see especially Won Lai Foon, "China-ASEAN and Japan-ASEAN Relations during the Post-Cold War Era", *Chinese Journal of International Politics* 1, no. 3 (Summer 2007): 373–404.

23. ASEAN, "Press Statement by the Chairperson of the ASEAN+China Summit, the ASEAN+Japan Summit, the ASEAN+Republic of Korea Summit, the ASEAN+India Summit, Bali, October 8, 2003" (Jakarta: ASEAN Secretariat, 2003).

24. ASEAN, "Chairman's Statement of the 8th ASEAN+Japan Summit, Vientiane, 30 November 2004" (Jakarta: ASEAN Secretariat, 2004).

25. ASEAN, "Joint Statement of the Ninth ASEAN-Japan Summit, Kuala Lumpur, 13 December 2005" (Jakarta: ASEAN Secretariat, 2005).

26. Julie Gilson, "Building Peace or Following the Leader? Japan's Peace Consolidation Diplomacy", *Pacific Affairs* 80, no. 1 (Spring 2007): 27–47.

27. *Asahi Shimbun*, 20 July 1997; *Yomiuri Shimbun*, 27 July 1997; *Asahi Shimbun*, 21 January 1998.

28. *Mainichi Shimbun*, 8 November 1997 and 3 March 1998.

29. Interview with a Cambodian Foreign Ministry official, 3 June 1998. See also *Nihon Keizai Shimbun*, 31 March 1998.

30. *Mainichi Shimbun*, 1 August 1998.

31. *Kokusai Kyoryoku Puraza*, May 1999, pp. 8–9.

32. Suppakarn Pongyelar, "The Implications of Japanese Engagement Policy towards Myanmar: 1988–Present", GSID Discussion Paper (Nagoya: Nagoya University, 2007).

33. Gaimusho, "Japan's Position Regarding the Situation in Myanmar, March 1997" (Tokyo: Ministry of Foreign Affairs, 1997).

34. Ian Holliday, "Japan and the Myanmar Stalemate: Regional Power and Resolution of a Regional Problem", *Japanese Journal of Political Science* 6, no. 3 (December 2005): 403–4.

35. Oishi Mikio and Fumitaka Furuoka, "Can Japanese Aid be an Effective Tool of Influence? Case Studies of Cambodia and Burma", *Asian Survey* 43, no. 6 (November/December 2003): 890–907.

36. Toshihiro Kudo, "Myanmar and Japan: How Close Friends Become Estranged", IDE Discussion Paper no. 118 (Chiba: Institute of Developing Economies, 2007), p.13.

37. Paulo Gorjao, "Japan's Foreign Policy and East Timor, 1975–2002", *Asian Survey* 42, no. 5 (September/October 2002): 754–71.

38. ASEAN Secretary-General, Surin Pitsuwan disclosed this information at the International Conference on the Fukuda Doctrine in Singapore, 3 November 2007.

39. Geoffrey Gunn, "Japan, Postcrisis Indonesia, and the Japanese Role in East Timor Development", in *Transglobal Economies and Cultures: Contemporary Japan and Southeast Asia*, edited by Rolando Tolentino, Ong Jin Hui and Hing Ai Yun (Manila: University of the Philippines Press, 2004), pp. 35–51.

40. Gaimusho, "The Preparatory Conference on Peace and Reconstruction in Aceh, 3 December 2002" (Tokyo: Ministry of Foreign Affairs, 2002).

41. See Rosalie Hall, "Civil-Military Cooperation in International Disaster Response: The Japanese Self-Defense Forces' deployment in Aceh, Indonesia", *Korean Journal of Defense Analysis* 20, no. 4 (December 2008): 383–400.

42. Gaimusho, *Diplomatic Bluebook 2003* (Tokyo: Ministry of Foreign Affairs, 2003), p. 44.

43. Gaimusho, "Japan Takes A More Active Role in the Mindanao Peace Process (Dispatch of Japanese Personnel to the International Monitoring Team), July 23, 2006" (Tokyo: Ministry of Foreign Affairs, 2006).

44. Gaimusho, "ASEAN-Japan Joint Declaration for Cooperation in the Fight against International Terrorism, November 2004" (Tokyo: Ministry of Foreign Affairs, 2004).

45. Gaimusho, "Co-Chair's Summary of Discussions and Recommendations, ASEAN-Japan Counter Terrorism Dialogue, 28–29 June 2006" (Tokyo: Ministry of Foreign Affairs, 2006).

46. David Fouse and Yoichiro Sato, "Enhancing Basic Governance: Japan's Comprehensive Counterterrorism Assistance to Southeast Asia" (Asia-Pacific Center for Security Studies, the United State Department of Defense, 2006).

47. John Bradford, "Japanese Anti-Piracy Initiatives in Southeast Asia", *Contemporary Southeast Asia* 26, no. 3 (December 2004): 480–505; Greg Chaikin, "Piracy in Asia: International Co-operation and Japan's Role", in *Piracy in Southeast Asia: Status, Issues, and Responses*, edited by Derek Johnson and Mark Valencia (Singapore: Institute of Southeast Asian Studies, 2005), pp. 122–42.

48. Gaimusho, "Kaizoku mondai no genjo, April 2001" (Tokyo: Ministry of Foreign Affairs, 2001).

49. Gaimusho, "Japan's Efforts to Combat Piracy and Armed Robbery against Ships, November 2001" (Tokyo: Ministry of Foreign Affairs, 2001).

50. It is said that Indonesia and Malaysia refused to join because of the decision to locate the Information Sharing Center in Singapore. See Noel Morada, "Institutionalization of Regional Order: Between Norms and Balance of Power", in *Regional Order in East Asia: ASEAN and Japan Perspectives*, edited by Jun Tsunekawa (Tokyo: National Institute of Defense Studies, 2007), pp. 37–38.

51. Yoichiro Sato, "Southeast Asian Receptiveness to Japanese Maritime Security Cooperation" (Asia-Pacific Center for Security Studies, the United State Department of Defense, 2007).

52. ASEAN, "External Trade Statistics, 2007" (Jakarta: ASEAN Secretariat, 2007).

53. Gaimusho, *Japan's ODA* (Tokyo: Ministry of Foreign Affairs, 2007).

54. For Japan's Indochina policy, see Gaimusho, "A New Dimension in Cooperation" (Tokyo: Ministry of Foreign Affairs) <http://www.mofa.go.jp/region/asia-paci/asean/relation/dimens.html.>.

55. Gaimusho, "Japan's Cooperation for the Mekong Subregion Development, November 2001" (Tokyo: Ministry of Foreign Affairs, 2001).

56. Masaya Shiraishi, "Mekon saburijon no jikken", in *Aratana chiikikeisei*, edited by Takehiko Yamamoto and Satoshi Amako (Tokyo: Iwanamishoten, 2007), pp. 67–92.

57. Gaimusho, "Japan's Cooperation to Initiative for ASEAN Integration (IAI), November 2001" (Tokyo: Ministry of Foreign Affairs, 2001).

58. On the Chiang Mai Initiative in 2000, see William Grimes, *Currency and Contest in East Asia: The Great Power Politics of Financial Regionalism* (Ithaca, NY: Cornell University Press, 2009), chap. 3.

59. Precise accounts for the abortive AMF can be found in Shigeko Hayashi, *Japan and East Asian Monetary Regionalism: Towards a Proactive Leadership* (London: Routledge, 2006) and Yong Wook Lee, *The Japanese Challenge to the American Neoliberal World* (Stanford: Stanford University Press, 2008). China's minimalist and passive role can be found in Hyoung-kyu Chey, "The Changing Political Dynamics of East Asian Financial Cooperation: The Chiang Mai Initiative", *Asian Survey* 49, no. 3 (May/June 2009): 450–67.

60. *Asahi Shimbun*, 22 October 1997; *Far Eastern Economic Review*, 27 November 1997.

61. *Nihon Keizai Shimbun*, 20 November 1997.

62. Saori Katada, "Japan's Counterweight Strategy: U.S.-Japan Cooperation and Competition in International Finance", in *Beyond Bilateralism: U.S.-Japan Relations in the New Asia-Pacific*, edited by Ellis Krauss and T.J. Pempel (Stanford: Stanford University Press, 2004), p. 186.

63. *Asahi Shimbun*, 21 December 1997.

64. *Japan Times*, 2 March 1998.

65. *Japan Times*, 5 October 1998.

66. Christopher Dent, *East Asian Regionalism* (London: Routledge, 2008), p. 156.

67. ASEAN, "The Joint Ministerial Statement of the ASEAN+3 Finance Ministers Meeting, Chiang Mai, Thailand, 6 May 2000" (Jakarta: ASEAN Secretariat, 2000).

68. Hidetaka Yoshimatsu, "Japan and Regional Governance in East Asia", in *Governance and Regionalism in Asia*, London: edited by Nicholas Thomas (Routledge, 2009), p. 72. See also Takashi Kiuchi, "The Future of ASEAN-Japan Financial Relations", in *ASEAN-Japan Cooperation* (Tokyo: Japan Center for International Exchange, 2003), pp. 108–24.

69. See especially Naoko Munakata, *Transforming East Asia: The Evolution of Regional Economic Integration* (Washington, DC: Brookings Institution Press, 2006).

70. Concerning the Nikai initiative, see Ministry of Economy, Trade and Industry, "Global Economic Strategy, April 2006" (Tokyo: Ministry of Economy, Trade and Industry, 2006). METI's rushing of the proposal without consulting the concerned ministries caused apprehension in Japan. *Asahi Shimbun*, 28 July 2006.

71. *Yomiuri Shimbun*, 24 August 2006; *Nihon Keizai Shimbun*, 12 November 2006. The so-called Nikai shock is said to have compelled the United States to push for the Asia-Pacific FTA.

72. ASEAN, "Joint Media Statement of the Thirteenth Consultations between the ASEAN Economic Ministers and the Minister of Economy, Trade and Industry of Japan (AEM-METI), Kuala Lumpur, 23 August 2006" (Jakarta: ASEAN Secretariat, 2006).

73. Jun Wada, "Higashiajia niokeru Nihon no kokusaibunkakoryu to bunkagaiko", in *Nihon no Higashiajia koso*, edited by Yoshihide Soeya and Masayuki Tadokoro (Tokyo: Keio gijuku daigaku shuppankai, 2004), pp. 59–109. For the Cultural Mission, see Tamotsu Aoki, "Imakoso takokukan bunkagaiko wo", *Chuo koron* (August 1998): 52–64.

74. On the Action Agenda, see Gaimusho, "ASEAN-Japan Multinational Cultural Mission's Action Agenda, 17 April 1998" (Tokyo: Ministry of Foreign Affairs, 1998).

75. Tadashi Yamamoto and Carolina Hernandez, "Social and Cultural Dimensions in East Asian Community Building", in *ASEAN-Japan Cooperation: A Foundation for East Asian Community* (Tokyo: Japan Centre for International Exchange, 2003), p. 172. For improved perceptions of Japan, see Bhubhindar Singh, "ASEAN's Perceptions of Japan: Change and Continuity", *Asian Survey* 42, no. 2 (March/April 2002): 276–96.

76. ASEAN, "Third Executive Report Progress of Implementation of the ASEAN-

196   Japan's ASEAN Policy

Japan Plan of Action" (Jakarta: ASEAN Secretariat, 2007) <http://www.aseansec.org/20462.htm>.

77. Regarding Japan's role in East Asia, see Eric Teo Chu Cheow, "Japan's Twin Challenges: Dealing with an ASEAN at the Crossroads and East Asian Regionalism", *Asia-Pacific Review* 10, no. 1 (May 2003): 30–43; Yeo Lay Hwee, "Japan, ASEAN, and the Construction of an East Asian Community", *Contemporary Southeast Asia* 28, no. 2 (August 2006): 259–75.

78. Lee Hsien Loong "Japan's Role in Southeast Asia", speech by Deputy Prime Minister of Singapore at the Japan Institute of International Affairs, Tokyo, 25 May 1999.

79. ASEAN, "Joint Statement on East Asia Cooperation, 28 November 1999" (Jakarta: ASEAN Secretariat, 1999).

80. Thus, given the longer history of Japan-ASEAN relations, it is China not Japan that is catching up. See, for instance, Brad Glosserman, "Japan-ASEAN Summit: Playing Catch Up with China?" *PacNet*, no. 52 (18 December 2003) and Bronson Percival, "Japan-Southeast Asian Relations: Playing Catch-Up with China", *Contemporary Connections* 8, no. 3 (13 October 2006). See also Injoo Sohn, "Learning to Co-Operation: China's Multilateral Approach to Asian Financial Co-Operation", *China Quarterly*, no. 194 (June 2008): 309–26 for China's learning process to be a reliable partner in East Asia.

81. See especially Evelyn Goh, ed., *Betwixt and Between: Southeast Asian Strategic Relations with the United States and China* (Singapore: Institute of Strategic and Defense Studies, 2005).

82. Gaimusho, "Japan's Co-operation to ASEAN (Japan's New Initiatives), 12 December 2003" (Tokyo: Ministry of Foreign Affairs, 2003).

83. ASEAN, "Joint Statement of the Ninth ASEAN-Japan Summit, Kuala Lumpur, 13 December 2005" (Jakarta: ASEAN Secretariat, 2005). Obviously ASEAN's and Japan's soft-balancing strategy against China is a founding factor. See especially Evelyn Goh, "Great Powers and Hierarchical Order in Southeast Asia", International Security 32, no. 3 (Winter 2007/08): 113–57 and Shotaro Yachi, *Gaiko no senryaku to kokorozashi* (Tokyo: Sankei shimbun shuppan, 2009): 146–47.

84. Gaimusho, "Japan-Indonesia Joint Statement: Strategic Partnership for Peaceful and Prosperous Future, 28 November 2006" (Tokyo: Ministry of Foreign Affairs, 2006).

85. Takaaki Kojima, *Japan and ASEAN: Partnership for a Stable and Prosperous Future* (Singapore: Institute of Southeast Asian Studies, 2006), p. 23.

86. Gaimusho, "Tokyo Declaration for the Dynamic and Enduring Japan-ASEAN Partnership in the New Millennium" (Tokyo: Ministry of Foreign Affairs, 2003) <http://www.mofa.go.jp/region/asia-paci/asean/year2003/summit/tokyo_dec.pdf>.

87. Gaimusho, "The Japan-ASEAN Plan of Action" (Tokyo: Ministry of Foreign Affairs, 2003) <http://www.mofa.go.jp/region/asia-paci/asean/year2003/summit/action.pdf.>.

88. ASEAN, "Third Executive Report Progress of Implementation of the ASEAN-Japan Plan of Action" (Jakarta: ASEAN Secretariat, 2007) <http://www.aseansec.org/20462.htm>.

89. See especially Richard Stubbs, "ASEAN Plus Three: Emerging East Asian Regionalism?" *Asian Survey* 42, no. 3 (2002): 440–55; Douglas Webber, "Two Funerals and a Wedding? The Ups and Downs of Regionalism in East Asia and Asia Pacific after the Asian Crisis", in *Comparative Regional Integration*, edited by Finn Laursen (Aldershot: Ashgate, 2003), pp. 125–57.

90. ASEAN, "Joint Statement on East Asia Cooperation, 28 November 1999" (Jakarta: ASEAN Secretariat, 1999); *Bangkok Post*, 29 November 1999.

91. *Nihon Keizai Shimbun*, 26 November 2000.

92. Gaimusho, "Towards an East Asian Community: Region of Peace, Prosperity and Progress, East Asia Vision Group Report 2001" (Tokyo: Ministry of Foreign Affairs, 2001) <http://www.mofa.go.jp/region/asia-paci/report2001.pdf.>.

93. ASEAN, "Press Statement by the Chairman of the 8th ASEAN Summit, the 6th ASEAN+3 Summit and ASEAN-China Summit, Phnom Penh, 4 November 2002" (Jakarta: ASEAN Secretariat, 2002).

94. ASEAN, "The Final Report of the East Asia Study Group, 4 November 2002" (Jakarta: ASEAN Secretariat, 2002).

95. ASEAN, "Press Statement of the Chairperson of the ASEAN+ China Summit, the ASEAN+ Japan Summit, the ASEAN + Republic of Korea Summit and the ASEAN + India Summit, Bali, Indonesia, 8 October 2003" (Jakarta: ASEAN Secretariat, 2003).

96. ASEAN, "Declaration of ASEAN Concord II, Bali, Indonesia, 7–8 October 2003" (Jakarta: ASEAN Secretariat, 2003). These three pillars synchronize with Japan's basic postures towards ASEAN since 1977.

97. ASEAN, "Chairman's Statement of the 8th ASEAN+3 Summit, 'Strengthening ASEAN+3 Cooperation', Vientiane, 29 November 2004" (Jakarta: ASEAN Secretariat, 2004). The critical role of Malaysia can be found in Chandran Jeshurun, *Malaysia: Fifty Years of Diplomacy, 1957–2007* (Kuala Lumpur: The Other Press, 2007), pp. 333–36.

98. *Straits Times*, 12 April 2005. For institutional balancing, see especially Kai He, *Institutional Balancing in the Asia Pacific* (London: Routledge, 2009), pp. 104–9.

99. Gaimusho, "Issue Papers prepared by the Government of Japan, 25 June 2004" (Tokyo: Ministry of Foreign Affairs, 2004).

100. ASEAN, "Kuala Lumpur Declaration on the East Asia Summit, Kuala Lumpur, 12 December 2005" (Jakarta: ASEAN Secretariat, 2005). Regarding Gaimusho's

intention to create a new institution in East Asia, see especially Hitoshi Tanaka, *Gaiko no chikara* (Tokyo: Nihon keizai shimbun shuppansha, 2009), pp. 162–69. Former Vice-Minister Yachi tried to persuade the United States to attend the EAS in 2005 but Washington refused to join. See Yachi, *Gaiko no senryaku*, p. 147.

101. See especially, Masayuki Tadokoro, "Nihon gaiko no zasetsu kara manabubekikoto", *Ronza*, November 2005, pp. 156–63.

102. Tang Siew-Mun, "Japan's Vision of an East Asian Community", *Japanese Studies* 26, no. 2 (September 2006): 209.

103. Takashi Shiraishi, "Higashiajia kyodotai: ASEAN jikuni tenkai", *Yomiuri Shimbun*, 4 September 2005.

104. For a different interpretation, see Anthony Smith, "Japan's Relations with Southeast Asia: The Strong Silent Type", in *Japan in a Dynamic Asia*, edited by Yoichiro Sato and Satu Limaye (Lanham, MD: Lexington Books, 2006), pp. 179–98.

6

TOWARDS A NEW
REGIONALISM IN EAST ASIA

International relations in Southeast Asia in the twenty-first century began to reflect a new phase, most notably in 2003, when the Association of Southeast Asian Nations (ASEAN) embarked on community building. Furthermore, ASEAN's extra-regional efforts resulted in the establishment of the East Asia Summit (EAS) in 2005. It was ASEAN's political will that indeed continued to be the hub of East Asian cooperation. Most significantly, in August 2007, the heads of member states signed the historic ASEAN Charter. With the strong foundation established by the charter, ASEAN is expected to manage the key challenges of regional integration, globalization and economic growth.

After several years of political instability, Japan also entered a new phase in domestic politics in 2009. The ruling Liberal Democratic Party (LDP) was doomed by its intraparty problems, especially after the Koizumi administration. The LDP changed its chairman three times, thereby appointing three prime ministers, within a period of three years, suggesting the need for a fundamental change in Japanese politics. Most importantly, the Japanese voters became disillusioned by a series of ineffectual prime ministers. The September 2009 general elections saw the Democratic Party of Japan (DPJ) come to power, ending the long-term political monopoly of the LDP. Adopting an alternative strategy, Prime Minister Yukio Hatoyama advocated the creation of an East Asian Community based on the political philosophy of "fraternity", although due to strained relations with the United States over military bases in Okinawa he was not able to pursue this for more than a year. Prime Minister Naoto Kan also announced Japan's new development strategy, which made East Asia one of the main target areas of foreign policy.

Thus, beginning in 2007, Japan-ASEAN relations have entered a new phase. The focus is on a new regionalism in East Asia where advanced countries and developing countries are required to act and work together to improve regional cooperation and integration. Whether a new ASEAN and a new Japan under the DPJ continue to serve as a hub of East Asian regionalism remains to be seen. In this last chapter, ASEAN's renowned quest for three-pillared community building and Japan's upgraded contributions to East Asian regionalism through sustainable Japan-ASEAN partnership will be explored.

THE CRITICAL YEAR 2007

ASEAN at 40

In the midst of turbulent globalization, ASEAN held the twelfth and thirteenth summits in Cebu, the Philippines and Singapore respectively in 2007. The Twelfth ASEAN Summit, held on 13 January, produced substantive outcomes that could generate momentum in ASEAN's community-building efforts. Most notably, ten ASEAN leaders agreed to shorten the target date for the establishment of an ASEAN Community from 2020 to 2015.[1] They expressed their intention to sign the ASEAN Charter, and several declarations were proposed to further strengthen political/security, economic and socio-cultural cooperation in the region. These included the Cebu Declaration Towards One Caring and Sharing Community, the ASEAN Convention on Counter Terrorism, the ASEAN Declaration on the Protection and Promotion of the Rights of Migrant Workers, and the ASEAN Commitment on HIV and AIDS.

Following suit, the Thirteenth ASEAN Summit, held on 20 November 2007 in Singapore, yielded milestone outcomes that could strengthen ASEAN's community-building efforts. Foremost among these was the signing of the long-awaited ASEAN Charter, which represented ASEAN's common vision and commitment to the development of an ASEAN Community with lasting peace, stability, sustained economic growth, shared prosperity and social progress.[2] The belief is that should the charter be carried out effectively, then it would result in a reinvigorated ASEAN. The charter, while compromised at best, reaffirms the essence of the ASEAN way, such as the principles of non-interference and consensus-based decision-making. While rejecting most of the controversial proposals by the Eminent Persons Group, ASEAN decided to institutionalize a human rights body. In a similar vein, through the Declaration on the ASEAN Economic Community (AEC) Blueprint, ASEAN leaders emphasized the importance of equitable economic development, the reduction of poverty and socio-economic disparities and urged that the benefits of economic integration be quickly available to all peoples of ASEAN through timely implementation of the provisions of the blueprint. To complement the AEC Blueprint, ASEAN also mandated the development of blueprints for the ASEAN Political Security Community and the ASEAN Socio-Cultural Community.

Having a charter is not in fact a new idea for ASEAN. Back in the early 1970s, the five founding member countries (Indonesia, Malaysia, the Philippines, Singapore and Thailand) did consider the possibility of developing some form of a constitutional document to formalize the establishment of ASEAN. This was in recognition of the fact that ASEAN was created out of a political rather than a legal document with the ASEAN Declaration that was signed in Bangkok on 8 August 1967. However, the discussions in the early 1970s did not result in a constitution. Now, as the association approaches its fortieth year, the ASEAN Charter is about to become a reality, since the charter is drafted in the form of a treaty, which requires ratification from all signatory states before it can enter into force. Most significantly, serving as the constitution of ASEAN, the charter formalizes the establishment of ASEAN as a fully fledged inter-governmental organization, moving it from its current state as a loosely organized regional entity.[3]

Needless to say, the fortieth anniversary of ASEAN saw some achievements and challenges. To begin with, ASEAN has achieved political cohesion on some regional and international issues. It has helped keep the peace among its members. It has adopted norms for interstate relations and managed to get others to accede to those norms. It has healed the divisions in Southeast Asia. Most of all, it has served as the core of regionalism in East Asia and the Asia-Pacific. However, ASEAN has fallen short of the ambitions that it has proclaimed for itself, particularly in terms of regional economic integration and regional identity.[4]

Japan's Belated Response

In May 2006 the reappraisal of the so-called Fukuda Doctrine suddenly came to the fore. The timing was doubly important. For one thing, Japanese foreign policy under the government of Junichiro Koizumi needed a fresh new start in its East Asian relations. On the other hand, the year 2007 marked the thirtieth anniversary of the Fukuda Doctrine as well as ASEAN's fortieth anniversary. As one newspaper editorial explained:

> Former Chief Cabinet Secretary Yasuo Fukuda finally indicated his intention to run in the party presidential race to select Koizumi's successor. Fukuda is driven by frustration about the Koizumi administration's disastrous performance in diplomacy with China and South Korea. While suggesting his disapproval of Koizumi's visits to Yasukuni Shrine, which have strained Japan's ties with its Asian neighbors, Fukuda referred to his father's diplomatic principles known as the Fukuda Doctrine.[5]

At the critical juncture, LDP's leader switched from Koizumi to a young promising leader, Shinzo Abe, with the main purpose of winning the forthcoming election. After forming his cabinet, Prime Minister Abe undertook a partial ASEAN tour, visiting only Malaysia and Indonesia in August 2007. In Indonesia, Abe delivered a policy speech, entitled "Japan and One ASEAN that Care and Share at the Heart of Dynamic Asia" in which he stressed three policies towards ASEAN: realization of the Economic Partnership Agreement; promotion of the Mekong region; and assistance in peace building. Furthermore, without referring to the Fukuda Doctrine, Abe underscored the importance of a closer relationship: "I mentioned earlier that ASEAN and Japan want to maintain and further nurture their 'care and share' relationship. ASEAN will, over the coming decade, be working to undergo a fundamental transformation. It aims at creating a community by 2015, and it will be critical that ASEAN continue[s] to sit in the driver's seat in the East Asia Summit and other regional cooperation frameworks that are expanding and overlapping, being both the hub and the driving force of East Asian cooperation. The development of ASEAN is therefore in and of itself in the interests of Asia and the interests of Japan. I am pleased to be able to take this opportunity to tell you that to advance these interests, in the years ahead Japan will continue to be unsparing in providing help."[6]

After one year, however, Abe suddenly gave up his premiership to the chagrin of many. When Yasuo Fukuda became the prime minister in September 2007, a Malaysian newspaper ran an article insinuating a change in Japan's ASEAN policy:

> With its adoption of a comprehensive approach to Southeast Asia instead of a primarily economic approach, the Fukuda Doctrine was widely perceived as marking a high point in Japanese relations with ASEAN. Whether Yasuo Fukuda can go beyond just countering China in Japanese relations with ASEAN and come out with something resembling his father's doctrine remains to be seen.[7]

Given the limited time and the lack of preparation, it was not conducive for Japan to announce a major policy doctrine. Nevertheless, in May 2008 Prime Minister Fukuda announced a "New Fukuda Doctrine" in which he highlighted the importance of Southeast Asia to Japan. He was taking a page from the historical Fukuda Doctrine articulated in 1977 by his father, the late Takeo Fukuda. Fukuda's speech entitled "When the Pacific Ocean Becomes an Inland Sea" was delivered at an international conference on the Future of Asia, organized by the *Nihon Keizai Shimbun* on 22 May. Comparing the Pacific Ocean to a vast inland sea, Fukuda appealed to attendees to work over the next thirty years to build a close network of nations in the Asia-Pacific region. In the speech, Fukuda discussed a policy proposal entitled the "Five Pledges to a Future Asia that Acts Together" in which he demonstrated a shared awareness of the issues and a spirit of cooperation with ASEAN. He pledged in this regard to support the creation of the ASEAN Community, to establish a Permanent Representative of Japan to ASEAN, and to cooperate in efforts to eliminate economic inequality in the region. Furthermore, with cooperation in the area of nontraditional security in mind, Fukuda proposed the creation of a system of "Disaster Management and Infectious Disease Control in Asia", which would aim to link emergency relief agencies in Asia into a network to support "diplomacy for disaster management cooperation" and provide effective responses to the problem of avian flu.[8]

Unlike the previous three doctrines of 1977, 1987 and 1997, however, the timing and place were not properly chosen. In particular, in not paying an official visit to the region, Fukuda's new doctrine was unconvincing to

ASEAN leaders, as post-Koizumi Japanese politics was not auguring well for conducting consistent foreign policy.[9] Accordingly, it was not surprising that the new Prime Minister was unable to undertake any top-level official visit to ASEAN.

THE POLITICAL PILLAR OF JAPAN-ASEAN RELATIONS

Simply due to its successively short-lived premiership, post-Koizumi LDP leadership was doomed and the change of the ruling party was expected to turn the tide. The new governments under Yukio Hatoyama and Naoto Kan, however, lasted less than a year due to mounting domestic and external problems, failure in the 2010 upper house elections and natural disasters in 2011. Nevertheless, synchronizing with ASEAN's three-pillars of community building, close political, economic and cultural relations have been maintained through the institutionalized framework, including summit meetings via ASEAN Plus Three (APT), the Foreign Ministers' Meeting, Economic Ministers' Meeting and the Japan-ASEAN Forum.[10]

Japan-ASEAN Summit

Although Japan has not been able to pay any top-level official visits to the region, Japan-ASEAN summit meetings take place almost every year, thanks to the APT summit meetings. After a one-year's absence, the tenth summit meeting in January 2007 was held in Cebu. The joint statement acknowledged the overall progress in the Plan of Action to implement the Declaration for the Dynamic and Enduring ASEAN-Japan Partnership in

TABLE 6.1
Japan-ASEAN Relations, 2007–11

	PM visit	Summit*	FMM	Forum	EMM	Finance
2007	Abe	12th, 13th	30th	23rd	14th	10th
2008			31st	24th	15th	11th
2009		14th	32nd	25th		12th
2010		15th	33rd	26th	16th	13th
2011		16th	34th	27th	17th	14th

Note: *ASEAN officially regards the 1997 summit as the first ASEAN-Japan summit. Accordingly, the 12th summit is counted as 10th.

the New Millennium adopted in Tokyo in December 2003 on the occasion of the thirtieth anniversary of Japan-ASEAN relations.[11] Both Japan and ASEAN acknowledged the establishment in March 2006 of the Japan-ASEAN Integration Fund (JAIF), Japan's fresh grant of $52 million to help bridge the development gap in ASEAN through the promotion of the Japan-ASEAN Comprehensive Economic Partnership (JACEP), Japan's assistance to the development of the Mekong region as well as the new initiative to expand its official development assistance (ODA) to the Mekong region for the next three years, and Japan's large-scale youth exchange initiative totaling $315 million over the next five years, which would include the invitation to 6,000 young people annually from ASEAN and other EAS member countries to Japan.

The eleventh meeting was held in November 2007. Both Japan and ASEAN reiterated the importance of the longstanding friendship between the two and reaffirmed the importance of the strategic partnership which has contributed to peace, stability and prosperity in the region. It was noted that 2007 marked the thirtieth Anniversary of the Fukuda Doctrine, which enshrines Japan's policy of a "heart-to-heart" relationship with ASEAN on the basis of an equal partnership. The joint statement underscored the steady progress made in the Plan of Action to implement the Declaration for the Dynamic and Enduring Japan-ASEAN Partnership in the New Millennium. Specifically, a joint statement was issued that welcomed the successful conclusion of the negotiations on the JACEP Agreement and the establishment of the Economic Research Institute of ASEAN and East Asia (ERIA), established to provide an intellectual foundation for the exchange of ideas and recommendations to further regional integration and strengthen partnerships between ASEAN and Japan.[12]

In November 2009, newly elected Prime Minister Hatoyama attended the Twelfth Japan-ASEAN Summit and explained Japan's Asian policy under the new government. At the summit meeting, Japan reaffirmed its continued commitment to help narrow the development gaps in ASEAN through various sub-regional development endeavours. Since the Japan East-Asia Network of Exchange for Students and Youths (JENESYS) Program commenced in 2007, some 5,600 ASEAN youth have visited Japan to promote mutual understanding of ASEAN and Japan. From 2009, Japanese students have been dispatched to visit ASEAN countries for the same purpose. Most importantly, the report of the ASEAN-Japan Eminent Persons Group submitted at the summit provided a set of action-oriented recommendations to strengthen the strategic partnership to achieve regional peace, stability and prosperity. The recommendations primarily address three critical concerns: (1) accelerating implementation of key activities in the existing ASEAN-Japan plan of action, (2) identifying priority activities to support implementation of the three pillars of the ASEAN Community, and (3) promoting new areas of cooperation.[13]

The Thirteenth Japan-ASEAN Summit was held on 29 October 2010 in Hanoi, Vietnam. The ASEAN leaders committed to strengthening a coordination and cooperation mechanism in Jakarta through the Committee of Permanent Representatives–Japan process. They stressed the importance of maintaining the JAIF to secure funding for the implementation of the ASEAN-Japan cooperative activities. Of note, ASEAN leaders welcomed Japan's support for ASEAN integration and narrowing the development gap based on the Japan-ASEAN Strategic Partnership, including Japan's contribution to the JAIF, the implementation of Japan's initiative to strengthen Asia's growth potential, and Japan's proposal to further promote "Japan-ASEAN Partnership for New Growth in Asia", through supporting the implementation of the Roadmap for an ASEAN Community 2009–15. Prime Minister Kan announced his keen intention to support ASEAN connectivity and promised to formulate a new declaration and a new plan of action.[14]

In November 2011 Japan and ASEAN held the 14th summit and adopted a joint declaration while promising to provide $26 billion worth of aid for development projects to strengthen regional integration. At an hour-long summit with the ASEAN leaders on the Indonesian island of Bali, Prime Minister Yoshihiko Noda expressed his commitment to boosting cooperation with the region over maritime security and safety amid China's increasing assertiveness at sea. In the joint declaration, Japan and ASEAN mapped out five strategies to promote peace, stability and prosperity in the region that included strengthening political-security cooperation in the region, intensifying cooperation towards ASEAN community building, enhancing ASEAN-Japan connectivity for consolidating ties between ASEAN and Japan, creating together a more disaster-resilient society, and addressing together common regional and global challenges. Japan also delivered a list of thirty-three "flagship" projects, expected to be funded by Japan's ODA, the Japan Bank for International Cooperation and private sector funds, in cooperation with international institutions such as the Asian Development Bank. Japan's assistance for ASEAN is aimed at boosting "connectivity" via better infrastructure in such fields as transport across borders and simplifying customs' procedures. These efforts to improve links within the region are part of ASEAN's vision to create an economic community by 2015.[15]

Foreign Ministers' Meeting and Japan-ASEAN Forum

At the ministerial level, Japan and ASEAN foreign ministers coordinate their regional policies through the ASEAN foreign ministers' meeting and the post-ministerial conference (PMC). In July 2008, for instance, the ASEAN PMC with Japan was co-chaired by Lao Deputy Foreign Minister Thongloun Sisoulith and Japan's Foreign Minister Masahiko Komura. The meeting welcomed the "New Fukuda Doctrine", in which Japan declared that Japan and ASEAN would be "partners thinking together, acting together and sharing a future vision". In this context, the meeting looked forward to the recommendations of the Japan-ASEAN Eminent Persons Group, which would chart the future course of Japan-ASEAN relations. The meeting welcomed the ratification by Japan of the JACEP, and looked forward to its early implementation. The meeting took note of Fukuda's declaration that the next thirty years would be the "thirty years of bridging Asian development gaps". In this regard, Japan pledged to support ASEAN's community-building efforts through strong support for the Initiative for ASEAN Integration. The meeting also stressed the need for closer cooperation in promoting energy efficiency, renewable energy, food security and combating infectious diseases. The meeting welcomed Japan's announcement that it would enhance ASEAN's pandemic reaction capacity by stockpiling an additional half a million doses of antiviral medication in each of the ASEAN countries. The meeting also discussed ways to strengthen cooperation in disaster management and relief. Japan's announcement of its intention to appoint an Ambassador for ASEAN was welcomed. This was acknowledged as a clear sign of Japan's commitment to ASEAN.[16]

In July 2009 the annual Japan-ASEAN Foreign Ministers' Meeting was held. The meeting appreciated Japan's assistance to narrow the development gap and support ASEAN integration based on the Japan-ASEAN Strategic Partnership. In this connection the following points are worth mentioning: (1) Japan's initiative to promote development of the Mekong Sub-region and the East Asia Growth Area; (2) the first Japan-

Mekong Summit scheduled to be held in the same year; (3) the "Growth Initiative towards Doubling the Size of Asia's Economy" to strengthen Asia's growth potential and expand domestic demand through such measures as ODA of up to $20 billion, a new line of trade insurance for infrastructure development amounting to $20 billion, and the facilitation of an additional $22 billion trade finance for two years; (4) the role of ERIA to develop policy recommendations, including a coherent master plan for promoting sub-regional development together with other relevant institutions; (5) Japan's financial contributions of $62 million to JAIF as emergency assistance to the ASEAN member states affected by the crisis; (6) the need to exert greater efforts to expand trade and investment in the region through the JACEP agreement; (7) the importance of strengthening an ASEAN identity through people-to-people exchange among ASEAN member states as well as between ASEAN and dialogue partners; (8) the ongoing exchanges under the Japan-East Asia Network of Exchange for Students and Youths (JENESYS) Program; (9) the importance of the ASEAN-Japan Center in promoting trade, investment, and tourism, as well as in raising public awareness of ASEAN; (10) the provision of a total of 500,000 courses of antivirals in each ASEAN country to tackle avian influenza as well as influenza A; (11) the importance of building the ASEAN Community based on universal values and norms.[17]

In July 2010 the ASEAN PMC with Japan was held. The conference noted the progress in the implementation of the Plan of Action, including cooperation in such areas as the environment, climate change, disaster management, health and welfare, pandemic diseases, counterterrorism, maritime issues, energy efficiency and people-to-people contact. The following were especially noted: (1) the continuation of the Japan-ASEAN Counter Terrorism Dialogue; (2) the enhanced cooperation in science and innovation and green development, noting ASEAN's proposal for a Japan-ASEAN green development promotion centre; (3) Japan's contribution to the Japan-ASEAN Integration Fund and Japan's assistance to narrow the development gap and support ASEAN integration based on the Japan-ASEAN Strategic Partnership; (4) Japan's proposal to further promote ASEAN-Japan cooperation towards economic growth by enhancing ASEAN connectivity; (5) the efforts for the early entry into force and effective implementation of the JACEP agreement, serving as a comprehensive framework to strengthen economic ties between ASEAN and Japan; (6) the Japan-ASEAN EPG Report on concrete measures to further advance the Japan-ASEAN strategic partnership; (7) the successful convening of the

Third Mekong-Japan Foreign Ministers' Meeting and "A Decade toward the Green Mekong" Initiative.[18]

The Japan-ASEAN Foreign Ministers' Meeting was held on 26 July 2011 in Bali, Indonesia. While reviewing the Japan-ASEAN Partnership, ASEAN evaluated Japan's various forms of cooperation with ASEAN — including connectivity assistance and anti-disaster cooperation — and witnessed progress in efforts for closer regional cooperation in the area of disaster management through the provision of support to the ASEAN Coordinating Center for Humanitarian Assistance on Disaster Management (AHA Centre). Japan's policy to assist the enhancement of ASEAN connectivity and a plan to establish an "ASEAN Wide–Area Professional Education Service Network" to train middle-level managers to attact private-sector investment were also highly evaluated. Importantly, both Japan and ASEAN agreed with the planned new Joint Declaration and Plan of Action to be adopted at the next Japan-ASEAN Summit Meeting in November 2011, while proposing a plan to set up a "Disaster Management Network for ASEAN Region", a comprehensive initiative geared towards strengthening ASEAN's disaster response capabilities through such measures as the establishment of an information-sharing system and the nurturing of human resources.[19]

In a similar vein, the ASEAN PMC+1 Session with Japan reviewed and discussed the progress of the implementation of the Tokyo Declaration for the Dynamic and Enduring ASEAN-Japan Partnership in the New Millennium and its Plan of Action. The ASEAN ministers commended their officials for the progress made in drafting the ASEAN-Japan Declaration and its Plan of Action (2011–15), and looked forward to the finalization of the two documents so that they could be submitted for their consideration and adoption during the 14th ASEAN-Japan Summit in Bali, in November this year. In particular, both ministers discussed the implementation of the ASEAN-Japan Plan of Action supported by the Japan-ASEAN Integration Fund (JAIF). They noted with appreciation Japan's further expanded priority areas of cooperation in JAIF encompassing economic partnership; the environment, climate change and disaster management; counterterrorism; health and welfare; maritime security, including piracy; and people-to-people exchanges. With respect to cooperation in disaster management and emergency response, the meeting reaffirmed Japan's assistance in efforts to narrow the development gaps through capacity building within the framework of the Initiative for ASEAN Integration and Other Sub-Regional Growth Areas. The meeting further welcomed Japan's commitment to funding implementation of the Master Plan on ASEAN Connectivity and the establishment of Japan's Task Force for ASEAN Connectivity, to coordinate with the ASEAN Connectivity Coordinating Committee.[20]

At the director's level, the Japan-ASEAN Forum (JAF) continues to play a part in promoting and smoothing Japan-ASEAN relations. The twenty-sixth JAF was held in Bali in October 2010 in an effort to boost ASEAN-Japan cooperation. The agenda included the discussion on the follow-up and implementation of Japan-ASEAN cooperation and other international issues that concern both parties, including the development of the regional architecture, the Korean Peninsula, and the Middle East peace process. As a follow up to the Thirteenth Japan-ASEAN Summit in Hanoi, Japan and ASEAN discussed the new elements to include in the upcoming Tokyo Declaration on the New Japan-ASEAN Partnership for the 21st Century and the New Japan-ASEAN Plan of Action. Some of these new elements included reinforcing the foundations for cooperation in the three pillars of ASEAN and Japan's support for the Implementation of the Master Plan on ASEAN Connectivity. Besides the new programmes and initiatives proposed by the Japanese, ASEAN also welcomed the continuation of the existing programmes, including the funding programme in the framework of JAIF and the JENESYS, as the prime mover of Japan-ASEAN partnership. By utilizing the assistance and cooperation with Japan, ASEAN is expected to accelerate the process of establishing the 2015 ASEAN Community.[21]

THE ECONOMIC PILLAR OF JAPAN-ASEAN RELATIONS

In response to the challenges of globalization wrought by increasing economic integration, developmental regionalism in East Asia is on the rise. In particular, ASEAN has been actively seeking two major goals: support for the IAI and free trade agreements with non-ASEAN countries. In 2009 ASEAN decided to upgrade its IAI work plan to expedite the region's economic integration. Reviewing the first work plan (2002–8), ASEAN found it conducive to narrowing the developmental divide. In fact, according to the review, there are 258 projects in the IAI Work Plan I, at various stages of implementation. Funding has been secured for 217 projects (84 per cent), of which 186 projects have been completed, 26 projects are under implementation and 4 projects are being planned for implementation. Some 5 projects have secured partial funding, 14 are in the matching process and 22 have yet to be funded.[22] Japan has been most actively supporting the IAI (see Table 6.2).

The second goal is concerned with free trade agreements with dialogue partners as exemplified by the Japan-ASEAN Comprehensive Economic Partnership (JACEP), in which Japan pledged to strengthen its economic assistance and cooperation with ASEAN. It should be noted here that the ratified JACEP in April 2008 is distinguished from traditional FTAs in that JACEP covers not only trade in products but also services and investment. Moreover, with FTAs as an integral part, JACEP also promotes trade facilitation measures and broad cooperation, including the improvement of investment conditions and technical cooperation. Accordingly, economic integration with ASEAN has become one of the fundamental elements of Japan's trade policy in East Asia.[23] The agreement was entered into force on 1 December 2009.

Declining Presence of Japanese Economy: Trade, Investment and Aid

Nevertheless, Japan's performance in economic cooperation with ASEAN is far from commendable (see Table 6.3). For instance, although the level of

TABLE 6.2
Contributions to IAI Projects

Donors	Number of Projects	Funding by Donors (US$)	Share (%)
Japan	47	8,085,311	34.8
Republic of Korea	7	5,125,127	24.2
India	5	3,272,066	15.4
Norway	2	1,528,502	7.2
EU	5	1,146,275	5.2
Australia	3	999,240	4.7
Denmark	1	622,395	2.9
New Zealand	2	412,650	1.9
China	1	200,000	0.9
Others*	11	566,176	2.6
Total	84	21,957,742	100.0

* Others include UNDP, ILO, World Bank, ASEAN Bankers Association and Hanns Seidel Foundation.
Source: ASEAN, "Status Update of the IAI Work Plan I (2002–2008)", Jakarta: ASEAN Secretariat, Annex 6, Table 5, 17 October 2009.

TABLE 6.3
Japan's Economic Relations with ASEAN, 2007–10 (US$ million)

	Trade	Investment	ODA
2007	182,790 (13.7%)	7,790 (10.6%)	612 (7.9%)
2008	208,917 (13.6%)	6,309 (4.8%)	−356 (–)
2009	158,385 (13.9%)	7,002 (9.4%)	881 (9.3%)
2010	213,080 (14.6%)	8,930 (15.6%)	901 (8.1%)

Sources: METI, *Tsusho Hakusho*, 2008–2011; JETRO, *Nihon no toshi*, 2008–2011; MOFA, *Japan's ODA*, 2008–2011.

Japan's investment in the region has remained consistently high, its trade with ASEAN since 2007 has fluctuated substantially due mainly to world economic conditions. Most seriously, despite the increasing expectation to catch up with China, Japan's ODA is in fact diminishing.[24]

In order to improve Japan's economic assistance, Japan decided to provide a Climate Change Program Loan to Indonesia in July 2008, as the first step in development loans based on the "Cool Earth Partnership".[25] Projects to improve the investment climate and energy-related cooperation are also in progress with Indonesia, and joint work is being carried out in areas such as disaster countermeasures, maritime safety in the Strait of Malacca, climate change and protection of the environment. In April 2009 Japan announced "the Growth Initiative towards Doubling the Size of Asia's Economy", which set aside $20 billion in ODA to boost domestic demand in Asian countries.[26]

If we look at Japan's foreign direct investment (FDI) at the country level, we can observe a transformative change. As explained superbly by Hamanaka, the change is Japanese investors' shift from the manufacturing sector to the service sector. In fact, Japan's FDI into ASEAN in manufacturing sectors, in which Thailand is the largest recipient, has been declining due in part to the country's political instability. In contrast, Japan's FDI into ASEAN in the service sector has been growing rapidly. A recent interesting phenomenon regarding Japan's service investment into ASEAN is its "Singapore Shift". The strategy of Japanese corporations supplying services to ASEAN countries through a commercial presence in Singapore has raised the expectation that the country will play the role of a hub in Southeast Asia.[27] This trend can be continued due to the yen appreciation in recent years.

Japan-ASEAN Economic Ministers' Meeting and AMEICC

Starting in 1992, Japan's Ministry of Economy, Trade and Industry (METI) has been coordinating regional economic policies with ASEAN. The fourteenth Japan-ASEAN Economic Ministers' Meeting (AEM-METI) was held in Makati City, in the Philippines, in August 2007. The meeting discussed various issues, including ASEAN-Japan trade and investment relations, progress of work under the JACEP framework, and ASEAN-Japan cooperation towards further economic development and integration in East Asia. At the same time, the AEM-METI Economic and Industrial Cooperation Committee (AMEICC) was held back-to-back with the AEM-METI meeting. The meeting noted the timely implementation of the AMEICC projects as well as the effective manner in which these projects were being implemented. The ASEAN ministers welcomed the progress of the ASEAN Brand Project, which had obtained funding from the JAIF, and the ASEAN Common Standard Curriculum, which had finalized its coordination process with the Senior Labor Official's Meeting.[28]

Similarly, the fifteenth meeting was held in Singapore, in August 2008, but the scheduled sixteenth meeting in 2009 was cancelled due to the Japanese minister's inability to attend. After a one-year absence, the sixteenth meeting was held in Da Nang, Vietnam, in August 2010, and major policy schemes were introduced. These included the Smart Community Initiative, Asian Sustainable Chemical Safety Plan, and Asia Knowledge Economy Initiatives. The Smart Community Initiative was planned to accommodate smart energy systems and various smart social infrastructures leading to sustainable society in the region, with support from the Japan Smart Community Alliance and the New Energy and Industrial Technology Development Organization through various projects. The Asian Sustainable Chemical Safety Plan would also contribute to developing sustainable society in the region. The Asia Knowledge Economy Initiatives include ongoing projects such as promoting "Green IT", assuring information security in business activities, establishing e-commerce infrastructure, and fostering IT professionals.[29]

Following the Nikai proposal of August 2006, METI's support for "ASEAN Plus Six" as part of open regionalism has been strengthened. Its new proposal of "Initial Steps" is a case in point. With recognition that the integration framework should be ASEAN Plus Six, it aims to promote the four working groups with the assistance of ERIA by studying the comparative research of the existing FTAs.[30] The new proposal emphasizes the promotion of four working groups, including the rules of origin, tariff nomenclature, customs procedures, and economic cooperation. It also points to the need to promote further discussion on a broader range of economic fields based upon seven pillars: (1) trade in goods; (2) customs procedures, trade facilitation and logistics; (3) economic cooperation; (4) industrial policy; (5) hard infrastructures and enhancement of connectivity; (6) investment and trade in services; and (7) movement of skilled labour. METI stresses the fact that promotion of liberalization and development alongside deeper integration will enable long-term sustainable growth in East Asia.

The seventeenth AEM-METI meeting was held in Manado, Indonesia, in August 2011. While emphasizing the importance of enhancing economic cooperation between ASEAN and Japan to deepen regional economic integration and narrow the development gap, both economic ministers welcomed the progress in the ongoing Japanese initiatives for improving the quality of economic growth in ASEAN, including the Asian Sustainable Chemical Safety Plan and the Asia Knowledge Economy Initiative. The topics they covered included the Smart Community Initiative, a bilateral offset credit mechanism, a supply-chain visibility initiative, support for small and medium enterprises, and intellectual property cooperation. Most importantly, the economic ministers agreed to task the senior officials with developing a road map for ASEAN-Japan economic relations in the next ten years, with support from the ASEAN Secretariat and the AMEICC. They affirmed that this road map should be considered with the objectives of, among others, promoting strategic partnerships to improve the business environment; facilitate and liberalize trade and investment; develop infrastructure, connectivity and human resources; and enhance the coordination of domestic policies and regulations.[31]

In a similar vein, at the AEM-METI Economic and Industrial Cooperation Committee (AMEICC), the ministers noted with appreciation the progress in implementing the AMEICC projects, especially those related to the further development of the least developed countries and the promotion of SMEs towards realizing the AEC. In addition, they appreciated follow-up activities to the Asian Sustainable Chemical Safety Plan, especially those on strengthening capacity building on risk-based chemical safety management and the work towards establishing the ASEAN Chemical Data Centre. They affirmed their commitment to further strengthening the economic partnership between ASEAN and Japan by implementing the proposed projects through AMEICC, especially for the enhancement of regional economic integration.[32]

THE CULTURAL PILLAR OF JAPAN-ASEAN RELATIONS

At the critical juncture of 1977, 1987, 1997, Japan's cultural policy towards ASEAN exhibited a major step forward, thereby maintaining the momentum in cultural cooperation. In particular, after reaching its target of 100,000 foreign students in 2003, Japan decided upon a new cultural exchange target of 300,000 students in 2008. In terms of Japan-ASEAN cultural cooperation, three dimensions are worth mentioning here.

First, ASEAN and Japan have placed emphasis on people-to-people contacts and cultural exchanges, particularly among youths and intellectuals, with a view to fostering a sense of togetherness, mutual respect and understanding of each other's traditions and values. Since the JENESYS was first implemented in January 2007, a variety of exchange activities involving various sectors have been conducted regularly. JENESYS is a 35-billion-yen youth exchange programme, inviting about 6,000 young people to Japan — mainly from the EAS member countries (ASEAN, China, Republic of Korea, India, Australia and New Zealand) — every year for five years after 2007. Through this programme approximately 26,993 youths have been received in Japan and 5,374 youths have been dispatched from Japan as of September 2010.[33]

At the Japan-ASEAN Summit in 2009, the following issues were stressed: ongoing exchanges under the JENESYS Programme which had received approximately 3,500 youths from ASEAN since May 2007; Japan's proposal was to invite young teachers under this programme. The meeting also appreciated the holding of "The Japan-ASEAN Students' Conference" scheduled in October 2009. The meeting shared the importance of a public outreach programme with a view to promoting public awareness towards ASEAN.[34]

Second, Prime Minister Abe announced the Asian Gateway Initiative in May 2007, envisioning Japan acting as a bridge between Asia and the world in the flow of people, goods, money, culture and information. The objectives of the Asian Gateway Initiative are threefold: (1) to incorporate Asia's growing and vibrant economy into Japan and to achieve new "creativity and growth"; (2) to play a responsible role in the development of Asia and its regional order; and (3) to create a "beautiful country" which is attractive, trustworthy and respected. To achieve these objectives, Japan is to carry out ten specific policies as priority factors in realizing the Asian Gateway Initiative: (1) change in aviation policy to achieve "Asian Open Skies", (2) implement a programme for streamlining trade measures, (3) restructure policy for foreign students in order for Japan to serve as a hub for a human resource network in Asia, (4) further open up universities to the world, (5) create a financial and capital market highly attractive to Asian customers, (6) transform agriculture into a successful growth industry during the time of globalization, (7) create an "Asian Gateway Special Zone", (8) implement policies in line with a comprehensive strategy for "creative industries", (9) promote Japan's attractiveness overseas, (10) strengthen Japan's central role in promoting regional study and cooperation for solving common problems.[35]

The third is ASEAN's expectations for Japan's role in East Asia. Should ASEAN and Japan constitute a core of promoting a new regionalism in East Asia, their mutual perceptions of each other need to be congenial. According to a recent opinion poll conducted by the Japanese government (see Table 6.4), it can be seen that history has diminished as a determining factor (Q1) and that ASEAN countries have a positive expectation of Japan's role (Q2 and Q3). However, ASEAN's expectations of China are much higher than for Japan (Q4 and Q5). Moreover, the public is not well informed about recent developments in the relationships between Japan and ASEAN countries (Q6).

JAPAN-ASEAN STRATEGIC PARTNERSHIP

As one observer put it, Japan has moved beyond economics to carve out a gradually more proactive role in the security affairs of Southeast Asia in the areas of multilateral security dialogue, peacekeeping missions, providing disaster relief and in combating piracy.[36] Let us look at two major areas in more detail in this section.

Dealing with Nontraditional Security: Counterterrorism and ReCAAP

In terms of nontraditional security issues, Japan views active counter-terrorism dialogues with ASEAN as most important. The Japan-ASEAN Counter Terrorism Dialogue, established in 2006, is a forum not only to exchange views about the current terrorism situation, but also to identify

TABLE 6.4
Opinion Poll on Japan, 2008

Q1 What do you think about the acts of Japan during World War II?						
	Indonesia	Malaysia	Philippines	Singapore	Thailand	Vietnam
Cannot forget	18.1%	26.7%	27.2%	23.1%	13.8%	11.9%
Not an issue now	69.5%	64.9%	59.0%	69.2%	68.2%	77.5%
Q2 Do you think Japan is a trustworthy friend for ASEAN countries?						
Yes	92.0%	91.2%	92.8%	91.8%	90.1%	97.4%
No	4.5%	2.7%	6.5%	4.0%	7.6%	1.8%
Q3 Do you think that Japan, as an Asian country, is playing an active role in the development of Asia?						
Yes	83.1%	88.4%	93.9%	72.4%	88.7%	97.8%
No	11.8%	8.1%	5.9%	24.5%	8.9%	1.6%
Q4 For ASEAN countries, which of the following is currently considered an important partner?						
Japan	37.9%	25.8%	32.7%	3.6%	25.3%	42.7%
China	12.8%	39.2%	8.6%	57.8%	42.7%	16.5%
US	22.3%	10.6%	45.0%	22.0%	13.0%	27.5%
Q5 For ASEAN countries, which of the following is currently considered to have the potential to be an important partner in the coming years?						
Japan	29.0%	19.1%	33.2%	4.0%	18.5%	32.2%
China	18.9%	39.6%	14.9%	48.2%	56.5%	21.7%
US	19.1%	3.2%	26.4%	3.1%	6.0%	22.7%
Q6 Are you aware of the fact that Japan has concluded or is negotiating economic partnership agreements with ASEAN countries?						
Yes	22.1%	48.9%	31.8%	55.7%	55.6%	29.0%
No	78.0%	51.1%	68.2%	44.3%	44.4%	71.0%

Source: Gaimusho, "Opinion Poll on Japan", Tokyo: Ministry of Foreign Affairs, 2008.

areas which need further cooperation. The past dialogues have formulated concrete projects that benefit counterterrorism efforts in the region, and which have been implemented by utilizing the JAIF. It has received high praise from ASEAN member states — including at the Japan-ASEAN Summit meeting in October 2009 — as a major framework for regional cooperation in counterterrorism.[37] As ASEAN integration makes steady progress, terrorism is considered to be the major impediment that could undermine ASEAN efforts to enhance "connectivity". Therefore, in the run up to 2015, continuous Japan-ASEAN cooperation in this regard is expected to be assured.

Through successive meetings — the second in September 2007 in Kuala Lumpur; the third in October 2008 in Luang Phabang, Laos; the fourth in August 2009 in Nha Trang, Vietnam and the fifth in June 2010 in Bali, Indonesia — the main problems were identified and the ways and means of resolving them were clarified. One of the spinoffs of Japan-ASEAN counterterrorism endeavours has been the adoption of the ASEAN Convention of Counter Terrorism in 2007.[38] Japan has implemented the following counterterrorism assistance:

1. Encouraged accession to international counterterrorism conventions and protocols and the implementation of relevant UN Security Council resolutions.
2. Extended technical assistance and relevant equipment. Held seminars and accepted trainees in the following areas: (a) immigration control, (b) aviation security, (c) port and maritime security, (d) customs cooperation, (e) export control, (f) law enforcement cooperation, (g) combating terrorist financing, (h) counter-CBRN (chemical, biological, radioactive and nuclear) terrorism, and (i) counterterrorism conventions and protocols.
3. Introduced a new assistance scheme, the Grant Aid for Cooperation on Counter-Terrorism and Security Enhancement from 2006. Providing JAIF support to the tune of $68 million since March 2006.
4. Hosted the ASEAN-Japan Counter-Terrorism Dialogue in June 2006 in Tokyo. Held a meeting every year to exchange views between Japan and ASEAN to strengthen counterterrorism cooperation in ASEAN by utilizing JAIF and Grant Aid for Cooperation on Counter-Terrorism and Security Enhancement.
5. Extended grant aid of approximately 861 million yen to Vietnam to improve customs functions at Haiphong Port through the Grant Aid for Cooperation on Counter-Terrorism and Security Enhancement in September 2009.
6. Extended grant aid of approximately 2.5 billion yen to Indonesia for "The Project for Airport Security System Improvement" and "The Project for Enhancement of Vessel Traffic System in Malacca and Singapore Straits (Phase 2)" through the Grant Aid for Cooperation on Counter-Terrorism and Security Enhancement in June 2010.[39]

As noted by many, Japan's most important contribution to security cooperation in Southeast Asia has been in its promotion of anti-piracy measures.[40] In fact, the Regional Cooperation Agreement on Combating Piracy and Armed Robbery against Ships in Asia (ReCAAP) — comprising fourteen members, which includes eight of the ten ASEAN countries, Japan, China South Korea, Bangladesh, India and Sri Lanka — started its main activities by establishing an Information Sharing Center (ISC) in Singapore in November 2006. ReCAAP and the ISC can be seen as building blocks to regional security cooperation as they bring together regional countries to address a common security challenge, to wit, piracy and armed robbery. ReCAAP does this through the sharing of information in three ways: the ISC–Focal Point Network; capacity-building to share best practices; and by engaging in cooperative arrangement activities with like-minded organizations to strengthen the focal points' ability to manage incidents at sea.[41]

The Japanese government took initiatives in developing a global maritime distress and safety system, conducting joint hydrological surveys and developing electronic hydrological maps of the straits. In this regard, the role of the Japan Coast Guard (JCG) has been critical. Its ships and aircraft regularly visit ASEAN states to assist local security forces through training and exercises in building their capacity to combat threats from piracy and maritime terrorism. In fact, in conducting a major joint exercise in the Strait of Malacca in February 2007, the JCG's non-military role has begun to bring about positive results. According to a recent survey, piracy in the Strait of Malacca and the Singapore Strait has been waning.[42]

Promoting Mekong Development

In January 2007 the Japan–Mekong Region Partnership Program was adopted with special emphasis on three goals: expansion of ODA to the Mekong region, bilateral investment agreements with Cambodia and Laos, and the Japan–Mekong region ministerial meeting. More specifically, Japan promised the following commitments: regarding the Mekong region as a priority area, Japan will expand its ODA to CLV (Cambodia, Laos, Vietnam) countries as well as to the region as a whole for the next three years. In addition, out of Japan's new assistance totaling $52 million for promotion of the Japan-ASEAN economic partnership, approximately $40 million will be allocated to the CLV. Of this amount, approximately $20 million will be used to assist the CLV "Development Triangle". In order to substantially expand joint assistance projects for the Mekong region, Japan will consult more closely with the rest of the ASEAN countries.[43]

Since April 2007 Japan has been implementing the Japan-Mekong Region Partnership Program, which rests upon the following three priority areas: (1) integrating economies of the region and beyond, (2) expanding trade and investment between Japan and the region, and (3) pursuing universal values and common goals of the region. Furthermore, at the Japan-Mekong Foreign Ministers' Meeting, held in January 2008 in Tokyo, approximately $20 million was declared for improving efficiency of logistics in the East-West Economic Corridor.[44] At the first meeting, a document of cooperation in the development triangle (Mekong-Japan Action Plan 63) was signed. In addition, a further $20 million was declared to aid in streamlining logistics of the East-West Economic Corridor. Japan agreed to reinforce ties with the Asian Development Bank, which is engaged in a range of regional cooperation activities in Asia, and to create new schemes to support sustainable development by promoting investment and energy conservation.[45] Based on the above commitment, in June 2009 Japan extended to the Philippines an ODA loan of around 45 billion yen to support the country's agriculture and logistics' infrastructure.

In November 2009, the first Mekong-Japan Summit Meeting between the heads of the governments of Japan and the Mekong region countries was held, where they shared the recognition of establishing a new partnership for a thriving common future and giving priority to the following areas: comprehensive development in the Mekong region; the environment/climate change; overcoming vulnerability; and expansion of cooperation and exchanges. Emphasizing the significance of the Mekong region as key to an open and transparent East Asian Community, Japan has continued to expand the policy of ODA to the CLV as well as to the Mekong region as a whole. Japan committed more than 500 billion yen of ODA for the Mekong region for the next three years.[46]

In October 2010 the second summit was held in Hanoi. While welcoming significant progress in the implementation of the Tokyo Declaration and Mekong-Japan Action Plan 63, the Japanese prime minister reiterated that Japan would continue its commitment to work with the countries of the Mekong region towards the goals set at the First Mekong-Japan Summit. The PM praised the self-help efforts made by the Mekong region countries. Especially noteworthy was the adoption of the Mekong-Japan Economic and Industrial Cooperation Initiative (MJ-CI) Action Plan, which focused on hard infrastructure, trade facilitation/logistics, enhancement of small and medium enterprises, supporting industries, entrepreneurship, the service sector and a new industrial sector based on recommendations from the business community.

It is expected that the MJ-CI Action Plan will promote business activities and narrow the development gap by resolving the "missing links" in the region under Action Plan 63. The leaders welcomed the outcome of the Mekong-Japan International Conference on the East-West Economic Corridor (EWEC) and the Southern Economic Corridor (SEC), co-hosted by Japan and Thailand in Bangkok in September 2010, and the workshop on the improvement of EWEC in Tokyo, in which participants stressed the importance of addressing both soft and hard infrastructure in order to make full use of the economic corridors and increase connectivity in the region.[47]

The Fourth Mekong-Japan Foreign Ministers' Meeting was held in Bali, Indonesia, on 21 July 2011. Reviewing Japan-ASEAN cooperation, foreign ministers considered both the Tokyo Declaration and Action Plan 63 as guidelines to successfully establish a new mutually beneficial partnership between Japan and the countries of the Mekong region. Major results of the partnership that were noted included progress in the implementation of the Master Plan on ASEAN Connectivity, positive synergy of Mekong-Japan cooperation, and the success of the Green Mekong Forum, co-hosted by Japan and Thailand. Japan's new initiative, the Disaster Management Network for the ASEAN Region — a comprehensive approach including the development of a regional information-sharing network through satellites, the deployment of experts and the running of training programmes in Japan — was also noted, together with Japan's efforts in public-private cooperation in the Mekong region, such as the Forum for the Promotion of Public-Private Cooperation in the Mekong Region, held in Tokyo on 14 December 2010.[48]

MAJOR ISSUES: WHITHER A NEW REGIONALISM IN EAST ASIA?

Japan, under the new government of the DPJ, has continued to stress the importance of promoting East Asian regionalism. Prime Minister Hatoyama announced his idea of forging the East Asian Community in

September 2009.[49] Nevertheless, the conventional view posits that East Asian regionalism could not be realized due to the polarization of the region. In fact, ever since concluding the ASEAN-China FTA in 2002, ASEAN's trade with China has been improving rapidly. Surpassing Japan's trade for the first time in 2009, China's presence and influence in the region has been enormously strengthened.[50] Japan is increasingly compelled to catch up to China in order to maintain its predominant role in East Asia.

Yet, it is still too early to conclude that Japan's ASEAN policy has become a function of Japan's reactive posture to China's growing influence in the region, or is synchronized with Japan's China policy. This could be explicated by recent developments in the APT and EAS's activities.

Evolution of ASEAN Plus Three (APT)

Entering its tenth year, the APT has made steady progress in the implementation of seventeen short-term and nine medium- and long-term recommendations of the 2002 East Asia Study Group, including the feasibility study for an East Asia Free Trade Area. Therefore, at the eleventh meeting, the APT adopted the Second Joint Statement on East Asia Cooperation and the APT Cooperation Work Plan (2007–2017).[51]

Of note, the year 2009 saw a major leap forward, as the twelfth APT in October in Cha-am Hua Hin, Thailand achieved commendable results. The following two developments were particularly noteworthy. The first was the adoption of the Chiang Mai Initiative Multilateralization (CMIM). As the joint statement explains, "We endorsed the agreement reached at the 12th ASEAN Plus Three Finance Ministers' Meeting on May 3, 2009

TABLE 6.5
ASEAN's Economic Relations with Japan and China, 2007–10 (US$ million)

	Japan		China	
	Trade	Investment	Trade	Investment
2007	173,062	8,828	171,118	1,684
2008	211,916	4,657	192,672	2,109
2009	160,863	5,308	178,185	1,509
2010	213,080	8,930	243,644	2,570

Source: ASEAN Statistical Yearbook, 2011.

in Bali to implement the CMIM with the total size of $120 billion by the end of 2009 and to set up an independent regional surveillance unit. We welcomed Thailand's offer to temporarily host such [a] unit. We also welcomed the agreement to establish the Credit Guarantee and Investment Mechanism (CGIM) with an initial capital of $500 million under the Asian Bond Markets Initiative (ABMI) to support the local currency-denominated corporate bond in our region. We welcomed China's contribution of $200 million to the CGIM." The second was the adoption of the Cha-am Hua Hin Statement on ASEAN Plus Three Cooperation on Food Security and Bio-Energy Development. As explained by the joint statement, "We noted progress in the East Asia Emergency Rice Reserve (EAERR) Pilot Project, which will expire on 28 February 2010. We welcomed the efforts to transform the EAERR into a permanent mechanism under the ASEAN Plus Three Emergency Rice Reserve (APTERR)."[52]

Furthermore, at the thirteenth APT Summit, held in Hanoi on 29 October 2010, the thirteen leaders reaffirmed that the APT process with ASEAN as the driving force would continue to be the main vehicle to achieve the long-term goal of building an East Asian Community and contributing to the sustainable development in the region. Especially noteworthy were tangible progress in the areas of financial cooperation and food security.[53]

The fourteenth APT Summit, held in Bali, Indonesia on 18 November, discussed present and future initiatives for enhancing regional cooperation on pressing issues such as food security, disaster management, economic integration and the global financial crisis. Expressing concern for the threat to food supplies caused by the recent floods in Southeast Asia, the APT countries agreed to work together to ensure the implementation of the food security measures outlined by the APT Emergency Rice Reserves (APTERR) agreement of October 2011. With respect to disaster management, the summit decided to launch the ASEAN Coordinating Centre for Humanitarian Assistance on Disaster Management. In addition, the APT countries praised the success of the October meeting of the East Asia Vision Group (EAVG II) that was held in Seoul, and commended Korea for its role in realizing the group's establishment. The APT countries also expressed their commitment to supporting the research of their respective representatives and experts in EAVG II. Regarding the debt crisis in Europe, the APT countries acknowledged the need to strengthen economic cooperation in the region and collectively called for a more active role by the

APT Macroeconomic Research Office (AMRO), the regional macroeconomic surveillance unit established in May. Finally, the APT countries stated that the 2012 APT summit would be held as a special anniversary summit, in commemoration of fifteen years since the APT was established, throughout which time regional cooperation has steadily advanced.[54]

The East Asia Summit: Searching for a Raison d'être

Since 2005 the EAS has been held almost every year. Table 6.6 suggests slow developments in East Asian regionalism. The second EAS, in Cebu on 15 January 2007, continued the cautious style of the first. The discussions

TABLE 6.6
Evolution of the APT and EAS

Date/location	APT	EAS
January 2007 Cebu	(1) Discussion on the second declaration (2) Discussion on APT cooperation	(1) Discussion on priority issues (2) Declaration on East Asian energy security
November 2007 Singapore	(1) The second declaration of East Asian cooperation (2) The Work Plan (2007–17)	(1) Discussion on regional and international issues (2) Declaration on climate change
October 2009 Hua Hin	(1) Discussion on regional and international issues (2) Statement on food and energy development	(1) Discussion on regional and international issues (2) Statement on EAS disaster management
October 2010 Hanoi	(1) Discussion on regional and international issues (2) Proposal for an East Asian Vision Group II	(1) Hanoi Declaration (2) Participation of the US and Russia (3) Discussion on regional cooperation
November 2011 Bali	(1) Macroeconomic Research Office (2) Emergency rice reserves agreement (3) Coordinating Centre for Humanitarian Assistance on Disaster Management	(1) Declaration on the principles for mutually beneficial relations (2) Declaration on ASEAN connectivity

covered much the same ground addressed in 2005, with an additional emphasis on energy efficiency and conservation and climate change, with a range of cooperative programmes and voluntary endeavours promoted. The discussion focused on energy issues, with the main tangible result being a Declaration on East Asian Energy Security, which calls for strengthened regional cooperation on energy security to ensure a stable and affordable energy supply into the future. Specifically, signatory countries should improve energy efficiency and reduce dependence on fossil fuels while proposing the creation of an ASEAN power grid and a trans-ASEAN natural gas pipeline. The Chairman's statement at the end of the summit also commended efforts like the restoration of Nalanda University in India and Japan's proposal for the establishment of an Economic Research Institute for ASEAN and East Asia.[55] Building upon the inaugural EAS, the participating countries of the second EAS identified five priority areas for cooperation, namely energy, finance, education, natural disaster mitigation and avian influenza.

The third summit, held in Singapore in November 2007, placed emphasis on developing dialogue on energy and climate change issues. The summit also endorsed establishing a new research body for the region, the Economic Research Institute for ASEAN and East Asia, known as ERIA. ERIA, a primarily Japanese-backed think tank, was launched in May 2008 and will be based initially at the ASEAN Secretariat in Jakarta. ERIA is expected to serve as both a policymaking and training forum and is also expected to be involved in infrastructure planning and the development of further plans for regional economic integration, particularly Japan's proposal for a Comprehensive Economic Partnership in East Asia. At this third EAS, Japan reiterated its continued efforts towards sustainable energy security and announced an environment cooperation initiative entitled "Towards a Sustainable East Asia". Japan also announced financial assistance to the tune of $2 billion towards capacity building for the prevention of pollution, launched a Japan-ASEAN dialogue on the environment, and announced the possible utilization of the JAIF for projects and the contribution of $10 billion to the Forest Carbon Partnership Facility of the World Bank. This resulted in the leaders of participating countries signing the Singapore Declaration on Climate Change, Energy and the Environment.[56]

Since the 2008 summit was postponed due to the domestic chaos in Thailand, the fourth EAS was held on 25 October 2009 in Cha-am Hua Hin, Thailand. The summit welcomed the entry into force of the ASEAN

Charter on 15 December 2008 and the signing of the Cha-am Hua Hin Declaration on a Roadmap to an ASEAN Community at the fourteenth ASEAN Summit in March 2009. While reaffirming that the EAS should continue to help build a prosperous and harmonious East Asia, with ASEAN as the driving force working in close partnership with other participants of the EAS, they acknowledged the importance of regional discussions to examine ways to advance the stability and prosperity of the Asia-Pacific region. In this connection, it is noteworthy that the EAS leaders endorsed the following: (1) the Philippines' proposal to invite the heads of other regional fora and organizations in the Asia-Pacific to future EAS meetings to discuss measures that will protect the region from future economic and financial crises and strengthen Asian economic cooperation, including through the possible establishment of an Asian Economic Community, and (2) Japan's proposal to reinvigorate the discussion towards building, in the long run, an East Asian Community based on the principle of openness, transparency and inclusiveness, and functional cooperation.[57]

The fifth EAS was held on 30 October 2010 in Hanoi, Vietnam. Commemorating the fifth anniversary of the EAS, all the members noted the significant achievements recorded so far, and stressed the importance of further strengthening the EAS process through reviewing the progress over the past five years, re-emphasizing the importance of the EAS in fostering dialogue and cooperation in the region, and reaffirming their commitments to further consolidating and strengthening the EAS. In this connection, the adoption of the Hanoi Declaration on the Commemoration of the Fifth Anniversary of the East Asia Summit is noteworthy. Finally, they welcomed the expressed interest and commitment of the Russian Federation and the United States in the EAS so as to engage more closely with the region, and formally decided to invite their leaders to participate in the EAS starting from 2011.[58] This new development suggests the fact that EAS is becoming a part of Asia-Pacific cooperation akin to APEC.

The sixth East Asia Summit, held in Bali in November 2011 concluded with the adoption of two key documents, namely the Declaration of the EAS on the Principles for Mutually Beneficial Relations and the Declaration of the 6th East Asia Summit on ASEAN Connectivity. The first declaration contains basic norms and common principles to guide conduct for EAS participating countries in promoting peace, stability and prosperity in the region. The second declaration includes connectivity as one of the key areas of cooperation, besides the existing five priorities, namely finance, energy, education, communicable diseases and disaster management. This declaration will *inter alia* support and facilitate further cooperation between ASEAN and other EAS participating countries in the connectivity initiative, the development of a regional public-private partnership development agenda, and greater engagement in people-to-people connectivity. Most noteworthy was the participation of the United States for the first time. The decision to join the EAS is part of a recalibration of United States' foreign policy vis-à-vis ASEAN-led multilateral institutions. This shift in policy reflects a broader attempt by the United States to re-engage with Southeast Asia and is equally related to China's growing influence in the Asia-Pacific. By joining the EAS, Washington is seizing an opportunity to reverse the perceived American disengagement from the region, which has allowed China to play a larger role in East Asian regional platforms.[59]

What is emerging from recent developments obviously runs counter to the conventional view on East Asian regionalism. As demonstrated by the issues of CMIM and EAERR, Japan's role has been critical in promoting APT cooperation. In other words, Japan does not dominate the EAS by merely opposing a China-centred APT. To further substantiate this, the following two cases are worthwhile examining.

The first is the Japan-China consultation for Mekong development, started in April 2008. The third meeting of the Japan-China Policy Dialogue on the Mekong Region was held in April 2010. At this meeting, both countries outlined their cooperation efforts in the Mekong region since the previous meeting in June 2009. The participants exchanged views on the possibility of Japan-China cooperation in the Mekong region. Both countries agreed there should be an exchange of views at various levels relating to concrete cooperation in overall aid policies, environmental conservation, public health and human resource development.[60]

The second case is the Japan-China Counter-Terrorism Consultations, started in January 2011. Both countries welcomed the first round of bilateral consultations with growing momentum to strengthen cooperation on global issues. They confirmed that they would cooperate more in counterterrorism efforts and that they would take an active and leading role in cooperating with each other in existing international and regional fora such as the ARF, APT, APEC, ASEM and EAS.[61]

The DPJ and New Asianism

The victory of the DPJ in the 2009 elections was an epoch-making event in the history of post-war Japanese politics. It meant that the two-party system had actually started to work, giving the voters the option of changing the government through elections. Accordingly, domestic and foreign policies ought to respond to the demands of a public that desires change. In fact, the DPJ's manifesto stressed the fact that Japan has hitherto been called a "faceless country", which has been the result of maintaining a passive diplomatic posture towards the world, based on a foreign policy constantly devoid of strength of will. The DPJ promised to change this negative stance, transforming Japan into an internationally oriented nation with a clear diplomatic will. A new path for Japan, as stipulated by the DPJ, is based on the following five initiatives: (1) stressing the importance of international cooperation and strengthening the functions of the United Nations, (2) building a relationship with the United States based on independence and equality, (3) making Japan truly an integral part of Asia, (4) rebuilding the defense structure to enable Japan to deal with new threats, and (5) conducting environmental diplomacy with the world.

Urged by public support for policy change, newly elected Prime Minister Hatoyama disclosed his initiative for a new Asianism.[62] Hatoyama's enthusiasm for the creation of an East Asian Community signalled the possibility of a partnership in East Asian regionalism, reflecting a foreign policy that sought a more autonomous role for Japan. It should be noted here that the DPJ's manifesto is akin to the alternative stream of Japanese foreign policy, if it is viewed alongside similar attempts by his grandfather, Ichiro Hatoyama, who initiated an anti-Yoshida foreign policy during the 1950s. At the Trilateral Summit in October 2009 in Beijing, for instance, Prime Minister Hatoyama stated that Japanese foreign policy had been thus far too dependent on the United States. This gave the impression that his East Asian Community idea would serve as a tool that would make it possible for Japan to pursue a more autonomous and independent foreign policy to the United States.[63]

In his proposal for the East Asian Community, Hatoyama clarified his position at the APEC meeting held in September 2009 by stating, "Japan will promote cooperation for the realization of an open community through diplomatic efforts underpinned by its alliance with the United States." While highlighting four key areas of cooperation in his concept for an East Asian Community, namely regional prosperity, the environment, protecting human life and maritime safety, Hatoyama explained the rationale for the new Asianism: "The concept behind my initiative for an East Asian Community stems from the philosophy of *yu-ai*. Within *yu-ai*, people respect the freedom and human dignity of others just as they respect their own freedom and human dignity. In other words, *yu-ai* means not only the independence of people but also their coexistence. I set this goal because reconciliation in the real sense of the word is not necessarily believed to have been achieved in the region."[64] However, before clarifying specific measures to realize the East Asian Community, Hatoyama was forced to step down due to the Futenma debacle and his financial problems.

Naoto Kan, who succeeded Hatoyama as prime minister in June 2010, has taken a more practical stance of pursuing the East Asian Community concept, while his government has further committed itself to APEC's development, serving as the host for the 2010 APEC meetings. Nevertheless, Prime Minister Kan continued to pursue his Asian policy locating the five pillars at its axis. The first of these pillars is the Japan-US alliance as the cornerstone of Japanese foreign policy; second, the new development of foreign relations with Asia; third, the promotion of economic diplomacy; fourth, the addressing of global issues, and; fifth, is Japan itself responding with precision to the security environment surrounding it.[65]

CONCLUSION

The fifth decade of Japan-ASEAN relations has started with continuity and change. Japan and ASEAN continue to recognize the importance of strategic partnership as the hub of East Asian regionalism. Yet, frequent changes in Japan's political leadership, together with disastrous earthquake and tsunami incidents in March 2011, has left the Japanese government unable to pursue top-level official engagement since 2007. It is unfortunate that Japan under the ruling Democratic Party has not as yet consolidated its firm domestic power base in order to pursue more consistent policies towards ASEAN and East Asia.

Despite the lagging role of political leaders, the ministerial level of Japan-ASEAN relations has been yielding major progress in the three areas of politico-security, the economy and sociocultural aspects. In other words, Japan's institutionalized ideas are still in operation, although ongoing synchronization of the three principles of regional policies is inevitably subject to change. In particular, significant progress has been achieved through APT cooperation in the areas of finance and agricultural cooperation. Suffice it to say, nurturing a new regionalism in East Asia depends a great deal on the strength of Japan's proactive ASEAN policy.

Notes

1. ASEAN, "Chairperson's Statement of the 12th ASEAN Summit, Cebu, 13 January 2007" (Jakarta: ASEAN Secretariat, 2007.
2. ASEAN, "Charter of the Association of Southeast Asian Nations, Singapore, 20 November 2007" (Jakarta: ASEAN Secretariat, 2007).
3. ASEAN, "Chairman's Statement of the 13th ASEAN Summit, Singapore, 20 November 2007" (Jakarta: ASEAN Secretariat, 2007).
4. On ASEAN's 40th anniversary, see Rodolfo Severino, "ASEAN at Forty: A Balance Sheet", in *Southeast Asian Affairs 2008* (Singapore: Institute of Southeast Asian Affairs, 2008), pp. 61–70; Shaun Narine, "Forty years of ASEAN: A Historical Review", *Pacific Review* 21, no. 4, (2008): 411–29; Chin Kin Wah, "ASEAN: Facing the Fifth Decade", *Contemporary Southeast Asia* 29, no. 3 (December 2007): 395–405. See also John Ravenhill, "East Asian regionalism: Much Ado about Nothing?" *Review of International Studies* 35, supplement 1 (2009): 215–35 for a pessimistic view.
5. *Asahi Shimbun*, 13 May 2006. For Japan-ASEAN relations during the fourth decade, see Julie Gilson, "Japan and Southeast Asia", in *Contemporary Southeast Asia*, 2nd ed., edited by Mark Beeson (New York: Palgrave Macmillan, 2009), pp. 208–19 and Kuunnavakkam V. Kesavan, "Japan and ASEAN: Their Changing Security Relations", ORF Occasional Paper, no. 22 (August 2011).
6. Shinzo Abe, "Japan and One ASEAN that Care and Share at the Heart of Dynamic Asia, 20 August 2007" (Tokyo: Ministry of Foreign Affairs, Japan, 2007).
7. *New Straits Times*, 10 October 2007. For an ASEAN official's view, see especially Surin Pitsuwan, "Fukuda dokutorin no konnichiteki imiwo kangaeru", *Kokusai Mondai*, no. 567 (December 2007): 46–54. At least three commemorative conferences on Japan-ASEAN relations were held in Kuala Lumpure, Singapore and Tokyo, which were indicative of public and academic anticipation for a new doctrine.
8. Yasuo Fukuda, "The Pacific Ocean Becomes an 'Inland Sea': Five Pledges to a Future Asia that 'Acts Together', 22 May 2008" (Tokyo: Ministry of Foreign Affairs, 2008).
9. Interview with a Cambodian governmental official in Phnom Penh, 12 August 2011.
10. See especially, ASEAN, "ASEAN-Japan 2010" (Jakarta: ASEAN Secretariat, 2010).

11. ASEAN, "Chairman's Statement of the Tenth ASEAN-Japan Summit, Cebu, Philippines, 14 January 2007" (Jakarta: ASEAN Secretariat, 2007); *Asahi Shimbun*, 15 January 2007.

12. ASEAN, "Chairman's Statement of the 11th ASEAN-Japan Summit, Singapore, 21 November 2007" (Jakarta: ASEAN Secretariat, 2007); *Yomiuri Shimbun*, 21 November 2007, evening issue.

13. ASEAN, "Chairman's Statement of the 12th ASEAN-Japan Summit, Cha-am Hua Hin, 24 October 2009" (Jakarta: ASEAN Secretariat, 2009); *Asahi Shimbun*, 25 October 2009.

14. ASEAN, "Chairman's Statement of the 13th ASEAN-Japan Summit, Hanoi, 29 October 2010" (Jakarta: ASEAN Secretariat, 2010).

15. ASEAN, "Chairman's Statement of the 14th ASEAN-Japan Summit, Bali, Indonesia, 18 November 2011" (Jakarta: ASEAN Secretariat, 2011).

16. ASEAN, "Joint Communiqué of the 41st ASEAN Ministerial Meeting, Manila, 24–25 July 2008" (Jakarta: ASEAN Secretariat, 2008).

17. ASEAN, "ASEAN Chairman's Statement on the ASEAN Post Ministerial Conference (PMC)+1 Sessions, Phuket, Thailand, 22 July 2009" (Jakarta: ASEAN Secretariat, 2009).

18. ASEAN, "ASEAN Chairman's Statement on the ASEAN Post Ministerial Conference (PMC)+1 Sessions, Hanoi, Vietnam, 22 July 2010" (Jakarta: ASEAN Secretariat, 2010).

19. ASEAN, "ASEAN Chairman's Statement on the ASEAN Post Ministerial Conference (PMC)+1 Sessions, Bali, Indonesia, 21–22 July 2011" (Jakarta: ASEAN Secretariat, 2011); *Asahi Shimbun*, 22 July 2011.

20. ASEAN, "Japan-ASEAN Forum, Bali, 26 November 2010" (Jakarta: ASEAN Secretariat, 2010).

21. ASEAN, "Status Update of the IAI Work Plan I (2002–2008)" (Jakarta: ASEAN Secretariat, 17 October 2009).

22. For JACEP, see especially Gregory Corning, "Between Bilateralism and Regionalism in East Asia: the ASEAN-Japan Comprehensive Economic Partnership", *Pacific Review* 22, no. 5 (December 2009): 639–65 and Mitoji Yabunaka, *Kokka no meiun* (Tokyo: Shinchosha, 2010), pp. 158–62.

23. *Yomiuri Shimbun*, 2 December 2008.

24. Regarding economic relations, see, Mitsuhiro Fukuyama, "Toward a New Japan-ASEAN Relationship in 2011", *RIETI Report*, no. 127 (February 2011); Hidetaka Yoshimatsu and Dennis Trinidad, "Development Assistance, Strategic Interests, and the China Factor in Japan's Role in ASEAN Integration", *Japanese Journal of Political Science* 11, no. 2 (2010): 199–219 and Thee Kian Wie, "Foreign Direct Investment from Northeast Asia to Southeast Asia", *Indonesia Quarterly* 38, no. 2 (2010): 188–212.

25. Gaimusho, "Financial Mechanism for 'Cool Earth Partnership'" (Tokyo:

Ministry of Foreign Affairs) <http://www.mofa.go.jp/mofaj/gaiko/oda/bunya/environment/cool_earth_e.html>.

26. Gaimusho, *Japan's ODA*, 2010, pp. 83–84.

27. See Shintaro Hamanaka, "Examination of the Singapore Shift in Japan's Foreign Direct Investment in Services in ASEAN", ADBI Working Paper 267, March 2011.

28. ASEAN, "Joint Media Statement of the Fourteenth Consultation between the ASEAN Economic Ministers and the Minister of Economy, Trade and Industry of Japan (AEM-METI), Makati City, Philippines, 25 August 2007" (Jakarta: ASEAN Secretariat, 2007); *Nihon Keizai Shimbun*, 25 August 2007, evening issue.

29. ASEAN, "Joint Media Statement of the 16th AEM-METI Consultations, Danang, Vietnam, August 26, 2010" (Jakarta: ASEAN Secretariat, 2010); *Nihon Keizai Shimbun*, 27 August 2010.

30. Mitsuhiro Fukuyama "Initial Steps toward Regional Economic Integration in East Asia (Japan's Proposal)", RIETI Policy Update 042, 23 February 2011.

31. ASEAN, "Joint Media Statements of the 17th AEM-METI Consultations, Manado, Indonesia, 13 August 2011" (Jakarta: ASEAN Secretariat, 2011).

32. *Nihon Keizai Shimbun*, 24 August 2011.

33. See especially, Kazuo Ogoura, *Japan's Cultural Diplomacy* (Tokyo: the Japan Foundation, 2009).

34. ASEAN, "Chairman's Statement of the 12th ASEAN-Japan Summit, Cha-am Hua Hin, Thailand, 24 October 2009" (Jakarta: ASEAN Secretariat, 2009).

35. Takumi Nemoto, "Asian Gateway Initiative", the Council for the Asian Gateway Initiative, 16 May 2007 <http://www.kantei.go.jp/foreign/gateway/kettei/070516doc.pdf>. See also Akira Ninomiya, "Ajia Getowei senryakukaigi gaegaku ryugakusei senryaku to UMAP no yakuwari", *Ajia Kenkyu* 54, no. 4 (October 2008): 56–69.

36. Bhubhindar Singh, "The Evolution of Japan's Security Role in Southeast Asia", *Round Table* 99, no. 409 (August 2010): 391.

37. ASEAN, "Chairman's Statement of the 12th ASEAN-Japan Summit". See also Taizo Watanabe and William Tow, "Trilateralism, Southeast Asia and multilateralism", in *Asia-Pacific Security*, edited by William Tow et al. (London: Routledge, 2007), pp. 125–38.

38. Gaimusho, "The 4th ASEAN-Japan Counter-Terrorism Dialogue, 13 August 2009" (Tokyo: Ministry of Foreign Affairs, 2009).

39. Gaimusho, "Japan's International Counter-Terrorism Cooperation, August 2010" (Tokyo: Ministry of Foreign Affairs, 2010).

40. See, for instance, Carlyle Thayer, "Southeast Asia: Patterns of Security Cooperation", *ASPI Strategy*, September 2010, pp. 1–68 and Lindsay Black, "Navigating the Boundaries of the Interstate Society: Japan's Response to

Piracy in Southeast Asia", in *Decoding Boundaries in Contemporary Japan*, edited by Glenn Hook (London: Routledge, 2010), pp. 79–100.

41. Joshua Ho, "Combating Piracy and Armed Robbery in Asia: Boosting Recaap's Role", *RSIS Commentaries*, no. 69, 2008. See also Gaimusho, "Tonanajia chiiki niokeru kaizokumondai no genjo to Nihon no torikumi, May 2010" (Tokyo: Ministry of Foreign Affairs, 2010).

42. James Manicom, "Japan's Role in Strengthening Maritime Security in Southeast Asia", NBR Special Report, no. 24, November 2010, pp. 31–41.

43. Gaimusho, "Mekong Partnership Program, January 2007" (Tokyo: Ministry of Foreign Affairs, 2007).

44. Masaya Shiraishi, "Japan and the Reconstruction of Indochina", in *New Dynamics between China and Japan in Asia*, edited by Guy Faure (Singapore: World Scientific, 2010), p. 154.

45. Gaimusho, "Chair's Statement, Mekong-Japan Foreign Ministers' Meeting, Tokyo, 16 January 2008" (Tokyo: Ministry of Foreign Affairs, 2008).

46. Gaimusho, "Tokyo Declaration of the First Meeting between the Heads of the Governments of Japan and the Mekong Region Countries: Establishment of a New Partnership for the Common Flourishing Future, 7 November 2009" (Tokyo: Ministry of Foreign Affairs, 2009); *Nihon Keizai Shimbun*, 8 November 2009.

47. Gaimusho, "Joint Statement of the Second Mekong-Japan Summit, Hanoi, Vietnam, 29 October 2010" (Tokyo: Ministry of Foreign Affairs, 2010).

48. Gaimusho, "Chairman's Statement of the Fourth Mekong-Japan Foreign Ministers' Meeting, 21 July 2011" (Tokyo: Ministry of Foreign Affairs, 2011).

49. *Straits Times*, 16 November 2009, *Asahi Shimbun*, 16 November 2009.

50. For the China factor, see especially Yul Sohn, "Japan's New Regionalism: China Shock, Values, and the East Asian Community", *Asian Survey* 50, no. 3 (2010): 497–519 and Christopher Dent, ed., *China, Japan and Regional Leadership in East Asia* (Cheltenham: Edward Elgar, 2008).

51. See ASEAN, "Chairman's Statement of the 10th ASEAN Plus Three Summit, Cebu, Philippines, 14 January 2007" and "ASEAN Plus Three Cooperation Work Plan 2007–2017, Singapore, 20 November 2007" (Jakarta: ASEAN Secretariat, 2007).

52. ASEAN, "Chairman's Statement of the 12th ASEAN Plus Three Summit, Cha-am Hua Hin, 24 October 2009" (Jakarta: ASEAN Secretariat, 2007).

53. ASEAN, "Chairman's Statement of the 13th ASEAN Plus Three Summit, Hanoi, Vietnam, 29 October 2010" (Jakarta: ASEAN Secretariat, 2010).

54. ASEAN, "Chairman's Statement of the 14th ASEAN Plus Three Summit, Bali, Indonesia, 18 November 2011" (Jakarta: ASEAN Secretariat, 2011).

55. ASEAN, "Chairman's Statement of the Second East Asia Summit, Cebu, Philippines, 15 January 2007" (Jakarta: ASEAN Secretariat, 2007).

56. ASEAN, "Chairman's Statement of the 3rd East Asia Summit, Singapore, 21 November 2007" (Jakarta: ASEAN Secretariat, 2007).

57. ASEAN, "Chairman's Statement of the 4th East Asia Summit, Cha-am Hua Hin, Thailand, 25 October 2009" (Jakarta: ASEAN Secretariat, 2009).

58. ASEAN, "Chairman's Statement of the East Asia Summit (EAS), Hanoi, Vietnam, 30 October 2010" (Jakarta: ASEAN Secretariat, 2010).

59. See ASEAN, "Declaration of the 6th East Asia Summit on ASEAN Connectivity, Bali, Indonesia, 19 November 2011" and "Declaration of the 6th East Asia Summit on the Principles for Mutually Beneficial Relations, Bali, Indonesia, 19 November 2011" (Jakarta: ASEAN Secretariat, 2011).

60. Gaimusho, "The First Japan-China Policy Dialogue on the Mekong Region, 25 April 2008" (Tokyo: Ministry of Foreign Affairs, 2008).

61. Gaimusho, "The 1st Japan-China Counter-Terrorism Consultations, 6 January 2011" (Tokyo: Ministry of Foreign Affairs, 2011).

62. *New York Times*, 1 September 2009. See also Daniel Sneider, "The New Asianism: Japanese Foreign Policy under the Democratic Party of Japan", *Asia Policy*, no. 12 (July 2011): 99–129 for DPJ's new Asian policy.

63. *Mainichi Shimbun*, 25 October 2009.

64. Yukio Hatoyama, "Japan's New Commitment to Asia: Toward the Realization of an East Asian Community, Singapore, 15 November 2009" (Tokyo: Ministry of Foreign Affairs, 2009).

65. Naoto Kan, "Japanese Diplomacy at a Historic Watershed, 20 January 2011" (Tokyo: Ministry of Foreign Affairs, 2011).

CONCLUSION

Our journey that has taken us to Japan and the Association of Southeast Asian Nations (ASEAN) is coming to an end. As is usually the case, the journey has had its ups and downs, with some pleasant surprises in coming to an understanding of the reality of Japan-ASEAN relations. The most profound change in post-war Japan's regional policy we have witnessed, is the fact that due to its proactive multilateralism, Japan could outgrow its low-profile posture or reactivity necessitated by the legacy of Japanese colonialism. Given the inherent limitation of Japanese foreign policy, Japan's ASEAN policy has traversed much further than expected. It is now safe to conclude that with the exception of China and South Korea, Japan has come to be accepted as a trustworthy and constructive partner in East Asia today.

In fact, ever since the Fukuda Doctrine laid the foundations in 1977, Japan's ASEAN policy has shown distinct features at critical junctures of Japan-ASEAN relations. The Takeshita Doctrine in 1987 consolidated the relationship during the late 1980s and mid-1990s and the Hashimoto Doctrine in 1997 began to expand the relations beyond Southeast Asia. Finally, the new Fukuda Doctrine in 2008 has attempted to nurture a new regionalism in East Asia, while at the same time retaining the essence of the Japan-ASEAN partnership. How has this unique relationship come about? Why has this relationship been sustained and developed? And most of all, whither the Japan-ASEAN partnership? By way of summary, first of all, let us put Japan's ASEAN policy into proper perspective.

JAPAN'S ASEAN POLICY AS AN ALTERNATIVE STREAM

As discussed at the outset of this study, Japanese foreign policy contains three major streams (see Figure 7.1). The mainstream, premised on

FIGURE 7.1
Outline of Japanese Foreign Policy Streams

	Mainstream	Intermediate Stream	Alternative Stream
Ideas	Dependence on US Economic Diplomacy ⇨ **Yoshida Doctrine** ⇨ Calder Model ⇨ Post-Yoshida Doctrine	A Sole Member of the West in Asia ⇨ Bridge-building ⇨ Asia-Pacific (APEC) ⇨ EAS	Autonomous Foreign Policy ⇨ Southeast Asia ⇨ **Fukuda Doctrine** (ASEAN) ⇨ East Asia (APT)
Institutions	MOFA LDP Keidanren	METI (MITI) Business Groups	MOFA (Asian Affairs Bureau) MOF
Orientations	Japan-US Bilateralism	Open Regionalism	Proactive Multilateralism

dependence on the United States and the pursuit of economic diplomacy, has proven effective as shown by the very fact that a defeated Japan became an economic great power in the middle of the 1960s. Even after the Cold War, Japan's alliance with the United States continues to constitute a cornerstone of Japanese foreign policy, although around the turn of the century the quest for grand strategy has become a post–Yoshida Doctrine national agenda.[1]

The second is the alternative stream, which emerged when anti-Yoshida group leader Nobusuke Kishi attempted to implement his autonomous foreign policy, particularly exemplified by his proposal for the Southeast Asian Development Fund in 1957. Following suit, Prime Minister Fukuda initiated an ASEAN-centred regional policy, thereby putting behind all the problems associated with the Yoshida Doctrine. After establishing a framework for Japan's autonomous foreign policy, the Asia Affairs Bureau of the Ministry of Foreign Affairs (MOFA) directed its proactive policy to consolidate the framework in 1987, and expanded it in 1997 and 2007–8. The change of the ruling party in 2009 underscored the importance of the alternative stream. And, together with the Ministry of Finance, Japan's proactive multilateralism has come to serve as a central element in promoting East Asian regionalism centred on the ASEAN Plus Three (APT).

The third stream, known as the intermediate stream, came to be recognized when Japanese policymakers hesitated to embrace an Asia-only regionalism. Stressing the inclusion of a sole member of the West in Asia and the role of bridge building, they found the more broadly defined region of the Asia-Pacific useful and acceptable to the United States. As the Ministry of Economy, Trade and Industry (METI)'s emphasis on Asia Pacific Economic Cooperation and East Asia Summit clearly suggests, the concept of "open regionalism" is the key to the intermediate stream, as shown by the East Asia Summit (EAS).

JAPAN'S PROACTIVE MULTILATERALISM

Among Japan's multilateral policies, its policy towards ASEAN seems to embrace a special feature. As our analysis of four distinct doctrines suggests, Japan's provision of policy ideas at critical junctures has been timely and proactive. It has been proactive in the sense that Japan has its own ideas, interests, and policy objectives. Japan is purposive and decisive, and has a clear conception of its national interests, thereby seeking to mobilize its citizens and national resources to attain its objectives.

Why has Japan's ASEAN policy become proactive and why is it important? Ever since Fukuda promised that "the government and people of Japan will never be sceptical bystanders in regard to ASEAN's efforts to achieve increased resilience and regional solidarity, but will always be with you as good partners, walking hand in hand with ASEAN", the foundation of Japan's multilateralism has been formulated. Thus, it is not coincidental that Japan's prime minister, supported by MOFA's Asian Affairs Bureau, announces its policy doctrine every ten years. As one scholar cogently put it, "The Japanese government has encapsulated its relations with Southeast Asia in a number of doctrinal pledges, from Fukuda senior to his son's tenure in 2007. Buffeted by domestic constraints, regional signs of acquiescence and changing international forces, the Japanese government knows that its future is attached to that of Southeast Asia as a whole."[2]

Since ASEAN Summit meetings deepen and widen regional cooperation, Japan's responses follow suit. For instance, Japan-ASEAN political cooperation was strengthened by the Japan-ASEAN Foreign Ministers' Meeting in 1978, which led to the establishment of the Post-Ministerial Conference in 1979. This led to support for the precarious Aquino regime in 1987, a constructive role in the Cambodian conflict, and the establishment of the ASEAN Regional Forum in 1994. Economic cooperation has been closely coordinated since the inception of regional industrial projects in 1977 and the agreement of brand-to-brand complementation in 1987. Most significantly, because of the 1977 Fukuda Fund, ASEAN's cultural cooperation has found its way, and has been substantially improved largely due to the two cultural missions in 1987 and 1997 by the Japanese government.

As a result of these proactive measures, we witnessed the synchronization of regional policies by Japan and ASEAN. As the evolution of Japan-ASEAN relations amply suggests, Japan's emphasis on political, economic and cultural cooperation gradually meshed into the three pillars of Japan's ASEAN policy. In turn, Japan's three pillars began to synchronize with ASEAN's community-building efforts in 2003, which exhibited ASEAN's determination to pursue political, economic and sociocultural communities. Thus, ASEAN's positive attitudes towards Japan have accrued. In the words of ASEAN's Director of Dialogue Partners, "as a reliable and dependable partner of ASEAN, Japan has been one of

ASEAN's most committed partners in capacity building and integration, as well as supporting a wide range of ASEAN's activities".[3]

THEORETICAL IMPLICATIONS

In explaining the origins and development of Japan's ASEAN policy, the following equation can be confirmed. Simply put, policy ideas are embodied in policymaking institutions, which in turn are likely to sustain the proactive nature of the proclaimed policy.

$$\textbf{Ideas} \implies \textbf{Institutions} \implies \textbf{Proactive Multilateralism}$$

To understand the impact of the institutionalized ideas on the policymaking process, the following two concepts are worth mentioning. The first concept of critical junctures answers the question of why Japan's doctrines were announced in 1977, 1987, 1997 and 2008. In fact, the promulgation of the Fukuda Doctrine was triggered by the pervasive anti-Japanese movements in Southeast Asia and the recognized failure of Japan's economic diplomacy. Takeshita's positive response to ASEAN in 1987 was mainly due to the critical change in ASEAN leadership and regional plight caused by political turmoil in the Philippines. Similarly, the Hashimoto Doctrine was a response to the challenge of globalization as epitomized by the East Asian financial crisis. Finally, it should be recalled that the reappraisal of the Fukuda Doctrine in 2006 had something to do with Japan's East Asian diplomacy. It was because of Koizumi's failure that a new style of Asian diplomacy was required by the Japanese and Southeast Asian policymakers.

The second is the concept of a focal point that explains well the question of why Japan continues to offer policy ideas to sustain its proactive multilateralism. As we have seen, the Takeshita Doctrine added new elements to the core principles of the Fukuda Doctrine. In a similar vein, the Hashimoto Doctrine offered policy reforms and the expansion of Japan-ASEAN relations. Thus, in conjunction with reiterating the previous doctrines, each prime minister formulates his own doctrine in consideration of the right time and the right place.

The third is the concept of institutionalization that explains well the sequence of Japan's ASEAN policy. The rivalry between MOFA and METI is a critical factor in embedding policy ideas to sustain proclaimed policies towards the region. Moreover, during the 1990s the role of the

MOF in the policymaking process had been enormously improved, thereby influencing the direction of Japan's regional policy. Depending on various contending ideas, Japan's ASEAN policy is inevitably subject to change at the critical junctures. Nevertheless, competition among major policymaking institutions is likely to strengthen each actor's motivations to offer better policy ideas, which ultimately leads to the maintenance of proactive multilateralism. In other words, ideas really matter when institutions utilize them in the quest for a greater leadership role in the region.

WHITHER JAPAN-ASEAN RELATIONS?

Upon analysing the development of Japan-ASEAN relations based on the idea-cum-institution framework, what is the prospect for the Japan-ASEAN partnership? The importance of the Japan-ASEAN partnership as the hub of East Asian regionalism is likely to continue, despite the growing perception of "Japan's soft power model not for emulation".[4] For one thing, even today it is widely recognized in Japan that "the Fukuda Doctrine as Japan's grand design is a rare case of success in Japanese foreign policy".[5] In this respect, the ASEAN Caravan of Goodwill in June 2011 augurs well for the stronger partnership. Another is the belief that the alternative stream has become an integral part of Japan's East Asian policy. Hence, ASEAN is a concept by which we measure Japan's contributions to East Asia.

As the contentious birth of EAS amply suggests, the issue of who belongs to East Asia remains a sensitive issue today. Given the diversity among the East Asian countries, this issue should not preoccupy the agenda for East Asian regionalism. Nevertheless, it would be commendable to start with the APT, as the issues of non-traditional security are the most critical agenda for the APT members.[6] Starting with the APT, regional cooperation could be expanded gradually in the Asia-Pacific region, where the United States could engage as security caretaker.

Given the unique nature and evolution of Japan-ASEAN relations as a novel form of promoting a new regionalism, can we apply its approach to other areas and regions? The essence of the doctrine can be applied not only to Southeast Asia but also to East Asia, albeit in a different form. Now that the East Asian Community is on the regional agenda, we will be able to utilize the lessons accrued from Japan-ASEAN experiences. For instance, the Japan-ASEAN partnership continues to serve by elevating existing ASEAN regimes into expanded and effective regimes, as exemplified by the Chiang Mai Initiative Multilateralization and East Asia Emergency Rice Reserve.[7] If a new regionalism in East Asia turns out to be successful, it will inject a new element into international relations of the region.

Suffice it to say, ASEAN is now at a crossroads in its development. Japan should try to fully understand ASEAN's present plight, as the region is of crucial strategic importance to Japan for economic, politico-security and cultural reasons.[8] As an ASEAN expert contends, "the relevant question facing bilateral cooperation between Japan and ASEAN especially under the 2011 Bali Declaration is whether the present political and other realities framing East Asia are conducive to more effective security cooperation between them. Japan and ASEAN should be able to find areas to enhance their security cooperation. The issue is how to proceed without unnecessarily rocking the East Asian security boat."[9]

Notes

1. Akio Watanabe, "Yoshida dokutorin to sonogo", *Kokusaiseiji*, vol. 155 (March 2009): 148–57.
2. Tamotsu Fukuda, "Nihon to ASEAN" in *Zero nendai Nihon no Judaironten*, edited by Toshihiro Minohara (Tokyo: Kashiwa shobo, 2011), pp. 105–25.
3. ASEAN, "Japan All Set to Strengthen Its Commitment and Partnership with ASEAN, with the Launch of the Japan Mission to ASEAN, 26 May 2011" (Jakarta: ASEAN Secretariat, 2011) <http://www.asean,org/26333.htm>.
4. Thomas Berger, "Japan in Asia: A Hard Case for Soft Power", *Orbis* 54, no. 4 (Fall 2010): 565–82.
5. Kenichi Ito, "Nihon gaiko to Higashiajia kyodotai koso", *Gaiko*, vol. 1 (September 2010): 64.
6. Satoshi Amako, *Ajia rengo enomichi* (Tokyo: Chikumashobo, 2010), p. 237.
7. Sueo Sudo, "Japan-ASEAN Partnership as a Hub of East Asian Regionalism", paper presented at the conference on East Asian Regionalism, Fudan University, March 2011.
8. Regarding Japan's political, economic and social policies, see especially Ken Jimbo, "Tonanajia eno senryakuinfura wo anzenhosho no toride ni", *Gaiko*, vol. 13 (2012): 96–104; Maaike Okano-Heijmans, "Japan's New Economic Diplomacy: Changing Tactics or Strategy?" *Asia-Pacific Review* 19, no. 1 (2012): 62–87; Nissim Kadosh Otmazgin, "Geopolitics and Soft Power: Japan's Cultural Policy and Cultural Diplomacy in Asia", *Asia-Pacific Review* 19, no. 1 (2012): 37–61.
9. Carolina Hernandez, "East Asian Security and Japan-ASEAN Cooperation", conference paper for the 9th Japan-ASEAN Dialogue, Tokyo, 13–15 March 2012.

BIBLIOGRAPHY

English Sources

Abe, Shinzo. "Japan and One ASEAN that Care and Share at the Heart of Dynamic Asia, August 20, 2007". Tokyo: Ministry of Foreign Affairs, Japan.

Acharya, Amitav. *Whose Ideas Matter? Agency and Power in Asian Regionalism*. Ithaca, NY: Cornell University Press, 2009.

Adiwoso-Suprapto, Ragi. "Indonesian Perceptions of Japan and Indonesian-Japan Relations". In *Presence and Perceptions: The Underpinnings of ASEAN-Japan Relations*, edited by Charles Morrison. Tokyo: Japan Center for International Exchange, 1986.

Akrasanee, Narongchai, ed. *ASEAN-Japan Economic Relations: Trade and Development*. Singapore: Institute of Southeast Asian Studies, 1983.

Antolik, Michael. "The Pattern of ASEAN Summitry". *Contemporary Southeast Asia* 10, no. 4 (March 1989): 362–74.

ASEAN National Secretariat, Malaysia. *Record of the Meeting of ASEAN Heads of Government*. Kuala Lumpur: ASEAN National Secretariat of Malaysia, 1977.

ASEAN Secretariat. *ASEAN Documents Series, 1967–1985*. Jakarta: ASEAN Secretariat, 1985.

———. *Twenty-Fourth ASEAN Ministerial Meeting and Post-Ministerial Conference with the Dialogue Partners*. Jakarta: ASEAN Secretariat, 1991.

———. *ASEAN Statistical Yearbook*, various issues.

ASEAN, the Way Forward: The Report of the Group of Fourteen on Asean Economic Cooperation and Integration. Kuala Lumpur: Institute of Strategic and International Studies, 1987.

Atarashi, Kinji. "Japan's Economic Cooperation Policy Towards the ASEAN Countries". *International Affairs* 61, no. 1 (1984/85): 109–27.

Baker, James A. *The Politics of Diplomacy: Revolution, War and Peace, 1989–1992*. New York: Putnam's, 1995.

Bartu, Friedemann. *The Ugly Japanese: Nippon's Economic Empire in Asia*. Singapore: Longman, 1992.

Basu, Dipak and Victoria Miroshnic. *Japanese Foreign Investment 1970–1998*. New York: Sharpe, 2000.

Berger, Thomas. "The Pragmatic Liberalism of an Adaptive State". In *Japan in International Politics*, edited by Thomas Berger, Mike Mochizuki, and Jitsuo Tsuchiyama. Boulder, CO: Rienner, 2007.

———. "Japan in Asia: A Hard Case for Soft power". *Orbis*, 54, no. 4 (2010): 565–82.

Black, Lindsay. "Navigating the Boundaries of the Interstate Society: Japan's Response to Piracy in Southeast Asia". *Decoding Boundaries in Contemporary Japan*, edited by Glenn Hook. London: Routledge, 2010.

Blechinger, Verena. "Flirting with Regionalism: Japan's Foreign Policy Elites and the East Asian Economic Caucus". In *Facing Asia: Japan's Role in the Political Economic Dynamism of Regional Cooperation*, edited by Verena Blechinger and Jochen Legewie. Munchen: Iudicium-Verl, 2001.

Bradford, John. "Japanese Anti-Piracy Initiatives in Southeast Asia". *Contemporary Southeast Asia* 26, no. 3 (2004): 480–505.

Calder, Kent. "Japanese Foreign Economic Policy Formation: Explaining the 'Reactive State'". *World Politics* 40, no. 4 (1988): 517–41.

———. "The Institutions of Japanese Foreign Policy". In *The Process of Japanese Foreign Policy: Focus on Asia*, edited by Richard Grant. London: Royal Institute of International Affairs, 1997.

Campbell, John. *Institutional Change and Globalization*, Princeton, NJ: Princeton University Press, 2004.

Caporaso, James. "International Relations Theory and Multilateralism: The Search for Foundations". *International Organization* 46, no. 3 (1992): 599–632.

Chaikin, Greg. "Piracy in Asia: International Co-operation and Japan's Role". In *Piracy in Southeast Asia: Status, Issues, and Responses*, edited by Derek Johnson and Mark Valencia. Singapore: Institute of Southeast Asian Studies, 2005.

Chantapan, Anoosorn. "Changing Patterns of Japan-ASEAN Relations (1967–1989)". PhD dissertation, Johns Hopkins University, 1993.

Cheow, Eric Teo Chu. "Japan's Twin Challenges: Dealing with an ASEAN at the Crossroads and East Asian Regionalism". *Asia-Pacific Review* 10, no. 1 (2003): 30–43.

Chey, Hyoung-kyu. "The Changing Political Dynamics of East Asian Financial Cooperation: The Chiang Mai Initiative". *Asian Survey* 49, no. 3 (2009): 450–67.

Chin Kin Wah. "ASEAN: Facing the Fifth Decade". *Contemporary Southeast Asia* 29, no. 3 (2007) 395–405.

Constantino, Renato. *The Second Invasion: Japan in the Philippines*. Quezon City: Karrel, 1989.

Corning, Gregory. "Between Bilateralism and Regionalism in East Asia:

The ASEAN-Japan Comprehensive Economic Partnership". *Pacific Review* 22, no. 5 (2009): 639–65.

Crone, Donald. "The ASEAN Summit of 1987: Searching for New Dynamism". *Southeast Asian Affairs 1988*, edited by M. Ayoob and Ng Chee Yuen. Singapore: Institute of Southeast Asian Studies, 1988.

Dent, Christopher, ed. *China, Japan and Regional Leadership in East Asia*. Cheltenham: Elgar, 2008.

———. *East Asian Regionalism*. London: Routledge, 2008.

Department of State. *Foreign Relations of United States 1952–1954*, vol. 14, pt. 2. Washington, DC: Government Printing Office, 1985.

Dobson, Hugo. *Japan and United Nations Peacekeeping*. London: Routledge Curzon, 2003.

Dobson, Wendy. *Japan in East Asia: Trading and Investment Strategies*. Singapore: Institute of Southeast Asian Studies, 1993.

Dosch, Jorn and Manfred Mols. "Thirty Years of ASEAN: Achievements and Challenges". *Pacific Review* 11, no. 2 (1998): 167–82;

Fouse, David and Yoichiro Sato. "Enhancing Basic Governance: Japan's Comprehensive Counterterrorism Assistance to Southeast Asia". Asia-Pacific Center for Security Studies, United States Department of Defense, 2006.

Fukuda, Yasuo. "The Pacific Ocean Becomes an 'Inland Sea': Five Pledges to a Future Asia that 'Acts Together', May 22, 2008". Tokyo: Ministry of Foreign Affairs.

Fukushima, Akiko. *Japanese Foreign Policy: The Emerging Logic of Multilateralism*. London: Macmillan, 1999.

———. "Japan's Perspective on Asian Regionalism". In *Asia's New Multilateralism*, edited by Michael Green and Bates Gill. New York: Columbia University Press, 2009.

Fukuyama, Mitsuhiro. "Initial Steps toward Regional Economic Integration in East Asia (Japan's Proposal)". RIETI Policy Update 042, 23 February 2011.

———. "Toward a New Japan-ASEAN Relationship in 2011". *RIETI Report*, no. 127, February 2011.

Funabashi, Yoichi. *Asia Pacific Fusion: Japan's Role in APEC*. Washington D.C.: Institute for International Economics, 1995.

———. *New Challenges, New Frontier: Japan and ASEAN in the 21st Century*. Singapore: Institute of Southeast Asian Studies, 2003.

Gilson, Julie. "Japan's Role in the Asia-Europe Meeting". *Asian Survey* 39, no. 5 (1999): 736–52.

———. "Complex Regional Multilateralism: 'Strategising' Japan's Response to Southeast Asia". *Pacific Review* 17, no. 1 (2004): 71–94.

———. "Building Peace or Following the Leader? Japan's Peace Consolidation Diplomacy". *Pacific Affairs* 80, no. 1 (2007): 27–47.

―――. "Japan and Southeast Asia". In *Contemporary Southeast Asia*, 2nd ed., edited by Mark Beeson. New York: Palgrave Macmillan, 2009.

Glosserman, Brad. "Japan-ASEAN Summit: Playing Catch Up with China?" *PacNet*, no. 52, 18 December 2003.

Goh, Evelyn, ed. *Betwixt and Between: Southeast Asian Strategic Relations with the United States and China*. Singapore: Institute of Strategic and Defense Studies, 2005.

―――. "Great Powers and Hierarchical Order in Southeast Asia". *International Security* 32, no. 3 (2007/08): 113–57.

Goldstein, Judith. *Ideas, Interests, and American Trade Policy*. Ithaca, NY: Cornell University Press, 1993.

Goldstein, Judith and Robert Keohane, eds. *Ideas and Foreign Policy: Beliefs, Institutions and Political Change*. Ithaca, NY: Cornell University Press, 1993.

Gordon, Bernard. *Toward Disengagement in Asia*. Englewood Cliffs: Prentice-Hall, 1969.

Gorjao, Paulo. "Japan's Foreign Policy and East Timor, 1975–2002". *Asian Survey* 42, no. 5 (2002): 754–71.

Green, Michael. *Japan's Reluctant Realism: Foreign Policy Challenge in an Era of Uncertain Power*. New York: Palgrave, 2001.

Grimes, William. *Currency and Contest in East Asia: The Great Power Politics of Financial Regionalism*. Ithaca, NY: Cornell University Press, 2009.

Gunn, Geoffrey. "Japan, Postcrisis Indonesia, and the Japanese Role in East Timor Development". In *Transglobal Economies and Cultures: Contemporary Japan and Southeast Asia*, edited by Rolando Tolentino, Ong Jin Hui, and Hing Ai Yun. Manila: The University of the Philippines Press, 2004.

Haacke, Jurgen. *ASEAN's Diplomatic and Security Culture*. London: Routledge Curzon, 2003.

Haddad, William. "Japan, the Fukuda Doctrine, and ASEAN". *Contemporary Southeast Asia* 2, no. 1 (June 1980): 10–29.

Hall, Rosalie. "Civil-military Cooperation in International Disaster Response: The Japanese Self-Defense Forces' Deployment in Aceh, Indonesia". *Korean Journal of Defense Analysis* 20, no. 4 (December 2008): 383–400.

Hamanaka, Shintaro. *Asian Regionalism and Japan: The Politics of Membership in Regional Diplomatic, Financial and Trade Groups*. London: Routledge, 2009.

―――. "Regionalism Cycle in Asia (-Pacific): A Game Theory Approach to the Rise and Fall of Asian Regional Institutions". ADB Working Paper Series on. Regional Economic Integration, no. 42, February 2010.

Hanggi, Heiner. *ASEAN and the ZOPFAN Concept*, Pacific Strategic Paper 4. Singapore: Institute of Southeast Asian Studies, 1991.

Hashimoto, Ryutaro. *Reforms for the New Era of Japan and ASEAN: For a Broader and Deeper Partnership*. Singapore: Institute of Southeast Asian Studies, 1997.

Hatakeyama, Kyoko and Craig Freedman. *Snow on the Pine: Japan's Quest for a Leadership Role in Asia*. Singapore: World Scientific, 2010.

Hatch, Walter and Kozo Yamamura. *Asia in Japan's Embrace: Building a Regional Production Alliance*. New York: Cambridge University Press, 1996.

Hatoyama, Yukio. "Japan's New Commitment to Asia: Toward the Realization of an East Asian Community, November 15, 2009, Singapore". Tokyo: Ministry of Foreign Affairs, 2009.

Hayashi, Shigeko. *Japan and East Asian Monetary Regionalism: Towards a Proactive Leadership*. London: Routledge, 2006.

Hellmann, Donald. "Japan and Southeast Asia". *Asian Survey* 64, no. 12 (1979): 1189–98.

———. "Japanese Politics and Foreign Policy: Elitist Democracy within an American Greenhouse". In *The Political Economy of Japan: The Changing International Context*, edited by Takashi Inoguchi and Daniel Okimoto. Stanford: Stanford University Press, 1988.

Hernandez, Carolina. "East Asian Security and Japan-ASEAN Cooperation". Paper presented at the 9th Japan-ASEAN Dialogue, Tokyo, 13–15 March 2012.

Ho, Joshua. "Combating Piracy and Armed Robbery in Asia: Boosting Recaap's Role". *RSIS Commentaries*, no. 69 (2008).

Holliday, Ian. "Japan and the Myanmar Stalemate: Regional Power and Resolution of a Regional Problem". *Japanese Journal of Political Science* 6, no. 3 (2005): 393–410.

Hook, Glen, Julie Gilson, Christopher Hughes, and Helen Dobson. *Japan's International Relations*. London: Routledge, 2001.

Hook, Glenn. "The Japanese Role in the Emerging Asia-Pacific Order". In *Facing Asia: Japan's Role in the Political Economic Dynamism of Regional Cooperation*, edited by Verena Blechinger and Jochen Legewie. Munchen: Iudicium-Verl, 2001.

Horie, Masahiko. "Peace Process and Japanese ODA for Cambodia". *Dokkyo International Review*, no. 10 (1977): 95–107.

Hughes, Christopher. "Japan's Subregional Security and Defence Linkages with ASEANs, South Korea and China in the 1990s". *Pacific Review* 9, no. 2 (1996): 229–50.

Ikehata, Setsuho and Lydia Yu Jose, eds. *Philippines-Japan Relations*. Manila: Ateneo de Manila University Press, 2003.

Ikema, Makoto. "Japan's Economic Relations with ASEAN". In *ASEAN in a Changing Pacific and World Economy*, edited by Ross Garnaut. Canberra: Australian National University Press, 1980.

Indorf, Hans. "The Kuala Lumpur Summit: A Second for ASEAN". *Southeast Asian Affairs 1978*, edited by Leo Suryadinata. Singapore: Institute of Southeast Asian Studies, 1978.

Inoguchi, Takashi. "Japan Goes Regional". *Japan's Asian Policy: Revival and Response*, edited by Takashi Inoguchi. London: Palgrave Macmillan, 2002.

Japan Center for International Exchange. *Presence and Perceptions: The Underpinnings of ASEAN-Japan Relations*. Tokyo: Japan Center for International Exchange, 1986.

Jeshurun, Chandran. *Malaysia: Fifty Years of Diplomacy, 1957–2007*. Kuala Lumpur: The Other Press, 2007.

JETRO. *Nihon no toshi*, various issues. Tokyo: JETRO.

Joesoef, Daoed. "Japan and ASEAN: Policies towards Promoting Closer Cooperation". In *Japan-Indonesia Cooperation: Problems and Prospects*, edited by the Center for Strategic and International Studies. Jakarta: CSIS, 1978.

Johnson, Chalmers. *Japan: Who Governs?* New York: Norton, 1995.

Jomo, K.S., ed. *The Sun Also Set*. Selangor: Institute for Social Analysis, 1983.

──────, ed. *Japan and Malaysia Development: In the Shadow of the Rising Sun*. London: Routledge, 1994.

Jorgensen-Dahl, Arnfinn. *Regional Organization and Order in South-East Asia*. London: Macmillan, 1982.

Kaifu, Toshiki. "Japan and ASEAN: Seeking a Mature Partnership for the New Age". *ASEAN Economic Bulletin* 8, no. 1 (1991): 87–94.

Katada, Saori. "Japan's Counterweight Strategy: U.S.-Japan Cooperation and Competition in International Finance". In *Beyond Bilateralism: U.S.-Japan Relations in the New Asia-Pacific*, edited by Ellis Krauss and T.J. Pempel. Stanford: Stanford University Press, 2004.

Kawashima, Yutaka. *Japanese Foreign Policy at the Crossroads*. Washington, DC: Brookings Institution Press, 2003.

Keohane, Robert. "Multilateralism: An Agenda for Research". *International Journal* 45, no. 4 (1990): 731–64.

Kerr, Paulin, Andrew Mack, and Paul Evans. "The Evolving Security Discourse in the Asia Pacific". In *Pacific Cooperation: Builidng Economic and Security Regimes in the Asia Pacific Region*, edited by Andrew Mack and John Ravenhill. St. Leonards: Allen & Unwin, 1994.

Kesavan, Kuunnavakkam V. *Japan's Relations with Southeast Asia, 1952–60*. Bombay: Somaiya, 1972.

──────. "Japan and ASEAN: Their Changing Security Relations". ORF Occasional Paper, no. 22, August 2011.

Khamchoo, Chaiwat. "Japan's Southeast Asian Policy in the Post-Vietnam Era 1975–1985". PhD dissertation, University of Washington, 1986.

──────. "Japan's Role in Southeast Asian Security". *Pacific Affairs* 64, no. 1 (1991): 7–22.

Khamchoo, Chaiwat and Bruce Reynolds, eds. *Thai-Japanese Relations in Historical Perspective*. Bangkok: Institute of Asian Studies, Chulalongkorn University, 1988.

Kiuchi, Takashi. "The Future of ASEAN-Japan Financial Relations". In *ASEAN-Japan Cooperation*, edited by the Japan Center for International Exchange. Tokyo: JCIE, 2003.

Kohno, Masaharu. "In Search of Proactive Diplomacy: Increasing Japan's International Role in the 1990s", CNAPS Working Paper, Center for Northeast Asian Policy Studies, the Brookings Institution, 1999 <www.brookings.edu/papers/1999/fall_japan_kohno.aspx>.

Koizumi, Junichiro. *Japan and ASEAN in East Asia: A Sincere and Open Partnership*. Singapore: Institute of Southeast Asian Studies, 2002.

Kojima, Takaaki. *Japan and ASEAN: Partnership for a Stable and Prosperous Future*. Singapore: Institute of Southeast Asian Studies, 2006.

Kudo, Toshihiro. "Myanmar and Japan: How Close Friends Become Estranged", IDE Discussion Paper no. 118. Chiba: Institute of Developing Economies, 2007.

Kudo, Toshihiro and Fumiharu Mieno. "Trade, Foreign Investment and Myanmar's Economic Development during the Transition to an Open Economy", IDE Discussion Paper Series No. 116. Chiba: Institute of Developing Economies, August 2007.

Langdon, Frank. *Japan's Foreign Policy*. Vancouver: University of British Columbia Press, 1973.

Lee Hsien Loong. "Japan's Role in Southeast Asia". Speech by Deputy Prime Minister of Singapore at the Japan Institute of International Affairs, Tokyo, 25 May 1999.

———. "The Future of East Asian Cooperation". Nikkei Net Interactive, the 11th International Conference on the Future of Asia, 25 May 2005, Tokyo.

Lee Poh Ping. "Malaysian Perceptions of Japan before and during the 'Look East' Period". *Asia Pacific Community*, no. 29 (1985): 97–108.

———. "ASEAN and the Japanese Role in Southeast Asia". In *ASEAN in the 1990s*, edited by Alison Broinowski. London: Macmillan, 1990.

Lee Yong Wook. *The Japanese Challenge to the American Neoliberal World*. Stanford: Stanford University Press, 2008.

Leifer, Michael. *The ASEAN Regional Forum*. Adelphi Paper 302. London, Oxford University Press, 1996.

Leong, Steven. "The East Asian Economic Caucus (EAEC): 'Formalized' Regionalism Being Denied". In *National Perspectives on the New Regionalism in the South*, edited by Bjorn Hettne et al. London: Macmillan, 2000.

Lim Teck Ghee. "Southeast Asian Perceptions of Japan and the Japanese". In *Japan as an Economic Power and Its Implications for Southeast Asia*, edited by K.S. Sandhu. Singapore: Singapore University Press, 1974.

Lincoln, Edward. "Japan's Role in Asia-Pacific Cooperation: Dimensions, Prospects, and Problems". *East Asia* 8, no. 4 (1989): 3–23.

Llewelyn, James. "Japan's Return to International Diplomacy and Southeast Asia: Japanese Mediation in *Konfrontasi*, 1963–66". *Asian Studies Review* 30, no. 4 (2006): 355–74.

Long, William. "Nonproliferation as a Goal of Japanese Foreign Assistance". In *Japanese Foreign Policy in Asia and the Pacific*, edited by Akitoshi Miyashita and Yoichiro Sato. New York: Palgrave, 2001.

Luhulima, C.P.F. "The Third ASEAN Summit and Beyond". *Indonesian Quarterly* 17, no. 1 (1989): 12–28.

Mackie, J.A.C. *Konfrontasi: Indonesia-Malaysia Dispute 1963–1966*. Kuala Lumpur: Oxford University Press, 1974.

Mahathir Mohamad. "Coexistence in Asia". Speech by the Prime Minister of Malaysia at the Kyushu-Asian Summit for Local Authorities in Kyushu, Japan, 21 October 1994.

———. *A Doctor in the House*. Kuala Lumpur: MPH Group Printing, 2011.

Manglapus, Raul. *Japan in Southeast Asia: Collision Course*. New York: Carnegie Endowment for International Peace, 1976.

Manicom, James. "Japan's Role in Strengthening Maritime Security in Southeast Asia". NBR Special Report, no. 24, November 2010.

Maswood, S. Javed. "Japanese Foreign Policy and Regionalism". In *Japan and East Asian Regionalism*, edited by S. Javed Maswood. London: Routledge, 2001.

Matsuzaki, Hideo. "Future of Japan-ASEAN Relations". *Asia Pacific Community*, no. 21 (1983): 11–22.

Md Nasrudin Md Akhir. "Five Decades of Malaysia-Japan Relations". In *Japan and the Asia Pacific*, edited by Md Nasrudin Md Akhir and Rohayati Paidi. Kuala Lumpur: Department of East Asian Studies, University of Malaya, 2009.

Mendl, Wolf. *Japan's Asia Policy: Regional Security and Global Interests*. London, Routledge, 1995.

Midford, Paul. "Japan's Leadership Role in East Asian Security Multilateralism". *Pacific Review* 13, no. 3 (2001): 367–97.

Ministry of Finance, Japan. *Financial Statistics of Japan*, various issues.

Ministry of Foreign Affairs, Japan. *Outline of Japan's Basic Policies and Japan-Singapore Relations*. Tokyo: Ministry of Foreign Affairs, 1977.

———. *Japan's ODA*. Tokyo: Ministry of Foreign Affairs, 2001–11.

Ministry of Foreign Affairs, Thailand. *Foreign Affairs Newsletter*, various issues.

Miyashita, Akitoshi. "Consensus or Compliance? Gaiatsu, Interests, and Japan's Foreign Aid". In *Japanese Foreign Policy in Asia and the Pacific*, edited by Akitoshi Miyashita and Yoichiro Sato. New York: Palgrave, 2001.

———. *Limits to Power: Asymmetric Dependence and Japanese Foreign Aid Policy*. Lanham, MD: Lexington Books, 2003.

Miyazawa, Kiichi. "New Era of the Asia-Pacific and Japan-ASEAN Cooperation". *ASEAN Economic Bulletin* 9, no. 3 (1993): 375–80.

Morada, Noel. "Institutionalization of Regional Order: Between Norms and Balance of Power". In *Regional Order in East Asia: ASEAN and Japan Perspectives*, edited by Jun Tsunekawa. Tokyo: National Institute of Defense Studies, 2007.

Munakata, Naoko. *Transforming East Asia: The Evolution of Regional Economic Integration*. Washington, DC: Brookings Institution Press, 2006.

Mutalib, Hussin. "At Thirty, ASEAN Looks to Challenges in the New Millennium". *Contemporary Southeast Asia* 19, no. 1 (1997): 74–85.

Nagesh, Narayana. *Japan's Economic Diplomacy in Southeast Asia*. New Delhi: Lancers Books, 1996.

Narine, Shaun. *Explaining ASEAN: Regionalism in Southeast Asia*. Boulder, CO: Rienner, 2002.

———. "Forty years of ASEAN: A Historical Review". *Pacific Review* 21, no. 4 (2008): 411–29.

Nemoto, Takumi. "Asian Gateway Initiative". Council for the Asian Gateway Initiative, 16 May 2007 <www.kantei.go.jp/foreign/gateway/kettei/070516doc.pdf>.

Nishihara, Masashi. *The Japanese and Sukarno's Indonesia: Tokyo-Jakarta Relations, 1951–1966*. Honolulu: University of Hawai'i Press, 1976.

———. "How Much Longer the Fruits of the 'Yoshida Doctrine'?". In *Korea and Japan: A New Dialogue across the Channel*, edited by Hahn Bae-ho and Yamamoto Tadashi. Seoul: Asiatic Research Center, Korea University, 1978.

Nishiyama, Takehiko. "International Relations in Southeast Asia". Mimeographed. n.d.

Oba, Tomomitsu. "Japan's Role in East Asian Investment and Finance". *Japan Review of International Affairs* 9, no. 3 (1995): 246–51.

Ogawa, Tadashi. "Origin and Development of Japan's Public Diplomacy". In *Routledge Handbook of Public Diplomacy*, edited by Nancy Snow and Phillip Taylor. London: Routledge, 2009.

Ogoura, Kazuo. "A Call for a New Concept of Asia". *Japan Echo* 20, no. 3 (1993): 37–44.

———. *Japan's Cultural Diplomacy*. Tokyo: Japan Foundation, 2009.

Ohama, Ikuo. "Materials on Japan-ASEAN Relations". In *Aspects of ASEAN*, edited by Werner Pfennig and Mark Suh. Munchen: Weltforum Verlag, 1984.

Oishi, Mikio and Fumitaka Furuoka. "Can Japanese Aid be an Effective Tool of Influence? Case Studies of Cambodia and Burma". *Asian Survey* 43, no. 6 (2003): 890–907.

Okamoto, Jiro. ed. *Trade Liberalization and APEC. London:* Routledge, 2004.

Okano-Heijmans, Maaike. "Japan's New Economic Diplomacy: Changing Tactics or Strategy?" *Asia-Pacific Review* 19, no. 1 (2012): 62–87.

Okazaki, Katsuo. "Japan's Foreign Relations". *Annals of the American Academy*, no. 308, November 1956.

Olson, Lawrence. *Japan in Asia*. New York: Praeger, 1970.

Otmazgin, Nissim Kadosh. "Geopolitics and Soft Power: Japan's Cultural Policy and Cultural Diplomacy in Asia". *Asia-Pacific Review* 19, no. 1 (2012): 37–61.

Owada, Hisashi. "Japan-ASEAN Relations in East Asia". Speech delivered at Hotel New Otani, Singapore, 16 October 2000 <http://www.jiia.or.jp/report/owada/Singapore>.

Parmer, Ronald and Thomas Reckford. *Building ASEAN: Twenty Years of Southeast Asian Cooperation*. New York: Praeger, 1987.

Percival, Bronson. "Japan-Southeast Asian Relations: Playing Catch-Up with China". *Contemporary Connections* 8, no. 3 (2006).

Pollard, Vincent. "ASA and ASEAN, 1961–1967". Asian Survey 10, no. 3 (1970): 244–55.

Pongelar, Suppakarn. "The Implications of Japanese Engagement Policy towards Myanmar: 1988–Present". GSID Discussion Paper. Nagoya University, 2007.

Pongpaichit, Pasuk et al., eds. *The Lion and the Mouse*. Bangkok: Chulalongkorn University, 1986.

Potter, David and Sueo Sudo. "Japanese Foreign Policy: No Longer Reactive?". *Political Studies Review* 1, no. 3 (2003): 317–32.

Pyle, Kenneth. *The Japanese Question: Power and Purpose in a New Era*. Washington, DC: AEI Press, 1992.

———. "The Primacy of Foreign Policy in Modern Japan". *Asian Policy*, no. 4 (2007): 208–211.

Ravenhill, John. "East Asian regionalism: Much Ado about Nothing?". *Review of International Studies* 35, supplement 1 (2009): 215–35.

Regnier, Philippe, ed. *Japan and Multilateral Diplomacy*. Aldershot: Ashgate, 2001.

Rix, Alan. "ASEAN and Japan: More than Economics". In *Understanding ASEAN*, edited by Alison Broinowski. London: Macmillan, 1982.

———. "Japan and the Region: Leadership from Behind". In *Pacific Economic Relations in the 1990s*, edited by Richard Higgott, Richard Leaver, and John Ravenhill. Boulder, CO: Rienner, 1993.

———. "Managing Japan's Aid: ASEAN". In *Japan's Foreign Aid: Power and Policy in a New Era*, edited by Bruce Keppel and Robert Orr. Boulder, CO: Westview, 1993.

Ruggie, John, ed. *Multilateralism Matters: The Theory and Praxis of an Institutional Form. New York:* Columbia University Press, 1993.

Sakuta, Eiji. "Japan-ASEAN Economic Relations". *Journal of Japanese Trade and Industry*, September-October 1986, pp. 10–14.

Samuels, Richard. *Securing Japan: Tokyo's Grand Strategy and the Future of East Asia*. Ithaca, NY: Cornell University Press, 2007.

Sato, Yoichiro. "Southeast Asian Receptiveness to Japanese Maritime Security

Cooperation". Asia-Pacific Center for Security Studies, United States Department of Defense, 2007.

Sato, Yukio. "Emerging Trends in Asia-Pacific Security: The Role of Japan". *Pacific Review* 8, no. 2 (1995): 267–82.

Seekins, Donald. *Burma and Japan since 1940: From 'Co-Prosperity' to 'Quiet Dialogue'*. Copenhagen: NIAS Press, 2007.

Sekiguchi, Sueo, ed. *ASEAN-Japan Economic Relations: Investment*. Singapore: Institute of Southeast Asian Studies, 1983.

Severino, Rodolfo. "ASEAN at Forty: A Balance Sheet". In *Southeast Asian Affairs 2008*, edited by Daljit Singh and Tin Maung Maung Than. Singapore: Institute of Southeast Asian Affairs, 2008.

Sheah, David Chee-Meow. "ASEAN and Japan's Southeast Asian Regionalism". In *Japan's Asian Policy*, edited by Takashi Inoguchi. New York: Palgrave Macmillan, 2002.

Shee Poon-Kim. "A Decade of ASEAN, 1967–1977". *Asian Survey* 17, no. 8 (1977): 753–70.

Shibusawa, Masahide. *Japan and the Asia Pacific Region*. London: Croom Helm, 1983.

Shimizu, Hiroshi and Hitoshi Hirakawa. *Japan and Singapore in the World Economy 1870–1965*. London: Routledge, 1999.

Shimizu, Sayuri. *Creating People of Plenty: The United States and Japan's Economic Alternatives, 1950–1960*. Kent, OH: Kent State University Press, 2001.

Shiraishi, Masaya. *Japanese Relations with Vietnam: 1951–1987*. Ithaca, NY: Cornell University Press, 1990.

———. "Japan and the Reconstruction of Indochina". In *New Dynamics between China and Japan in Asia*, edited by Guy Faure. Singapore: World Scientific, 2010.

Sikkink, Kathryn. *Ideas and Institutions: Developmentalism in Argentina and Brazil*. Ithaca, NY: Cornell University Press, 1991.

Singh, Bhubhindar. "ASEAN's Perceptions of Japan: Change and Continuity". *Asian Survey* 42, no. 2 (2002): 276–96.

———. "The Evolution of Japan's Security Role in Southeast Asia". *Round Table* 99, no. 409 (2010): 391–402.

Smith, Anthony. "Japan's Relations with Southeast Asia: The Strong Silent Type". In *Japan in a Dynamic Asia*, edited by Yoichiro Sato and Satu Limaye. Lanham, MD: Lexington Books, 2006.

Sneider, Daniel. "The New Asianism: Japanese Foreign Policy under the Democratic Party of Japan". *Asia Policy*, no. 12 (2011): 99–129.

Soesastro, Hadi. "The Institutional Framework for APEC: An ASEAN Perspective". In *APEC: Challenges and Opportunities*, edited by Chia Siow Yue. Singapore: Institute of Southeast Asian Studies, 1994.

Sohn, Injoo. "Learning to Co-Operation: China's Multilateral Approach to Asian Financial Co-Operation". *China Quarterly*, no. 194 (2008): 309–26.

Sohn, Yul. "Japan's New Regionalism: China Shock, Values, and the East Asian Community". *Asian Survey* 50, no. 3 (2010): 497–519.

Solidum, Estrella. *Towards a Southeast Asian Community*. Quezon City: University of the Philippines Press, 1974.

———. *The Politics of ASEAN: An Introduction to Southeast Asian Regionalism*. Singapore: Eastern University Press, 2003.

St John, Ronald. "Japan's Moment in Indochina". *Asian Survey* 35, no. 7 (1995): 668–81.

Stubbs, Richard. "ASEAN Plus Three: Emerging East Asian Regionalism?" *Asian Survey* 42, no. 3 (2002): 440–55.

———. "ASEAN at Twenty: The Search for a New Consensus". In *Regionalism in Asia: Critical Issues in Modern Politics*, edited by See Seng Tan. London: Routledge, 2009.

Sudo, Sueo. "From Fukuda to Takeshita: A Decade of Japan-ASEAN Relations". *Contemporary Southeast Asia* 10, no. 2 (1988): 119–43.

———. "The Politics of Thai-Japanese Trade Relations". In *Thai-Japanese Relations in Historical Perspective*, edited by Chaiwat Khamchoo and Bruce Reynolds. Bangkok: Institute of Asian Studies, Chulalongkorn University, 1988.

———. *The Fukuda Doctrine and ASEAN: New Dimensions in Japanese Foreign Policy*. Singapore: Institute of Southeast Asian Studies, 1992.

———. *Evolution of ASEAN-Japan Relations*. Singapore: Institute of Southeast Asian Studies, 2005.

———. "Japan's ASEAN Policy: Reactive or Proactive in the Face of a Rising China in East Asia?" *Asian Perspective* 33, no. 1 (2009): 137–58.

———. "Japan-ASEAN Partnership as a Hub of East Asian Regionalism". Paper presented at the Conference on East Asian Regionalism, Fudan University, March 2011.

Suehiro, Akira. "The Road to Economic Re-entry: Japan's Policy toward Southeast Asian Development". *Social Science Japan Journal* 2, no. 1 (1999): 85–105.

Sumitwongse, Kusuma. "Thirty Years of ASEAN: Achievements through Political Cooperation". *Pacific Review* 11, no. 2 (1998): 183–94.

Suriyamongkal, Marjorie. "The Politics of Economic Cooperation in the Association of Southeast Asian Nations". PhD dissertation, University of Illinois, 1982.

Takeshita, Noboru. "Opening Statement". Meeting of the ASEAN Heads of Government and the Prime Minister of Japan. Jakarta: ASEAN Secretariat, 1987.

———. "Japan and ASEAN: Thinking Together, Advancing Together". *ASEAN Economic Bulletin* 6, no. 1 (1989): 125–33.

Talalla, Albert. "A Pre-Summit Evaluation". In *The Association of Southeast Asian Nations: After 20 Years*, edited by Hans Indorf. Washington, DC: Woodrow Wilson International Center for Scholars, 1988.

Tamura, Hajime. "ASEAN and Japan on the Eve of the 21st Century". *ASEAN Economic Bulletin* 4, no. 1 (1987,): 114–18.

Tan, Gerald. *ASEAN Economic Development and Cooperation*. Singapore: Times Academic, 1996.

Tanaka, Shoko. *Post-War Japanese Resource Policies and Strategies: The Case of Southeast Asia*. Ithaca, NY: China-Japan Program, Cornell University, 1986.

Tang Siew Mun. "Japan's Vision of an East Asian Community". *Japanese Studies* 26, no. 2 (2006): 199–210.

———. "The Fukuda Doctrine: Historical Relic or Enduring Wisdom?" In *Japanese Relations with ASEAN since the Fukuda Doctrine*, edited by Lee Poh Ping and Md Nasrudin Md Akhir. Kuala Lumpur: Japan Studies Program, University of Malaya, 2009.

Tang, James. "ASEAN-Japan Relations: Literature Review and an Agenda for Further Research". Proceedings of an Intra Universities Seminar on ASEAN-Japan Relations, Bandung, Padjadjaran University, 1990.

Tanino, Sakutaro. "Japan and the United States". In *U.S.-Japan Relations: New Attitudes for a New Era*, edited by Center for International Affairs. Cambridge, MA: Center for International Affairs, Harvard University, 1984.

Tarling, Nicholas. *Regionalism in Southeast Asia*. London: Routledge, 2006.

———. *Southeast Asia and the Great Powers*. London: Routledge, 2010.

Thayer, Carlyle. "Southeast Asia: Patterns of Security Cooperation". *ASPI Strategy*, September 2010.

Togo, Kazuhiko. *Japan's Foreign Policy 1945–2009: The Quest for a Proactive Policy*. Boston: Brill, 2010.

Tomoda, Seki. "Japan's Search for a Political Role in Asia". *Japan Review of International Affairs* 6, no. 1 (1992): 43–60.

Tsurutani, Taketsugu. *Japanese Policy and East Asian Security*. New York: Praeger, 1981.

United Nations Educational, Scientific, and Cultural Organization. *UNESCO Statistical Yearbook*, various issues.

Uno, Sosuke. "Engine for Development: Japan-ASEAN Cooperation toward Peace and Stability". *Speaking of Japan*, November 1988.

Wakamiya, Yoshibumi. *The Postwar Conservative View of Asia*. Tokyo: LTCB International Library Foundation, 1998.

Wan, Min. *Japan between Asia and the West*. Armonk: Sharpe, 2001.

Watanabe, Taizo and William Tow. "Trilateralism, Southeast Asia and multilateralism". In *Asia-Pacific Security*, edited by William Tow et al. London: Routledge, 2007.

Weatherbee, Donald. *International Relations in Southeast Asia: The Struggle for Autonomy*. Lanham, MD: Rowman & Littlefield, 2005.

Webber, Douglas. "Two Funerals and a Wedding? The Ups and Downs of Regionalism in East Asia and Asia Pacific after the Asian Crisis". In *Comparative Regional Integration*, edited by Finn Laursen. Hampshire: Ashgate, 2003.

Wee Mon-cheng. *Chrysanthemum and the Orchid: Observations of a Diplomat*. Times Academic, 1975.

Wee Nib-cheung, "How Can Japan Assist the Industrial Projects in ASEAN Countries". *Look Japan*, 10 July 1977.

Weinstein, Franklin. *Indonesian Foreign Policy and the Dilemma of Dependence*. Ithaca, NY: Cornell University Press, 1976.

Wendt, Alexander. *Social Theory of International Politics*. Cambridge: Cambridge University Press, 1999.

Wie, Thee Kian. "Foreign Direct Investment from Northeast Asia to Southeast Asia". *Indonesia Quarterly* 38, no. 2 (2010): 188–212.

Won Lai Foon. "China-ASEAN and Japan-ASEAN Relations during the Post-Cold War Era". *Chinese Journal of International Politics* 1, no. 3 (2007): 373–404.

Wong, Any. *Japan's Comprehensive National Security Strategy and its Economic Cooperation with the ASEAN Countries*. Hong Kong: Chinese University of Hong Kong, 1991.

Yamamoto, Tadashi and Carolina Hernandez. "Social and Cultural Dimensions in East Asian Community Building". In *ASEAN-Japan Cooperation: A Foundation for East Asian Community*, edited by Japan Center for International Exchange. Tokyo: Japan Center for International Exchange, 2003.

Yano, Toru. "Toward a Reorientation of Asian Policy: The Fukuda Doctrine and Japanese-US Cooperation". In *Encounter at Shimoda: Search for a New Pacific Partner*, edited by Herbert Passin and Akira Iriye. Boulder, CO: Westview Press, 1979.

Yasutomo, Denis. *Japan and the Asia Development Bank*. New York: Praeger, 1983.

———. *The Manner of Giving: Strategic Aid and Japanese Foreign Policy*. Lexington, MA: Lexington Books, 1986.

———. *The New Multilateralism in Japan's Foreign Policy*. New York: St. Martin's, 1995.

———. "Japan's Multilateral Assistance Leadership: Momentum or Malaise?" In *Facing Asia: Japan's Role in the Political Economic Dynamism of Regional Cooperation*, edited by Verena Blechinger and Jochen Legewie. Munchen: Iudicium-Verl, 2001.

Yeo Lay Hwee. "Japan, ASEAN, and the Construction of an East Asian Community". *Contemporary Southeast Asia* 28, no. 2 (2006): 259–75.

Yoshikawa, Yoko. "War Reparations Implementation, Reparations-Secured Loans and a Treaty of Commerce". In *Philippines-Japan Relations*, edited by Setsuho

Ikehata and Lydia Yu Jose. Manila: Ateneo de Manila University Press, 2003.

Yoshimatsu, Hidetaka. "Japan and Regional Governance in East Asia". In *Governance and Regionalism in Asia*, edited by Nicholas Thomas. London: Routledge, 2009.

Yoshimatsu, Hidetaka and Dennis Trinidad. "Development Assistance, Strategic Interests, and the China Factor in Japan's Role in ASEAN Integration". *Japanese Journal of Political Science* 11, no. 2 (2010): 199–219.

Ysu Yun Hui, ed., *Japan and Singapore*. Singapore: McGraw-Hill, 2006.

Yueng, C.K. "Japan's Role in the Making of the Asia-Pacific Economic Cooperation (APEC)". In *Japanese Foreign Policy in Asia and the Pacific*, edited by Akitoshi Miyashita and Yoichiro Sato. New York: Palgrave, 2001.

Yuzawa, Takeshi. *Japan's Security Policy and the ASEAN Regional Forum*. London: Routledge, 2007.

Japanese Sources

Amako, Satoshi. *Ajia rengo enomichi* [The road to an Asian Union]. Tokyo: Chikumashobo, 2010.

Aoki, Maki. "Chiikibunkakyoryoku womeguru bunka sesshoku" [Cultural contacts through regional cultural cooperation]. In *Sengo Nihon no Kokuksai bunka koryu*. Tokyo: Keiso shobo, 2005.

Aoki, Tamotsu. "Imakoso takokukan bunkagaiko wo" [Now is the time for multilateral cultural diplomacy]. *Chuo koron*, August 1998, pp. 52–64.

Arai, Toshiaki. *ASEAN to Nihon* [ASEAN and Japan]. Tokyo: Nicchu shuppan, 2003.

Asashi, Yasushi. *Nintai to kibo: Kambojia no 560nichi* [Perseverance and hope: 560 days in Cambodia]. Tokyo: Asahi Shimbunsha, 1995.

Edamura, Sumio. "Fukuda dokutorin no tanjo" [The birth of the Fukuda Doctrine]. *Gaiko Foramu*, November 2008, pp. 82–87.

———. "Hatsuno Nihon ASEAN shuno kaigi" [The first Japan-ASEAN Summit Meeting]. *Gaiko Foramu*, December 2008, pp. 70–75.

———. "Indoneshia-Filipin to Manila supichi" [Indonesia-the Philippines and Manila Speech]. *Gaiko Foramu*, January 2009, pp. 9–95.

Ezaki, Masumi. *Keizaimasatsu kaisho no taisaku*" [Measures to resolve economic frictions]. Tokyo: Sekaiseikei bunka kenkyusho, 1983.

Fukuda, Takeo. *Kaiko kyujunen* [Ninety years recollections]. Tokyo: Iwanami shoten, 1995.

Fukuda, Tamotsu. "Nihon to ASEAN [Japan and ASEAN]". In *Zero nendai Nihon no Judaironten*, edited by Toshihiro Minohara. Tokyo: Kashiwa shobo, 2011.

Gaimusho [Japan's Ministry of Foreign Affairs]. *Waga gaiko no kinkyo* [Current state of Japanese diplomacy]. Tokyo: Okurasho insatsukyoku, 1972–1986.

———. *Deta nimiru Nihon to ASEAN* [Japan and ASEAN seen from data]. Tokyo: Ministry of Foreign Affairs, 1982.

———. *Gaiko seisho* [Diplomatic bluebook]. Tokyo: Okurasho insatsukyoku, 1987–2011.

———. *Waga kuni no seifukaihatsuenjo* [Japan's official development assistance]. Tokyo: Okurasho insatsukyoku, 1972–2000.

Goto, Kanichi. *Kindai Nihon to Indoneshia* [Modern Japan and Indonesia]. Tokyo: Hokuju shuppan, 1989.

Hatano, Sumio, ed. *Ikeda-Sato seikenki no Nihon gaiko* [Japanese diplomacy during the Ikeda-Sato administration]. Kyoto: Mineruva shobo, 2004.

Hatano, Sumio and Susumu Sato. *Gendai Nihon no Tonanajia seisaku 1950–2005* [Contemporary Japan's Southeast Asian policy, 1950–2005]. Tokyo: Wasedadaigaku shuppanbu, 2007.

Hirata, Keiko. "Gaiko" [Diplomacy]. In *Akusesu Nihonseiji ron*, edited by Hiroshi Hirano and Masaru Kono. Tokyo: Nihon keizai hyoron sha, 2003.

Hoshiro, Koji. "Tonanajia kaihatsukaigi no kaisai to Nihon gaiko" [The Ministerial Conference for the Economic Development of Southeast Asia and Japanese Diplomacy]. *Kokusaiseiji*, no. 144 (2006): 1–15.

Ihara, Nobuhiro. "ASEAN setsuritsukatei saiko: Genkameikoku no taiIndoneshia fushin ni chumokushite" [Rethinking the process of establishing ASEAN: focus on the original member countries' mistrust of Indonesia]. *Kokusaiseiji*, no. 164 (2011): 115–28.

Ikeda, Tadashi. *Cambodia wahei enomichi* [Toward a peace settlement in Cambodia]. Tokyo: Toshi shuppan, 1996.

Ikegami, Mana. "Taietsu keizaienjo niokeru Nihongaiko" [Japanese diplomacy in its economic assistance to Vietnam]. *Hogakuseiji Ronkyu* 85 (2010): 61–90.

Imagawa, Eiichi and Hiroshi Matsuo, *Nikka haiseki* [Boycotting the Japanese goods]. Tokyo: Nikkei shinsho, 1973.

Imagawa, Yukio. *Cambodia to Nihon* [Cambodia and Japan]. Tokyo: Rengo shuppan, 2000.

Inoue, Toshikazu. *Nihon no gaiko* [Japanese diplomacy]. Tokyo: Shinzansha, 2005.

Intarathai, Khoontong. *ASEAN to Nihon* [ASEAN and Japan]. Tokyo: Yazawa shobo, 1982.

Iokibe, Makoto, ed. *Sengo Nihon gaikoshi* [A diplomatic history of postwar Japan]. Tokyo: Yuhikaku, 1999.

Ishii, Kazuo. *Nihon no Boeki 55nen* [55 years of Japanese trade]. Tokyo: JETRO, 2000.

Ishii, Risako. "Posuto reisenki Indoshina niokeru Nihon no enjogaiko" [Japan's aid policy toward Indochina in the post-Cold War period]. *Kokusaikankeiron Kenkyu*, no. 20 (2004): 83–113.

Ishii, Yoneo and Toshiharu Yoshikawa. *Nittai Koryu Yonhyakunenshi* [Four hundred years of Japan-Thailand relations]. Tokyo: Kodansha, 1987.

Ito, Kenichi. "Nihon gaiko to Higashiajia kyodotai koso" [Japanese diplomacy and the East Asian Community]. *Gaiko* 1 (September 2010): 60–67.

Ito, Shigeyuki. *Ajia to Nihon no miraichitsujo* [Future order of Asia and Japan]. Tokyo: Toshindo, 2004.

Ja, Yan-hyon. "1977nen Fukuda Takeo shusho Tonanajia rekiho to Nihon no Tonanajia seisakukeisei" [Prime Minister Takeo Fukuda's Visit to Southeast Asia in 1977 and the formation of Japan's Southeast Asian policy]. *Kokusaikankeiron Kenkyu*, no. 22 (2004): 65–95.

Japan External Trade Organization [JETRO]. *Kaigaishijo hakusho*. Tokyo: JETRO, 1983.

Jeong, Kyong-ah. "60nendai niokeru Nihon no Tonanajia kaihatsu" [Japanese Policy of Southeast Asian Development during the 1960s]. *Kokusaiseiji*, no. 126 (2001): 117–31.

Jimbo, Ken. "Tonanajia eno senryakuinfura wo anzenhosho no toride ni" [Building the maritime security infrastructure of ASEAN: Japan's new engagement in Southeast Asia]. *Gaiko* 13 (2012): 96–104.

Kaneko, Masashi. "Nihon no paburikku dipuromashi [Japan's public diplomacy]". In *Paburikku dipuramashi*, edited by Masashi Kaneko and Mitsuru Kitano. Tokyo: PHP kenkyusho, 2007.

Karu, Hiroshi. "Kanminkyoryoku niyoru kokusaikyoryoku suishin no ichihosaku" [An attempt to promote international cooperation by public-private cooperation]. *Shakaikagaku Tokyu*, no. 117 (1994): 253–75.

Kato, Kazuhide. "Kambojia funso to Nihon gaiko" [Cambodia conflict and Japanese diplomacy]. *Kokusaishogaku Ronshu* 13, no. 3 (2002): 35–69.

Keidanren. *Keidanren sanjunenshi* [Thirty years of the Federation of Economic Organizations]. Tokyo: Keidanren, 1978.

Kohama, Hirohisa. *ODA no Keizaigaku* [Economy of ODA]. Tokyo: Nihon hyoronsha, 1998.

Kohno, Masaharu. *Wahei kosaku* [Peace settlement]. Tokyo: Iwanami shoten, 1999.

Kono, Masaru. "Gaiko seisaku" [Foreign policy]. In *Gendai Nihon no seiji*, edited by Ikuo Kume and Masaru Kono. Tokyo: Hosodaigaku kyoiku shinkokai, 2011.

Kosaka, Masataka. *Saisho Yoshida Shigeru* [Premier Shigeru Yoshida]. Tokyo: Chuokoronsha, 1968.

———. "Nihon gaiko no bensho" [The dialectics of Japanese diplomacy]. In *Koza kokusai seiji*, edited by Tadashi Aruga et al. Tokyo: Tokyodaigaku shuppankai, 1989.

Kume, Kunisada. "Nihon no Tonanajia gaiko to ASEAN" [Japan's Southeast Asian diplomacy and ASEAN]. In *ASEAN womeguru kokusaikankei*, edited by Tatsumi Okabe. Tokyo: Nihon kokusaimondai kenkyusho, 1977.

Kwon Yongseok. *Kishiseikenki no Ajiagaiko* [Asian diplomacy of the Kishi Administration]. Tokyo: Kokusai shoin, 2008.

Lee Kuan Yew. "Watashi no rirekisho [My resume]". *Nihon Keizai Shimbun*, 1–30 January 1999.

Mahathir Mohamad. "Watashi no rirekisho [My resume]". *Nihon Keizai Shimbun*, 1–30 November 1995.

Miyagi, Taizo. *Sengo Ajia chitsujo no mosaku to Nihon* [In search of postwar Asian order and Japan]. Tokyo: Sobunsha, 2004.

———. "Sengo Nihon no chiiki chitsujo koso" [Postwar Japan's search for regional order]. In *EU to Higashiajia no Chiikikyodotai*, edited by Masaharu Nakamura and Yves Schemeil. Tokyo: Jochidaigaku shuppan, 2012.

Miyake, Wasuke. *Gaiko ni shori wanai* [No victories in diplomacy]. Tokyo: Fuyosha, 1990.

Monbu Kagaku sho [Ministry of Education and Science]. Monbukagakusho hakusho [White paper on education and science], various issues.

Murayama, Tomiichi. *Tenmei no 561 nichi* [Doomed 561 days]. Tokyo: Besuto serazu, 1996.

Nagai, Yonosuke. *Gendai to senryaku* [Contemporary strategy]. Tokyo: Bungei shunju, 1985.

Nakae, Yosuke. "Nihon no tai Tonanajia gaiko" [Japan's Southeast Asian policy]. *Keidanren Geppo*, October 1977, pp. 24–27.

———. "Nihon to ASEAN no shinjidai" [A new age of Japan and ASEAN]. *Keizai to Gaiko*, September 1977, pp. 2–15.

———. "Ajia gaiko no genjo to tenbo" [Current state and prospects of Asian diplomacy]. *Keizai Kyoryoku*, no. 130 (1978): 7–10.

———. *Ajia gaiko: Do to sei* [Asian diplomacy: Dynamics and tranquility]. Tokyo: Sotensha, 2010.

Nakamura, Keiichiro. *Miki seiken 747 nichi* [747 Days of the Miki Administration]. Tokyo: Gyoseimondai kenkyusho, 1981.

Nakayama, Taro. *Ajia wa 21seiki ni dougokuka* [How Asia evolves in the 21st century]. Tokyo: TBS Buritanika, 1997.

Ninomiya, Akira. "Ajia Getowei senryakukaigi gaegaku ryugakusei senryaku to UMAP no yakuwari" [The role of foreign student strategy and UMAP as planned by the Asia Gateway Strategic Committee]. *Ajia Kenkyu* 54, no. 4 (2008): 56–69.

Nishiyama, Takehiko. "Fukuda sori no Tonanajia rekiho" [Prime Minister Fukuda's Visit to Southeast Asia]. *Gaiko Jiho*, October 1977, pp. 3–10.

———. "Nihon-ASEAN Foramu" [The Japan-ASEAN Forum]. *Keizai to Gaiko*, May 1977, pp. 36–40.

———. "Nihon-ASEAN Foramu dainikai kaigo no kaisai" [The Second Japan-ASEAN Forum]. *Keizai to Gaiko*, December 1977, pp. 11–15.

Nobori, Amiko. "Tonanajia niokeru Nihonimeji to Nihongaiko" [Japan image and Japanese diplomacy in Southeast Asia]. In *Imeji nonakano Nihon*, edited by Yutaka Oishi and Nobuto Yamamoto. Tokyo: Keiogijukudaigaku shuppankai, 2008.

Nozoe, Fumiaki. "Tonanajia kaihatsukakuryokaigi kaisai no seijikeizaikatei" [The political and economic process of initiating the Ministerial Conference on Economic Development in Southeast Asia]. *Hitotsubashi Hogaku* 8, no. 1 (2009): 61–99.

Ochi, Michio. *Chichi Fukuda Takeo* [Fukuda Takeo: My father]. Tokyo: Sankei bizinesu, 1973.

Ono, Naoki. *Nihon no tagaikodo* [External behavior of Japan]. Kyoto: Mineruba shobo, 2011.

Owada, Hisashi. *Gaiko towananika* [What is diplomacy]. Tokyo: NHK Shuppan, 1996.

Oyane, Satoshi. "Keizai gaiko [Economic diplomacy]". In *Nihon seiji*, edited by Keiichi Tako. Osaka: Osakadaigaku shuppankai, 2005.

———. *Kokusai rejimu to Nichi Bei no gaiko koso* [International regimes and Japanese and American diplomatic ideas]. Tokyo: Yuhikaku, 2012.

Pitsuwan, Surin. "Fukuda dokutorin no konnichiteki imiwo kangaeru [Fukuda Doctrine: Impact and implications on Japan-ASEAN relations]". *Kokusai Mondai*, no. 567 (2007): 46–54.

Sato, Torao. *Filipin to Nihon* [The Philippines and Japan]. Tokyo: Saimaru shuppan, 1994.

Sengo Nihon kokusaibunkakoryu kenkyukai. *Sengo Nihon no kokuksai bunka koryu* [Postwar Japan's international cultural exchanges]. Tokyo: Keiso shobo, 2005.

Shibusawa, Masahide and Shiro Saito, eds. *Tonanajia no Nihon hihan* [Southeast Asian criticism over Japan]. Tokyo: Saimaru shuppan, 1974.

Shimabayashi, Takaki. "Indoshina sogokaihatsu foramu nitaisuru aratana igizuke" [A new significance of the Forum for Comprehensive Development of Indochina]. *Tonanajia*, no. 41 (2012): 61–81

Shimizu, Hiroshi. *Shingaporu no keizaihatten to Nihon* [Economic development of Singapore and Japan]. Tokyo: Komonzu, 2004.

Shimomura, Yasutami. "Nihon noenjo ga ASEAN no keizaihatten ni oyoboshita eikyo" [The Effects of Japanese assistance on ASEAN economic development]. In *ASEAN no Keizai hatten to Nihon*, edited by Takatoshi Ito. Tokyo: Nihon hyoron sha, 2004.

———. *Kaihatsuenjo seisaku* [Development assistance policy]. Tokyo: Nihon keizai hyoron sha, 2011.

Shiraishi, Masaya. "Mekon saburijon no jikken" [The experiment of the Mekong

Subregion]. In *Aratana chiikikeisei*, edited by Takehiko Yamamoto and Satoshi Amako. Tokyo: Iwanamishoten, 2007.

Sonoda, Sunao. *Sekai, Nihon, Ai* [The World, Japan, love]. Tokyo: Daisan seikei kenkyusho, 1983.

Sudo, Sueo. *Kokka no taigaikodo* [External behavior of the state]. Tokyo: Tokyodaigaku shuppankai, 2007.

Suharto. "Watashi no rirekisho [My resume]". *Nihon Keizai Shimbun*, 1–30 January 1998.

Suzuki, Shizuo. "1970 nendaizenhan no Tonanajia niokeru hannichi no ronri" [The logic of anti-Japanese movements in Southeast Asia in the early 1970s]. In *Tonanajia to Nihon*, edited by Toru Yano. Tokyo: Kobundo, 1991.

Tadokoro, Masayuki. "Nihon gaiko no zasetsu kara manabubekikoto" [What we should learn from Japan's diplomatic failure]. *Ronza*, November 2005, pp. 156–63.

Tanaka, Hitoshi. *Gaiko no chikara,* [Power of diplomacy]. Tokyo: Nihon keizai shimbun sha, 2009.

Tanaka, Tatsuo. *Sekai ni tobu* [Around the world]. Tokyo: Kodansha, 1981.

Tanaka, Yasutomo. "Posuto Betonamu no Tonanajia anteikaseisaku toshiteno Fukuda dokutorin" [The Fukuda doctrine as the stabilizing policy in the post-Vietnam Southeast Asia]. Ajia Kenkyu 45, no. 1 (1999): 29–60.

Tomoda, Seki. "Nichietsu gaiko kankeijuritsu no keii to shomondai" [The evolution and problems of Japan-Vietnam diplomatic normalization]. In *Nihon to Ajia*, edited by Ajiadaigaku Ajia kenkyusho. Tokyo: Ajiadaigaku Ajia kenkyusho, 1995.

Tsusho Sangyo sho [Ministry of International Trade and Industry: MITI]. *Tsusho hakusho* [White paper on trade]. Tokyo: Ministry of Economy, Trade and Industry, n.d.

———. *ASEAN sangyo kodoka bijon* [A vision for upgrading ASEAN industries]. MITI, 1993.

———. *Keizaikyoryoku no genjo to mondaiten* [Current state and problems of economic cooperation]. Tokyo: Okurasho insatsukyoku, 1969–2000.

Wada, Jun. "Higashiajia niokeru Nihon no kokusaibunkakoryu to bunkagaiko" [Japan's international cultural exchanges and cultural diplomacy]. In *Nihon no Higashiajia koso*, edited by Yoshihide Soeya and Masayuki Tadokoro. Tokyo: Keio gijuku daigaku shuppankai, 2004.

Wakatsuki, Hidekazu. "Fukuda dokutorin: Posuto reisengaiko no yoboenshu" [The Fukuda Doctrine: A precursor of post–Cold War diplomacy]. *Kokusaiseiji*, no. 125 (2002): 197–217.

———. *Zenhoi gaiko no jidai* [The age of omnidirectional diplomacy]. Tokyo: Nihonkeizai hyoron sha, 2005.

Watanabe, Akio. *Ajia Taiheiyo no Kokusaikankei to Nihon* [Asia-Pacific International Relations and Japan]. Tokyo: Tokyodaigaku shuppankai, 1992.

———. "Yoshida dokutorin to sonogo" [The Yoshida Doctrine and after]. *Kokusaiseiji* 155 (2009): 148–57.

Yabunaka, Mitoji. *Kokka no meiun* [The fate of state]. Tokyo: Shinchosha, 2010.

Yachi, Shotaro. *Gaiko no senryaku to kokorozashi* [Diplomatic strategy and determination]. Tokyo: Sankei shimbun shuppan, 2009.

Yoshikawa, Yoko. *Nihhi baishogaiko kosho no kenkyu* [A study of Japan-Philippine reparation negotiations]. Tokyo: Keiso shobo, 1991.

Index

Organization for Economic
    Cooperation and Development,
    20, 176
Owada, Hisashi, 4, 7n7, 71, 132

P

Paris agreement in 1991, 132
Paris Peace Accord, 47
peacekeeping operation (PKO),
    158–59
Peru, hostage crisis in, 150
Philippine armed forces, 118
Philippines, 40–41
    diplomatic rupture between
        Malaysia and, 35
PKO. *See* peacekeeping operation
    (PKO)
Plaza Agreement, 120
"plus 3 *vs.* plus 6" rivalry, 188
PMC. *See* Post-Ministerial
    Conferences (PMC)
political relations, reinforcing
    foreign ministers' meeting, 111–13
    Japan-ASEAN forum, 113–14
    Japan's security role and ASEAN
        regional forum, 114–20
    prime ministers' visits to ASEAN,
        108–11
politico-military environment of
    Southeast Asia, 92
post–Cold War
    era in 1990, 140
    foreign policy, 10
    international environment, 21
    Japanese foreign policy, 10
    period, 104, 115
Post-Ministerial Conferences (PMC),
    78, 207
post–Vietnam War era, 57
post-war Japanese foreign policy, 2,
    18

Prawiro, Radius, 67
proactive foreign policy, Fukuda
    Doctrine as, 18–19
proactive multilateralism, 4, 24–26
pro-China Pol Pot regime, 66
pro-Yoshida Doctrine group, 3
Pyle, Kenneth, 28n13

Q

"quiet diplomacy" characterization,
    10

R

Rahman, Tengku Abdul, 39
reactive foreign policy, 11–14
"reactive state" model, 20
ReCAAP. *See* Regional Cooperation
    Agreement on Combating Piracy
    and Armed Robbery against
    Ships in Asia (ReCAAP)
"Reforms for the New Era of Japan
    and ASEAN for a Broader and
    Deeper Partnership," 150
Regional Conference on Combating
    Piracy and Armed Robbery
    against Ships, 167
Regional Cooperation Agreement on
    Combating Piracy and Armed
    Robbery against Ships in Asia
    (ReCAAP), 168, 219
    counterterrorism and, 216–19
regional cooperation scheme,
    framework of, 67
regional institution building, 24
regionalism in Japanese foreign
    policy, 2
regional-level multilateralism, 20
regional multilateralism, 26
Regional Studies Promotion Program,
    89
reluctant realism, 14–16

ABOUT THE AUTHOR

Sueo Sudo is a professor of Nanzan University, Nagoya, Japan. He received his PhD from the Department of Political Science, the University of Michigan in 1987. Before taking his current position, he was a research fellow at Chulalongkorn University in Bangkok, a fellow at the Institute of Southeast Asian Studies in Singapore and a professor at Saga University in Saga Prefecture, Japan. His research interests are ASEAN and Japan-ASEAN relations. He has published various books in English and Japanese, including *The Fukuda Doctrine and ASEAN* (ISEAS, 1992), *The Structure of Southeast Asian International Relations* (1996 in Japanese), *International Relations of Japan and South East Asia* (2002), *Evolution of ASEAN-Japan Relations* (ISEAS, 2005) and *External Behavior of the State* (2007 in Japanese).

www.ingramcontent.com/pod-product-compliance
Lightning Source LLC
Chambersburg PA
CBHW060153280326
41932CB00012B/1741